FOOTBALL FIELDS AND BATTLEFIELDS

FOOTBALL FIELDS AND BATTLEFIELDS

THE STORY OF EIGHT ARMY FOOTBALL PLAYERS AND THEIR HEROIC SERVICE

JEFF MILLER

Skyhorse Publishing

Skyhorse Publishing books may be purchased in bulk at special discounts for sales promotion, corporate gifts, fund-raising, or educational purposes. Special editions can also be created to specifications. For details, contact the Special Sales Department, Skyhorse Publishing, 307 West 36th Street, 11th Floor, New York, NY 10018 or info@skyhorsepublishing.com.

Skyhorse® and Skyhorse Publishing® are registered trademarks of Skyhorse Publishing, Inc.®, a Delaware corporation.

Visit our website at www.skyhorsepublishing.com.

10 9 8 7 6 5 4 3 2 1

Library of Congress Cataloging-in-Publication Data is available on file.

Cover design by Tom Lau
Cover and spine photo credit: AP Images

Print ISBN: 978-1-5107-3041-0
Ebook ISBN: 978-1-5107-3042-7

Printed in the United States of America

Physical qualities may well determine the destiny of the intellect. To emphasize these truths I had carved on the stone portals of the gymnasium these words:

"Upon the fields of friendly strife
Are sown the seeds
That, upon other fields, on other days
Will bear the fruits of victory"

—Douglas MacArthur, United States Military Academy
Class of 1903, academy superintendent 1919–1922

TABLE OF CONTENTS

Introduction

SINGING FIRST

While the cadets of the United States Military Academy at West Point and the midshipmen of the United States Naval Academy at Annapolis continued to huddle together and shiver in their respective corners of Lincoln Financial Field's lower bowl, many of the announced gathering of 70,844 who'd come to south Philadelphia for the 104th chapter of the storied college football rivalry between Army and Navy on the first Saturday of December 2003 had long since fled the premises as the game's final seconds ticked down. Navy's starting quarterback, Craig Candeto, had ceded custody of his helmet to some member of the team's equipment staff a few series earlier. The Midshipmen's No. 2 quarterback, Aaron Polanco, had even completed a cameo appearance under center and since given way to third-stringer Lamar Owens. The Middies approached the line of scrimmage for 3rd down and 4 yards to go at their 49-yard line. Owens took the snap, faked an inside handoff, and broke toward the left side of his offensive line. Army linebacker Tom Farrington sniffed out the play early. A reserve throughout his four years on the team who most often played on special teams, Farrington took off in hot pursuit of Owens, came through Navy's line essentially untouched, and lunged at him with both hands. His right hand managed to barely clip Owens's right ankle, bringing down the Navy quarterback one yard short of the first down.

A first down would have stopped the game clock by college rules—at least until the first-down chains along the sideline could be reset. With neither coaching staff interested in using any of its remaining timeouts, the final seconds ticked away. Navy won, 34–6, for an outcome that was widely expected. The Midshipmen were favored by 22.5 points according to the betting line established in Las Vegas. For Army's Black Knights, the 28-point defeat was actually a mathematical improvement; their 58–12 loss to Navy a year earlier was the most lopsided in series history. The '03 Middies finished their regular season with an 8–4 record—their first winning season since 1997—and were bound for their first postseason bowl since 1996. More important to the legion of Naval Academy grads, Navy had won the triangular gridiron competition with Army and Air Force for the first time since 1981. The Commander-in-Chief's Trophy would finally return to Annapolis, Maryland.

Losing was all too familiar to Army's players. They lost every game that they played that season, all 13 of them. The vast majority of college football teams that play in the NCAA's top classification—known now as the Football Bowl Subdivision (FBS) but called Division I-A in 2003—have played a maximum of 12 regular-season games beginning with the 2002 season. West Point played 13 games in 2003 through a scheduling anomaly. That allowed Army to become the first team in the long history of major college football to finish 0–13.

Navy's victorious head coach, Paul Johnson, left the sideline soon after receiving a chilled shower courtesy of Candeto and two teammates, who dumped a half-full cooler of ice water on him, per the custom whose roots trace to the National Football League's 1984 New York Giants. Johnson began his soaked saunter toward midfield, seeking to engage in a football tradition that's much older than the sideline shower—exchanging a handshake, and possibly pleasantries, with the opposing coach. Johnson had walked no more than a handful of steps off Navy's sideline when he was first greeted by someone associated with Army football and offered congratulations. That was Ryan Kent, a senior "sniper" (Army's vernacular for an outside linebacker then) and three-year starter who played his high school football only a few minutes from Philadelphia in the small New Jersey town of Woodbury.

Tradition, at least for Army-Navy football, also called for the competitors to stand in front of their respective student bodies and sing the two alma maters. The losing team always goes first; hence, "singing second" is a year-long goal for both squads. The football playing members of West Point's Class of 2004, seniors that day in Philadelphia, enjoyed the pleasure of singing second after the Navy game only once. That happened when they were sophomores, following Army's 26–17 victory in 2001 just up South 11th Street in Lincoln Financial Field's predecessor, Veterans Stadium.

As more frigid fans left "The Linc," Army players gathered in front of the Corps of Cadets, seated in the stadium's northwest seats. And they didn't simply crowd around the stadium wall like impatient shoppers on Black Friday. They lined up in formal rows, standing at attention. The nearby West Point marching band began to play, and the players—some with tears in their eyes—began to sing. The final lines:

> E'er may that line of gray . . . Increase from day to day . . .
> Live, serve, and die, we pray, West Point, for thee.

The alma mater reflects West Point's three-word motto: Duty, honor, and country. "Those hallowed words reverently dictate what you ought to be, what you can be," General Douglas MacArthur told the cadets in May 1962—sixty-three years after he had initially arrived there as a wide-eyed freshman from Wisconsin—when accepting the Thayer Award for lifetime service to the academy. "They are your rallying point to build courage when courage seems to fail, to regain faith when there seems to be little cause for faith, to create hope when hope becomes forlorn."

Kent, Farrington, and all of the Army football players then crossed the field and stood behind the exultant Navy players, who sang second. The Black Knights then made their way to their locker room—as the day's designated home team, they occupied the quarters normally held by the Temple Owls—left to ponder a season that they had approached with enthusiasm and promise. Farrington and Kent were two of the eight fourth-year seniors—or *firsties* in West Point parlance—who played that day for Army. The Navy roster, in contrast, featured fifteen seniors. Only three of Army's seniors started on offense or defense—Kent (outside linebacker), Brian Hill (inside linebacker), and Clint Woody (receiver). A fourth, Anthony Zurisko, was Army's first-string placekicker.

Four starters among eight seniors from the 51 inter-collegiate football "candidates" who had reported to West Point during the summer of 2000 as freshmen, or *plebes*. The process of welcoming freshman football players to Army, Navy, and Air Force is vastly different from what's practiced at other universities that play major collegiate football. The "mainstream" teams award football scholarships to about 25 promising players each year with a maximum of 85 allowed on scholarship at any time. (The math indicates someone's going to be displeased along the way.) Army, Navy, and Air Force don't award athletic scholarships; each newly enrolled student receives free tuition for the balance of his or her stay (pending academic eligibility), and some are invited to participate in intercollegiate athletics—corps sports, in West Point lingo.

Varsity football has long held a storied place in the history of the United States Military Academy. The Army Cadets claimed national championships in 1944, '45, and '46, their games attracting a huge national audience. In two of those seasons, a West Point football player was recognized as the best in the nation, with the awarding of the Heisman Trophy to Felix "Doc" Blanchard in 1945 and Glenn Davis in 1946; they were nicknamed "Mr. Inside" and "Mr. Outside," respectively, for their running styles. Army's clashes during the 1940s with another college football program that was hugely popular from coast to coast, Notre Dame, were staged at the nation's most well-known sports venue, Yankee Stadium in New York, and were among the most memorable sporting events of the mid-twentieth century. The stature of an Army football player both on the field and off is symbolized by words long attributed to General George C. Marshall during World War II: "I want an officer for a secret and dangerous mission. I want a West Point football player." The George C. Marshall Foundation can't verify if the general actually said that, but the words now appear on a plaque that's fixed to the wall near where Army players run out onto the field at the academy's long-time football home, Michie Stadium. Every Army football player touches that plaque on his way onto the field before each game. The practice is considered such a revered, imperative aspect of West Point football that a reproduction of the plaque is brought to each away game, so the tradition can continue.

While Army doesn't award football scholarships, it isn't a stretch to conclude that most of the high school seniors who seek to play football for the Black Knights decide to enroll at the academy primarily for that very reason. For many, Army represents their only opportunity to play major college football beyond walking on elsewhere and hoping to earn an athletic scholarship. Enrolling at West Point means committing the first five years after graduation to being an active-duty army officer and, for those who elect to leave the service at that point, the subsequent three years to duty in the reserves. Political writer Bill Kauffman, in a 1999 contribution to *The American Enterprise*, cited a survey taken of cadet candidates for West Point's Classes of 1998–2002 during their first days of summer military training—a kinetic mutation of freshman orientation appropriately called Beast Barracks—in which fewer than 20 percent of the males identified a desire to become an army officer as their primary reason for enrolling at West Point. Consider what military service distills to according to John McCain and co-author Mark Salter, as stated in *13 Soldiers: A Personal History of Americans at War*:

Scared kids. That is what combat mostly comes down to in the end. Scared kids fighting and killing other scared kids. The main objective of a soldier's training is to show him how to act while he is afraid, how to use a rifle and bayonet and his hands to kill a man he is afraid will kill him. A soldier's training is supposed to be intense and unpredictable and realistic so that even if actual combat isn't a familiar experience when you confront it—even though fear is choking your throat, even though your hands are shaking and your legs trembling, even though you are confused, shocked, terrorized, even though you want to run away—you still know how to fight, how to do your job, and you will still follow orders, you will still kill your enemy if you can.

How and why did the original 51 Army football frosh of 2000 become eight who played against Navy in 2003? Reasons for such significant Army football attrition were many. They were related to factors particular to attending a military academy (such as deciding after arrival at West Point that you didn't *really* want to be an army officer) to enrolling at a college whose academic demands are often equated to those found at an Ivy League school (in autumn 2003, the *Princeton Review* named West Point as the most selective college in the United States, having accepted only 1,300 of the 13,000 applicants). What often shakes up and shakes out any college sports team's roster is a change of head coaches. All of those affected the gridiron hopefuls among West Point's Class of 2004.

Those who lost an appetite—or at least a tolerance—for the prospect of future military service likely could trace their figurative about-face to the events of September 11, 2001. Each member of West Point's Class of 2004 had agreed to attend the academy during peacetime. Each tuition-free academic year at West Point is valued between $50,000 and $65,000. A cadet in good standing can pack up and, in civilian terms, withdraw from the university anytime during the first two years and not be liable for any financial restitution to the US government or service as an army officer. That all changes the night before a cadet's third year begins. The juniors report to Thayer Hall and stand, right hands raised, for the affirmation ceremony. That is a blood oath without the blood. From that day forward, any cadet with a change of heart toward military service will be informed before his or her exit how much of a bill is due to Uncle Sam. And there's a military commitment, but for two years as a soldier instead of being an officer. The Class of 2004 was the first student assemblage brought to West Point that, in the wake of 9/11, had the opportunity to decline a military obligation that could lead to armed conflict. The academy, asked to provide numbers on how many '04 cadets left between 9/11 and the affirmation ceremony in August 2002, stated no such tally exists. One Army football staffer who was there then estimated that ten players in the combined Classes of 2004 and 2005 left school before their affirmation obligations because of 9/11. Academy records show 1,200 West Point hopefuls walked into Michie Stadium on that first day of Beast Barracks in 2000. That included 63 high school valedictorians and 39 salutatorians, 222 who were either class president or student-body president, 500 who captained one or more high school athletic teams. The Class of 2004's graduation roll numbered 960, right at 80 percent.

Eight football seniors endured the humbling, disheartening record 13th attempt at victory during the 2003 season that was unfulfilled. Hall of Fame football coach Bill Parcells (an Army assistant coach from 1966–1969) famously stated during his NFL coaching term, "You are what your record says you are." The eight players' previous football seasons at West Point were unfortunately similar to 2003 when defined by the cold reality of wins and losses. The Black Knights finished 1–10 in 2000, 3–8 in 2001, and 1–11 in 2002. Their combined, four-year mark was 5–42. Five of those firsties arrived at West Point following a year's stay at the academy's prep school in Fort Monmouth, New Jersey. They were South Jersey's Kent; Farrington from greater Pittsburgh; Josh Davis from New Smyrna Beach, Florida near Daytona Beach; Brad Waudby from the town of Oakland in North Jersey; and Zurisko from little Springdale, Pennsylvania near Pittsburgh. The other three were 2000 high school graduates who came straight to the academy, located on the banks of the Hudson River about 50 miles north of New York City: Hill from Port Orange, Florida next door to New Smyrna Beach; Peter Stewart from the north end of Houston, Texas's urban sprawl; and Woody from rural Hayesville, North Carolina.

Those eight could have waved goodbye to West Point after what initially appeared to be five years of peacetime military service were replaced by likely war-zone deployments. Five-hundred and thirty-nine days after graduation day, on May 29, 2004, the class suffered its first wartime casualty about 7,000 miles from West Point. Even in electing to remain at the academy, those eight could have walked away from a football program that drained valuable time and energy that could be have directed toward other pursuits—like studies. Those eight were convinced another victory lay just ahead. Those eight didn't want to be defined by the steady stream of football defeats year after year.

This book attempts to depict their experiences both at the United States Military Academy—as football players and as cadets—and during the years that followed their departures from West Point in 2004. I visited with each multiple times—from late 2004 through early 2018—as well as with their families, friends, West Point peers, fellow US Army officers, and superiors; I've been to West Point, Fort Hood, Fort Riley, Fort Rucker, Fort Sill, Fort Benning, Fort Leavenworth, Fort McPherson, Fort Monmouth, and Camp Merrill. I hope what follows is a compelling and enlightening journey.

Chapter One

"THE *PLACE* OF ALL *PLACES*"

The clatter of cleats was all that could be heard as junior quarterback Ryan Kent and the rest of the Woodbury High football team, physically drained and emotionally spent, boarded their buses for the short ride back to campus from nearby Paulsboro on the first Saturday of December 1997. But for the Thundering Herd, the trip of maybe 10 minutes felt like 10 hours. South Jersey high school football's Montagues and Capulets had just staged an encore to their annual regular-season engagement, which once required the intervention of twelve local police departments when hometown pride escalated far beyond trash talk. This meeting decided the champion of South Jersey's Group 1, the Garden State's version of a state title, and Paulsboro had won yet again. That gave Paulsboro's Red Raiders six consecutive group championships, and it wasn't like they simply played above their heads every postseason. The 16–12 victory was Paulsboro's 62nd straight, the most ever for a New Jersey high school football team. Before Paulsboro's championship run began, the previous four group titles were captured by Woodbury.

The headline in the following Monday's *Philadelphia Daily News* read, "Woodbury Can't Overcome Powerhouse Rival Paulsboro." For Kent, it might as well have stated "World Ends." At 6-foot and 190 pounds, Kent was the deft operator of Woodbury's option offense and felt an unreasonable

1

amount of responsibility for the defeat, as quarterbacks are wont to do. He threw a first-quarter interception, at best a jump ball of a pass, which was returned for a touchdown. He soon after came inches from answering that with a touchdown of his own on a 78-yard burst around left end that ended with him struggling to maintain his balance over the final 20 yards and being pulled down inside Paulsboro's 1-yard line. Surely, the Herd would score from there. But the Red Raiders' defense stiffened, and the promising series ended with Kent buried beneath a pile of defenders in the backfield. Any blame that Kent was intent on self-inflicting on the morose ride home failed to account for the loss of the Herd's star running back, Lamar Sturdivant, seven plays into the game to injury, or for Kent throwing a fourth-down touchdown pass on the game's opening possession. He would, as a senior in the fall of 1998, have one more chance to lead Woodbury to a state championship, and probably one more chance to end the haunting Paulsboro streak.

Woodbury had become Kent's hometown by choice. He was born in Michigan, his parents divorcing when he was a few months old. His mother, Dawn, and his stepfather, Bill Livingston, moved to south Jersey when Kent was about to enter the eighth grade. He could have remained in small-town Michigan with his father, David, and his stepmother, Lynne, who'd been in his life since he could remember, or he could relocate with the Livingstons. There was no right or wrong choice. Young Kent was greatly attracted by the activity that would lay across the Delaware River in Philadelphia, only minutes from home in south Jersey. Goodbye to the Tigers, Lions, Pistons, and Red Wings. Hello to the Phillies, Eagles, Sixers, and Flyers.

Woodbury is a bedroom community of about 10,000. For four days during the Revolutionary War, British General Charles Cornwallis headquartered in a house on what today is Broad Street. James Lawrence, born in 1781, grew up in Woodbury; that's significant because it was Lawrence who, during the War of 1812, futilely cried, "Don't give up the ship!" just before his *USS Chesapeake* went down. The Woodbury of the late 1990s was still small enough where every student walked to school. Lunch period meant hustling to a nearby convenience store or picking up a couple of slices at a pizza parlor.

When Woodbury and Paulsboro met again in late September 1998, the Raiders' behemoth of a winning streak was indeed still breathing, at 63 games. Herd fans arrived at the Woodbury field adjacent to the high school with high hopes despite their team having lost its first game of the season, by one point. Some bravely carried the signs that featured the letter "P" circled with a slash through it, signs that the Red Raiders fans were all too familiar with and ignored. But if the Herd were to slay mighty Paulsboro, they likely would do it without one of their standout linemen. Senior Jadie Barringer III had injured his knee a few weeks earlier, and most Woodbury players were certain Barringer would have trouble that day simply walking, no less playing in a football game.

But, hey, Woodbury is almost Philly, and Philly is *Rocky*, and, like Rocky Balboa, Barringer arrived in the locker room before the game on a dead sprint. The rest of the day played out like a football movie that Woodbury players and fans had waited years to enjoy. The final score was 14–13 Herd, thanks to a Paulsboro PAT that sailed wide right with about five minutes to play and a 31-yard Raiders field-goal attempt that did likewise in the closing seconds after the kicking unit scurried onto the field since Paulsboro was out of timeouts. Seconds later, Kent cradled a ball and cried into the shoulder of a teammate as a scene that resembled New Year's Eve in Times Square appeared to play out around them. He composed himself a few minutes later to appear on a local telecast, proclaiming, "The happiness is indescribable."

Woodbury and Paulsboro predictably qualified for the playoffs again. Another championship matchup failed to materialize with Glassboro's upset of Paulsboro in the semifinals, and at least some Herd fans confessed to being relieved that the Red Raiders were out of the way. After Woodbury beat Glassboro, 21–6, to claim its first group title since 1991, many of those same fans considered the championship victory second in importance to the win over Paulsboro two months earlier. Kent scored on a 76-yard run the first time that he touched the ball. After the game, his mind returned to that disconsolate ride back from Paulsboro a year earlier. "Ever since then, I made a promise to myself to get back to the championship game and leave with a different feeling," he said, according to the *Star-Ledger* of Newark, New Jersey.

Barringer's primary contribution that day, other than simply showing up, was a crushing blow on Glassboro's quarterback that knocked him from the game. (He later compared the hit to "running over a mannequin.") Four years earlier, the outgoing Barringer was one of the eighth graders who openly welcomed newcomer Kent from Michigan. His father is African American, the first to serve on Woodbury's city council, and his mother Italian. The two boys' friendship grew to where the Livingstons referred to Barringer as their fourth son. He was a regular in basketball tournaments held behind the Kents' home on American Street. He accompanied the Livingstons to the Jersey shore. Kent, when a student at West Point, would mail Army football game tickets to the Barringers.

Woodbury's 1999 yearbook featured Kent as the boy who was "Most Attractive" and who had the "Most School Spirit." (His contributions to both ending the Paulsboro streak and winning the group championship somehow didn't earn him the title of the boy who was "Most Athletic." That accolade went to Paris Minor, a running back who earned a football scholarship to the University of Maine.) As a youngster, Kent seemingly could never run short of energy and wasn't easily deterred. If knocked down while playing, he popped right up and returned to his business. For that quality, Dawn Livingston referred to him as her "Weeble." He also didn't accept defeat well. David Kent didn't allow any of his sons—two by his first marriage and two by his second—to easily beat him in backyard sports. Ryan's distaste for defeat was developed early.

Kent attracted little attention from collegiate offensive coordinators despite his unquestionable success at running an option attack, which primarily ran the ball rather than pass. He was considered too short to stand out for a major-college team. The offensive line coach at the nearby University of Delaware, a successful program in Division I-AA for decades, offered him a scholarship. Kent prepared to sign with the Blue Hens, even adding a Delaware T-shirt to his wardrobe, until word came that Delaware's quarterback coach chose to sign a different signal-calling prospect. That negated the offer that had been extended to Kent. West Point, a rare major-college team whose offense employed the option, was among the other schools that had recruited Kent earlier. Army's point of contact was Bob Shoop, who joined head coach Bob Sutton's staff going into the 1998 season and left soon afterward for Boston College. In the midst of Shoop's departure from the academy, his recruiting files apparently weren't smoothly assimilated into the rest of the staff paperwork. Kent, awkwardly turned away by Delaware, was no longer on Army's recruiting radar as the time period for officially signing college football prospects began on the first Wednesday of February 1999. He soon after was brought back to the staff's attention thanks to a phone call from Kent's determined stepfather. Livingston subsequently took Kent on a trip to West Point and met with Sutton. It turned out that one of Army's formal football recruits had changed his mind about attending the academy, which left an enrollment slot available. Sutton invited Kent to fill the slot but to enroll that fall not at West Point but at the academy's prep school in Fort Monmouth, located about 90 minutes east of Woodbury near the Jersey shore.

Sutton's suggestion to precede arrival at West Point with a year at the prep school was a common recommendation for incoming football players. Army, in addition to not attaching free tuition to athletic prowess, doesn't participate in the common collegiate sports practice of red-shirting, in which an athlete can be held out of formal competition for one season without that counting against the maximum of four years' eligibility. Most football players at major universities will take a red-shirt year, typically as an incoming fresh-man, and play four seasons over the course of five academic years. That allows the athlete the benefit from an extra year of sports instruction and physical maturation while also spreading the academic load over five years. Given the rigors of the four-year academic gauntlet at West Point, even football recruits with solid high school transcripts often elect to attend the prep school since its emphasis on the core courses of math and English will provide another year of foundation before facing the challenges of the academy environment. Kent accepted Sutton's recommendation and agreed before returning home to enroll at Fort Monmouth; he was also relieved to see that West Point cadets didn't live in buildings like the army barracks that he'd seen in the movies.

* * *

The coaches at Shaler Area High School, located in the hills just north of Pittsburgh, were well acquainted with Tom Farrington's athletic prowess before he stepped onto the tree-laden campus in 1995. For one, he'd impressed them with his drive and intensity no matter the sport. (Farrington later summed up his pigskin predilection: "I just love to hit. To me, it's the best part of football.") The coaches were also pleased with his blood lines. Farrington's father, Tom Sr., had long been involved in local high school athletics, first as a game official and later as a supervisor of officials. Tom Sr. was a carpenter, quiet and driven to succeed no matter the task—and a Pittsburgh Steelers season-ticket holder. He was considered a man's man and served as both hero and best friend to his only child. Wife Theresa was a hospital nurse who became a school nurse when young Tom began playing junior high sports. That way, she could attend as many of his games as possible.

Shaler Area High opened in the fall of 1971, the product of a court-ordered merger of four schools that served adjoining boroughs. Farrington played football and basketball for the Titans, earning a spot on the latter's varsity as a freshman. He went on to start three seasons at safety and shared the position of running back as a senior in the one-back, run-and-shoot offense under head coach Frank Rocco, who'd been a back-up quarterback at Penn State. As a 6-foot-1, 195-pound senior, Farrington also started on the basketball team as a slightly undersized center.

As Shaler Area's 1998 football team retreated to the school gym to practice one rainy, late-summer day, the players took notice of the various championship banners—and noted the lack of representation of the football team. They promised that day that the '98 Titans would contribute to the banner collection. Contribute they did. Shaler won the school's first conference championship and added the school's first-ever playoff win in football. With Shaler's top rusher missing that game with a sprained ankle, Farrington rumbled for 132 yards in the convincing 31–6 victory over Ringgold. He was named to the *Pittsburgh Post-Gazette* north edition's "Fabulous 22" postseason team.

Basketball season likewise held significant promise for Shaler. The Titans won their first six games and were led by junior sharpshooter Yuri Demetris, who was extremely accurate from the perimeter. Farrington, playing center, could score both from the outside and bull his way through taller defenders inside. Demetris was the lone Titan who attracted the attention of

NCAA Division I basketball coaches and would eventually play for nearby Pitt, but Shaler head coach Howie Ruppert considered Farrington his best player. Ruppert was from Staten Island, had served as an assistant coach at Division I's Seton Hall in New Jersey and Duquesne in Pittsburgh, and shared in Farrington's appetite for blue-collar skills on the court. Ruppert liked that Farrington reveled in rebounding, made the pass that led to the pass that led to a basket. He also liked that Farrington drew charges.

Farrington was averaging 18 points per game, second on the team to Demetris, when Shaler Area's basketball team made the drive south of downtown Pittsburgh, winding along the south bank of the Monongahela River to West Mifflin for a non-conference game in mid-December. Shaler held a comfortable lead in the closing minutes when tempers began raging. Farrington's temperature rose when he saw a West Mifflin player punch one of his teammates. Soon after, he was involved in a loose-ball scramble that escalated into a scuffle. A West Mifflin player spat in Farrington's face, and the two got into it. Coaches from both benches ran onto the court to calm their players, but not before Farrington was assessed a technical foul. The pushing and shoving continued; Farrington was t'ed up a second time, which disqualified him from the remainder of the game and would prevent him from playing in the Titans' next game.

Ruppert dispatched assistant coach Roger Depew to take Farrington down a nearby hallway to calm him. Depew then escorted him to the Titans' locker room, located one floor below the court at the end of a small, winding staircase. Shaler won, 72–57, and the teams didn't exchange handshakes afterward. Depew returned to the court to retrieve the team camera while Farrington continued to seethe. In a building that he was unfamiliar with, Farrington threw a punch with his right hand, thinking he was going to strike a locker, and soon after let out an ungodly scream. His fist instead went through an office door window that was reinforced by wire mesh. His hand was shredded by the combination of glass and metal. The alarmed Depew arrived seconds later and wrapped Farrington's blood-soaked right wrist in what was available—the player's jersey.

The rest of the Titans contingent, just then making its way down the stairway, was jolted by Farrington's screams. He came running up the stairs, and Ruppert was horrified at what appeared to be a nearly severed hand. Ruppert grabbed Farrington's right hand, squeezed it as hard as he could, got a towel to replace the jersey, and had Farrington lay down. Ruppert frantically phoned an old Staten Island friend who was a local orthopedic surgeon and worked with baseball's Pittsburgh Pirates. Patrick DeMeo immediately referred him to Mark Baratz, a nationally renowned hand specialist at nearby Allegheny General Hospital. Baratz waited until the following morning to operate. He reconnected nerves and muscles and essentially saved young Farrington's right hand, though the prospect for full recovery was unknown. With all the tubes and attachments connected as Farrington lay in a hospital bed, the hand resembled that of a marionette. A physician's assistant told the Farringtons it was possible the hand would never return to normalcy, that the lack of full mobility could leave it in a claw-like condition. Farrington quietly told his parents, "They don't know me."

News of the episode soon hit the local sports pages given the Shaler basketball team's standing as one of the area's best and a potential contender for state honors, and Farrington explained to the *Post-Gazette*: "Sometimes you get so much adrenaline in you." In mid-January, the inevitable was confirmed: Farrington wouldn't be playing anymore basketball for Shaler. Toward the end of the season, the healing reached the point where he came to practice and at least fooled around some on the court.

Much of the football recruiting interest in Farrington abated in the weeks following the incident in West Mifflin. That left one NCAA Division I-A school that was still considering Farrington, hand issue and all. West Point wasn't ready to give up on him. He was invited to visit the academy over Super Bowl weekend in late January. Farrington's hand was still early in the healing process when he traveled to West Point by himself. His predicament made for some awkward interaction with his fellow recruits since he didn't want to extend his heavily bandaged right hand during introductions. Some of the other prospects were confused when Farrington kept his right hand stuffed in his coat pocket and instead offered his left for a handshake.

Maladroitness aside, Farrington thoroughly enjoyed the time that he spent with his student host, Clay Daniels, who would be the Black Knights' starting quarterback during the 1999 season. The recruits checked in at the nearby Bear Mountain Inn—they ordinarily would have stayed at the stately Thayer Hotel just inside the academy's main gate, but that was under renovation—and then were treated to dinner and arcade games at a Dave & Buster's down at the Palisades Center Mall in West Nyack. On Sunday morning, the culmination of the recruits' weekend was breakfast with Bob Sutton in the officers' club followed by private meetings with the coach in a downstairs room. In that room, Sutton offered Farrington the opportunity to play Army football following a year at the prep school. Farrington said he would think about it. He didn't think all that long; a week later, he told his father that he was "just going to do it" and sign with the Black Knights. Farrington's parents had essentially left the decision to him, happy to offer advice but primarily there to listen. The decision brought with it a coalescence of joy and relief. "It's pretty neat there," Farrington told the *Post-Gazette*. "The place is amazing, and the people there are a lot like me. It's just a good deal. My life is planned out."

The hand healed enough for Farrington to enjoy one additional experience as a high school athlete, playing in a summer all-star football game for players from schools north of Pittsburgh, held at Fox Chapel High. Most of the participants simply saw the invitation as the cherry atop a successful high school gridiron career; Farrington viewed it as an opportunity to prove the hand injury wasn't an impediment to future athletic endeavors. The week of on-site practice preceding the game was generally meant to meld the players from various high schools into offenses and defenses that could at least somewhat function together for 60 minutes. Farrington treated the drills as a referendum of his football worth and attacked them with zeal. With a little too much zeal for the coaches and some of his teammates, the latter vexed by the kid from Shaler Area who tried to knock off their heads. Farrington must not have set his sights on Anthony Zurisko, a slightly-built kicker from Springdale High, located in the modest town of the same name. Early in the week, Zurisko asked Farrington if he was going to West Point. Yes, he replied. "I'm going, too," Zurisko said. In the game's closing minutes with the outcome already decided, Farrington was true to his personal athletic doctrine of always playing to the final whistle. When the opposing quarterback, Pitt-bound Rod Rutherford, lined up as a receiver, Farrington was convinced a pass was coming Rutherford's way—and made sure to break it up with a jarring hit. On the game's final play, Farrington recovered a botched center-quarterback exchange and felt like he'd done all that he could in one game to assure any onlookers that he had plenty more football to play despite the injury.

* * *

Josh Davis made the same recruiting trip as Tom Farrington—he wondered if the left-handed handshakes were an expression of cockiness—along with his father, Mike. They traveled from Volusia County, Florida, which is located almost halfway down the state's east coast and is best known as home of the Daytona International Speedway. The Davises lived toward the county's southern end in the sleepy town of New Smyrna Beach. Ponce de Leon is said to have come traipsing through there in 1513. New Smyrna, as it's most-often known, is a haven for surfers and fishermen, attractive to many who simply want to sit back and enjoy sunrise and surf. Mike Davis had lived all across Florida, from St. Petersburg to Jacksonville to Orlando, when he settled in New Smyrna with wife Cheryl, son Josh, and daughter Nicole in 1993.

Davis didn't fit the physical mold of the typical New Smyrna surfer, though he did ride some waves. As a sophomore, he pushed 300 pounds while standing about six feet. He was a member of the New Smyrna Beach High Barracudas' weight-lifting team, was a heavyweight wrestler, and began a three-year run as starting center for the football Cudas. That was the first time that Davis was allowed to play organized football; his size had prevented him from participating in New Smyrna's youth league. As a 310-pound senior, he helped the Barracudas finish the regular season 9–1—earning their first playoff berth since 1972—and was named to the state sportswriters' Class 4A all-state second team. Later that school year, Davis lifted a combined 765 pounds to finish second among heavyweights in the state Class 4A meet; that total would have won the competition in the state's largest classification, Class 6A.

Had Davis stood at least 6-foot-2, he probably would have attracted the attention of major college football programs. He did spark interest from the South Carolina staff of head coach Brad Scott, but Scott was fired after going

1–10 in 1998. Lou Holtz came out of coaching retirement to take over the Gamecocks, and South Carolina's recruitment of Davis ended. His two best options for earning a football scholarship were from Division I-AA schools—The Citadel and Western Kentucky. That was until Army assistant coach Darrell Hazell (a Minnesota Vikings assistant during the 2017 season) came through Volusia County and invited Davis to visit West Point.

Davis scheduled his three recruiting trips to be made within one week in late January 1999, beginning at Western Kentucky. The Hilltoppers' head coach, Jack Harbaugh, was the patriarch of the football family that includes sons John (then a Philadelphia Eagles assistant and the Baltimore Ravens' head coach since 2008) and Jim (the Ravens' starting QB in 1998; he coached the San Francisco 49ers to the 2013 Super Bowl and has been Michigan's head coach since 2015). Davis's visit to Western included a stop at Harbaugh's home and a film session of sorts; the two of them watched old footage of Jim playing youth football. Jim Harbaugh had previously visited New Smyrna on behalf of his father to spend time with Davis and teammate Manny Robles, and received something of a lukewarm reception from the two recruits. That was because they didn't recognize him. They were subsequently informed of their unintentional snubbing of an NFL quarterback by one of their aghast coaches. The two kids scrambled for the door to catch up with Harbaugh but were too late. Before Davis left dinner and home movies at the Harbaughs, he made a verbal commitment to Western Kentucky. He went ahead with the trips to The Citadel and West Point, joined only during the latter by his father.

Davis wasn't surprised to encounter snow and frigid temperatures on the banks of the Hudson. Despite the meteorological jolt, he was awed by the academy's ambience, the combination of physical beauty and history. He wasn't the first to be smitten with the surroundings upon his maiden visit to West Point. Such was the case in 1839 when a reluctant first-year enrollee arrived from Ohio. Ulysses Hiram Grant—somehow nominated for admission as "Ulysses S. Grant," which made for a much more patriotic moniker later on as the nation's 18th President—futilely hoped some manner of travel mishap would prevent him from reporting on time for the academy's academic year. By late September, he wrote to a cousin, R. McKinstry Griffith, and extoled the beauty of the United States Military Academy: "So far as it regards natural attractions it is decidedly the most beautiful place that I have ever seen; here are hills and dales, rocks and river; all pleasant to look upon. . . . In short this is the best of all places—the *place* of all *places* for an institution like this." Visitors often shared such wonderment. Charles Dickens said of West Point: "It could not stand on more appropriate ground, and any ground more beautiful can hardly be."

Davis's student host was Neil Ravitz, a three-year starter on the offensive line and one of the captains of Army's 1998 team. After the Friday night fun at Dave & Buster's, the Davises strolled out to a patio in the frigid night and discussed the evening's events and, more importantly, Josh's impending decision. At Western Kentucky, he could enjoy "mainstream" college life and play for a team that could compete for a Division I-AA playoff berth. Army was his only "big-time" football opportunity, albeit with a program that appeared to be years from competing for even a minor bowl invitation. Mike noted what a West Point degree would mean in ten, fifteen years. Josh, with two days remaining in the visit, had essentially made up his mind.

On Saturday, the recruits visited the superintendent's house and toured the football facilities. Davis was informed along the way of West Point's restrictions on weight, that football linemen received exemptions since players of their size were needed to compete in major college football. The occasional conflict between holding firm to rules that were set to produce the best military officers possible and the ability to compete in major college athletics had existed for decades. Without such waivers for cadets who were too heavy and/or too tall to meet academy regulations, Army would be hard-pressed to field football linemen or basketball players who could go toe-to-toe with counterparts from other major college teams. The philosophical clash sometimes extended to include academic qualifications, all the way back to Douglas MacArthur's tenure as West Point superintendent beginning in 1919. MacArthur, himself a baseball player at the academy, was convinced fielding successful intercollegiate teams by recruiting top-notch athletes would enhance the academy's national standing. Such enthusiasm wasn't always shared by West Point's academic board.

The two Davises got on the phone with Cheryl back in Florida and informed her of Josh's intent to formally sign with Army. She was apprehensive and asked Mike if he'd steered their son into making that enormous commitment, one that extended well beyond the football field. Mike tried his best to assure her that Josh's decision was his own. Josh took the phone and delivered the same message. On Sunday morning, Davis took his seat across from Bob Sutton and was offered a West Point appointment and football slot after a year at Fort Monmouth. He signed right there and then; the public signing in early February for what's referred to as National Signing Day—which actually begins a signing period—was for the benefit of any local media back in Florida. "I'll be fighting for a spot in my freshman year," Davis told the *Orlando Sentinel*. "I plan on starting by my sophomore year."

* * *

Like Davis, Brad Waudby Jr. couldn't play in just any youth football league because of his size. He began playing in the first grade in his hometown of Oakland—a bedroom community located about 30 miles west of New York City and popular with the metropolitan area's big-league athletes—but was denied reentry two years later because of his weight. His family took him to play with a cousin 15 miles away in Clifton, where there was no weight limit, but all parties soon tired of the travel time.

Young Brad lived with his family on the second floor of the funeral home that his father operated, which certainly proved to be a conversation starter. His family moved into the home in 1976, when his father became its caretaker; Bradford Sr. bought the business in 1983, and the Waudbys moved into a "regular" house when Brad was in the fifth grade. He certainly was no different from other boys who enjoyed helping their fathers at work. Brad would remove the sympathy cards from floral arrangements after services, straighten chairs, and vacuum. And ask questions: "Dad, what did he die from?" Brad would accompany his father on body removals and got to where he'd help embalm. Bradford would occasionally chastise his son for making too much noise upstairs when Brad had one of his school friends over, and there was the time that Brad tried out a new fishing rod by casting it down from a second-floor catwalk and hooked it on a table decoration that shattered. Given such eccentricities of Waudby home life, Bradford was perplexed when his son was frightened during his first sleepover at someone else's house: "What are you crying about? You live with dead people below you!" And Bradford didn't want his only son following him in the business: "I want you to have a life."

Waudby's athletic interest grew to include baseball, especially pitching. He was throwing 70 miles per hour as an eighth grader and played with the sons of former New York Yankees second baseman Willie Randolph (Andre) and New York Giants defensive tackle Jim Burt (Jim Jr.). Mothers of opposing players weren't comfortable having their sons step into the batter's box against Waudby and sometimes asked his coach for proof that he was young enough to play in that league.

Waudby was finally able to formally return to football at home as a 240-pound freshman at Oakland's Indian Hills High School, and he continued pitching during his first two years with the Braves. Having played relatively little organized football compared to his teammates, Waudby was intimidated by their knowledge of the game and became discouraged. He wasn't particularly strong for his size but had quick feet, which led the coaching staff to initially place him exclusively on the offensive line. It didn't help that his freshman coach was a high-energy Bronx native who'd played pro football. Gene Prebola, who scored the first winning touchdown in the history of the Oakland Raiders, rode the inexperienced freshman relentlessly because he recognized the challenges that Waudby would face down the road as a varsity player. The 1995 freshman Braves lost only one game, which was to their next-door neighbor, arch-rival Ramapo. The Braves won their league championship during Waudby's junior and senior seasons and qualified for the playoffs in 1998, going out in the first round. He suffered a chipped finger one season that should have sidelined him for a significant amount of time according to the team doctors. Waudby's father didn't understand that conclusion, noting that his son was neither a quarterback nor a receiver, and had him cleared to play by other doctors. Waudby returned to action soon after with no problem.

Waudby also competed in the discus and the shot put for Indian Hills' track and field team coached by . . . Gene Prebola. Waudby and a couple of his track teammates—all football linemen—incurred Prebola's wrath after one road meet by leaving without a parent, a violation of a team rule. The following Monday, Prebola made the offenders follow their throwing practice by running 100-yard dashes with only a brief rest period between runs. Waudby really struggled and began to complain. His fellow detainees warned him to keep quiet, else their coach might increase their punishment. No such punitive augmentation was necessary; the boys never pulled that stunt again.

Waudby was a first-team all-league offensive lineman and named third-team all-Bergen County that year as chosen by *The Record* of Hackensack at both lineman and tight end. The biggest college programs to initially show interest in him were Boston College, Syracuse, and Rutgers. When he received a recruiting letter from West Point, his father, an Air Force veteran, was floored and urged his son to accept an invitation to play Army football—all of 36 miles northeast of Oakland—if given the opportunity. His mother, Nancy, was hesitant, given the post-graduate military commitment. On the drive home to New Jersey from a summer football camp at BC, Bradford diverted from the most direct route back to Oakland for one that conveniently went down the main road toward West Point. Nancy chided her husband: "Don't put ideas in his head." The idea was already there; Brad agreed to attend the prep school with the hope of playing football for Army's Black Knights.

* * *

Among the 98-member Springdale High Class of 1999, Anthony Zurisko was selected as the most athletic boy. He played soccer, basketball, and football. On the football team, he was a receiver and a kicker, his career at the former ending after he injured a finger while making a catch. From that point on, Zurisko's football focus was on being the kicker for the Dynamos—the nickname came from having two power plants in town. His kicking motion was atypical. Most kickers have a follow-through that results in the kicking leg raised high and figuratively bisecting the goalposts. Zurisko's right leg remained relatively low after connecting with the ball and pulled to his left. His peers contended he was defying the laws of physics. No one complained about his aberrant approach when his 35-yard field-goal attempt sailed straight through the uprights in the closing seconds against conference-rival Duquesne High for a 15–14 win during his senior season.

Springdale is located about 15 miles northeast of downtown Pittsburgh amid the hills along the north bank of the Allegheny River. It's just across the river from Oakmont, home of the august country club that has hosted PGA Tour major tournaments since the 1920s. The Dynamos usually compete in the state's smallest enrollment classification, and a big night for the students, if they elected not to head into Pittsburgh, usually meant hanging out at a friend's house or going to the bowling alley. Zurisko's father, Damian, worked in town at the PPG plant. He also earned money on the side as a football back judge until Anthony became a junior in high school and the father felt guilty for missing games played by the eldest of his three sons.

During the winter of Zurisko's junior year of high school, Army's Bob Shoop visited Springdale and met with the Dynamos' kicker. Zurisko told his parents that night about meeting with the Black Knights assistant, and his father was ecstatic. As a senior, Zurisko was recruited by Pitt, Syracuse, Temple, and West Virginia, visiting most of those campuses. The best scholarship offers, however, were to begin his college football career with a partial scholarship that could become a full ride if merited by his performance. He didn't take a recruiting trip to West Point, but his guidance counselor, Joanna Tano (with a son who was a Naval Academy graduate), made sure Zurisko was aware that four years' tuition-free education at the United States Military Academy would in no way be connected with how many field-goal attempts that he could convert. And Damian made sure Anthony was clear on the post-graduate military commitment. Nancy Zurisko urged her son to apply to West Point even if he wasn't sold on attending. If he was accepted, she said, he'd then at least have a decision to make. When Shoop phoned to offer a slot at the prep school, Zurisko didn't hesitate: "I'm ready."

* * *

A few weeks after Signing Day 1999 passed, a change of personnel at the United States Military Academy took place that would greatly impact the future Army football careers of Ryan Kent, Tom Farrington, Anthony Zurisko, Josh Davis, and Brad Waudby. A replacement for retiring West Point athletic director Al Vanderbush was introduced on April 22. The choice of academy superintendent Lieutenant General Daniel Christman was Rick Greenspan, the AD at Illinois State for the previous six years. Christman was predictably enthusiastic in describing Greenspan: "I am absolutely convinced he is the right person to lead Army's intercollegiate sports program into the twenty-first century." For most major college athletic programs, football serves as the financial and public-relations bell cow. So, Army fans were wise to study the kind of football program that Greenspan had cultivated at Illinois State. The school competes in NCAA Division I-AA in football. Illinois State's Cardinals finished the 1998 season 8–4 under third-year coach Todd Berry, the program's first winning finish in five years, and qualified for the I-AA playoffs.

Chapter Two

CONDOS BY THE BEACH

Though Tom Farrington recovered from the calamitous hand injury enough to play in a summer all-star game, the possibility that West Point would conclude at the relative last minute that he wasn't physically able to attend the prep school was never far from his mind during the summer of 1999. His parents drove him from Pittsburgh to Fort Monmouth on the day before prep school students were scheduled to report for their version of West Point's Beast Barracks military orientation. After the Farringtons returned to their hotel room after dinner, Tom pensively checked the family's home answering machine to see if any messages had rendered their trip unnecessary. There was no such depressive directive. Nine months after the accident, Farrington's greatest issue with the hand was his lack of control over the pinkie finger. During the prepsters' first days learning the basics of military protocol, his unconstrained digit prompted some quizzical looks from superiors when he saluted. Farrington resorted to taping some of his fingers together, but that proved problematic for other tasks and was quickly abandoned.

Anthony Zurisko's parents made a similar drive from greater Pittsburgh. At dinner the night before the prepsters reported, their son didn't seem to be himself. If Zurisko had any last-minute misgivings, he didn't state them then or the following morning when the incoming students reported to Fort Monmouth. They and their families gathered in a reception area, when a school representative read off the students' names and the cadet hopefuls walked off. The day was filled with instruction in basic tasks, like facing movements and routine exercises with a robust amount of verbal "encouragement" from the supervising officers. Students and families were reunited at 5 p.m. in a parking lot, the prepsters having been liberated from any hair atop their heads and issued identical T-shirts. Families were told they had 10 minutes to visit before the students would move on and begin their prep year. The Zuriskos struggled to find their son amid the congregation of white shirts and shorn skulls. The 10 minutes felt like two. The Zuriskos had planned to stay over one more night near Fort Monmouth, but instead drove right back to Springdale.

The prepsters were housed in two three-story barracks in a back corner of the post. Brad Waudby was disappointed the dorm rooms didn't resemble the "condos by the beach" that were described during recruitment. It was almost cruel for the sweating prep cadets to stand at attention in formation during their first days of the late summer and look overhead to see the prop planes carrying advertising banners over the nearby shore. Fort Monmouth approached the 1999 football season without a head coach. The team's previous coach, Mike Bender, left after only one season to work in the NFL's European league. Athletic director Bob Mueller determined he lacked sufficient time to identify a suitable replacement and decided to do the job himself for the upcoming season. The position, however, wasn't new to him. Mueller was first employed at the prep school in 1969, which was located then at Fort Belvoir in Virginia, soon after he finished graduate school at Ithaca College in New York. He'd been drafted into the army and asked his football coach at Ithaca, Dick Lyon, if there were any immediate coaching opportunities at West Point. There weren't, but Lyon helped Mueller land the head coaching job at the prep school. Mueller coached the prepsters for only the one season, determining early on that he much preferred overseeing a football program that featured more than one academic class of players. He spent the next four years coaching at two high schools in the northeast before returning to the prep school's football program in 1974, holding that job through 1986 (the operation moved to Fort Monmouth in 1975) and then concentrating on being athletic director.

The prep school's 1999–2000 class numbered 232. Enrollment at Fort Monmouth was capped at about 240, with a typical class sending slightly fewer than 200 on to the academy. According to West Point, 11 percent of the average academy graduating class since 1951 has consisted of prep school grads, while occupying 25 percent of senior leadership positions of the Corps of Cadets. West Point's prep school was meant to be a transition to academy life without duplicating what the students would face upon their arrival on the banks of the Hudson. While the military training, conducted by actual officers instead of older students, resembled what they would experience at West Point, prep school students could earn privileges that far exceeded those that were available at the academy.

The incoming students—primarily high school graduates, though some older civilians decide to take a crack at admission to West Point—endured three weeks of basic training, one of those weeks conducted about an hour away from the school at Fort Dix. When the school year began, academics consisted of study in the core courses of math and English that figured to benefit them once they arrived at West Point. Students typically took two sections of math—one hour of instruction and one of lab work—plus two hours of English. There were also sessions called "student success," as well as an additional afternoon instruction period. Students reported to mandatory study halls Sunday through Thursday nights. If a student struggled in a particular class, he or she would be scheduled for an additional study session on Friday evening.

Mueller and his staff—which included recently-commissioned Neil Ravitz, Josh Davis's recruiting host among the graduate assistants—worked with a football roster of 60, 44 of whom were recruited to play on the team. Two Jersey boys were selected as team captains—Ryan Kent representing the offense and linebacker Jeremy Campbell from Montclair for the defense. Kent's competition at quarterback featured Andre McLeod from Monroe, New York (only 15 miles from West Point); Adam Rafalski from Bel Air, Maryland; and Thomas Roberts from Cincinnati, Ohio. Each ran the option in high school. New York's *Daily News* hailed McLeod as the best option quarterback in New York State as a senior. Rafalski led a football renaissance at his high school, which had not qualified for the playoffs in fifteen seasons. Roberts, reared by a single mother who became a police officer, captained his football, basketball, and baseball teams at Hughes High next door to the University of Cincinnati. He considered accepting a partial athletic scholarship to play baseball for Notre Dame or Stanford before choosing West Point.

Roberts roomed with Tom Farrington. On their first night together, Farrington discovered that Roberts preferred having a veritable soundtrack of his personal music in order to feel comfortable. Farrington was willing to accept that, except when it was time for them to turn in for the night. The band played on, so to speak. Farrington politely asked Roberts to turn off his music. Roberts turned off what was playing—and promptly turned on something else, which was Otis Redding's soulful "Sittin' on the Dock of the Bay." All Farrington could do was giggle, and the roommates forged an immediate bond.

For years, the prep school football team faced junior varsity squads from major college programs located in the region, like Maryland or Rutgers, until such programs were phased out nationally. Subsequent opposition was provided by junior colleges and other prep schools located within a relatively short drive. Fort Monmouth's 1999 schedule included powerful Nassau Community College, Milford Academy (quarterbacked by Farrington's signal caller at Shaler Area, Chris Siegle), Princeton's junior varsity, West Point's own junior varsity and—not coincidentally the final game of the season—the prep school from the Naval Academy. The prepsters finished 4–5. On their visit to West Point, they lost to the junior varsity, 42–34. But they brought a 31–14 triumph back from Annapolis for the highlight of their season. Kent and McLeod emerged to receive the most playing time under center. They essentially shared the starting duties and sometimes shuttled in and out during the same series. Roberts eventually shifted to defensive back and found a new football home there.

At Fort Monmouth, young men and women who hoped to become West Point cadets were first introduced to the physical fitness test given to all members of the army: the APFT. The test consisted of three parts, each needing to be passed to continue as a student in good standing, since physical conditioning was one of the bedrock emphases of the institution. The cadet was directed to do pushups for two minutes, sit-ups for two minutes, and then run two miles. Passing grades varied by age and gender within four age groups beginning at age seventeen and running through age thirty-six. The bar for men 17–21 was set at 35 pushups, 47 sit-ups, and completing the run within 16:36. A prepster who failed to pass the test when administered in the fall was granted a second opportunity in the spring, with failure endangering his or her appointment to the academy. All passed.

Kent initially seethed at the difference between the life he was living as a first-year college student, with its voluminous military constraints, and what his former Woodbury classmates enjoyed elsewhere. He soon learned that life as a prep schooler was a veritable breeze compared to what awaited him on the banks of the Hudson. Kent signed out most Friday afternoons after the football season ended and was a drive of only about 90 minutes from lounging on his familiar couch at home. Anthony Zurisko's parents made the drive of five-and-a-half hours to attend the prep team's two home games. As weeks went by, Zurisko's calls home often included mention that this student or that student had quit. Prepsters who lived in New Jersey or nearby states like Kent, Zurisko, Farrington, and Brad Waudby often brought home team-mates who weren't afforded the same geographical luxury. Waudby loaded as many classmates as possible into his Chevy Blazer. Roberts visited with Kent and the Livingstons in south Jersey. Zurisko took home Bo Reynolds, a West Point legacy from Alabama. Josh Davis's roommate was from Wyoming and about half his size. Bernard Gardner was an avid hunter and fisherman and was soon given the nickname "Bean" by a preponderance of classmates for his diminutive size. Gardner was a high school wrestler and sometimes exhibited his mat mentality in the pair's barracks room, jumping atop Davis for no apparent reason.

The introduction to military instruction for Waudby, the team's starting right guard, didn't begin smoothly. In some ways, his first months at Fort Monmouth resembled his baptism to Indian Hills football under Gene Prebola. One NCO, in particular, seemed intent on making Waudby's life miserable. Some fellow prepsters were unsparing in their ridicule of Waudby's size and often told him that he'd never make it out of Fort Monmouth and up to West Point. It was more than Waudby could handle, and he was ready to resign during the first semester. He contacted Rutgers and asked if any football scholarships were available for the coming academic year. It didn't help to hear, like Kent did, about high school friends enjoying their weekends at their colleges while he often spent Saturday nights catching up on homework. Waudby's father wanted his son to make his own decision about sticking it out at Fort Monmouth but was dead set against a transfer. He told young Brad not to make a decision while he was angry. Waudby typed a letter of resignation and printed it. Bo Reynolds, a defensive lineman who'd dreamed of playing for Army's Black Knights as a child, roomed across the hall and dropped by just as Waudby's letter came off the printer. With the ink barely dry, Reynolds read the letter, ripped it into small pieces, and yelled, "Bullshit! Screw those people saying that shit!"

Twenty-seven of the prep school students, or almost 12 percent, were female. They were received by their male counterparts with varying degrees of acceptance, skepticism, or contempt. Skepticism and contempt were fueled when one of the young women became emotional when failing to complete routine tasks, such as immediately learning where the student's barracks room was located. An officer would quickly spit out the floor and room numbers outside the barracks with a cadet candidate expected to race to said room, drop off belongings, and report back that the room was secure. If that wasn't performed correctly, the student's entire company dropped for punitive pushups. For one female, the pressure of the situation grew exponentially when she was unable to do that multiple times. She broke into tears, only drifting further from the proper reply, leading to more pushups.

At West Point, Bob Sutton's 1999 Black Knights stood at 3–4 with four games remaining—including both of their clashes that would help decide the Commander-in-Chief's Trophy, which Army had not won since the 1996 season that concluded with the team's most recent bowl trip. The closing stretch got off to a discouraging start; the Cadets' 28–0 loss at Air Force was their third straight in the series with the Falcons and their second shutout defeat in three weeks. The following Saturday at Memphis, Army crossed midfield only once in the second half and fell 14–10 to clinch Sutton's third consecutive losing finish. Next up was the Cadets' final appearance of the season at Michie Stadium, a 26–14 loss to Houston. That left the 100th meeting with Navy, at the Vet in Philadelphia. Navy sophomore quarterback Brian Madden, who grew up in the shadow of Fort Sill in Oklahoma, torched Army for 177 rushing yards in the Midshipmen's 19–9 victory. The Cadets aided Navy's cause with four turnovers.

Following the season-ending loss, Sutton and athletic director Rick Greenspan were among the West Point athletic personnel who spent that Saturday night at a Marriott in downtown Philadelphia, a long-standing academy practice. The next morning, Greenspan called Sutton and asked him to come see him in his suite. Sutton dutifully complied, finding his boss surrounded by his family in his accommodations. Greenspan recognized the environment wasn't conducive for his conversation topic and told Sutton that they should go for a walk. On a nearby street corner, Greenspan told Sutton that he was making a coaching change. The dismissal was announced from West Point the following day. Sutton's nine seasons at the Army helm ranked second in academy history to the eighteen of the vaunted Earl "Red" Blaik, which included the three consecutive national championships from 1944–1946. When detailing rationale for Sutton's dismissal, Greenspan went beyond the boilerplate lamentation of too many losing seasons and the just-completed campaign having spiraled toward the finish with losses in the final four games. He cited Army's offense in particular as being unsatisfactory. Of the 114 teams that competed in Division I-A football in 1999, the Cadets ranked 78th in total offense despite a rushing attack that ranked 5th thanks to the option alignment. Greenspan said he wasn't ready to name Sutton's replacement, that he had a "number" of people to consider and the academy had already visited with "some people."

The following week, Army's search was over, with a predictable result. The relatively new athletic director had hired the coach from his previous stop, having already witnessed the coach's success first hand. Rick Greenspan and Todd Berry were vocationally reunited. Berry, a thirty-nine-year-old Oklahoman, was a second-generation football coach who dramatically improved Illinois State's fortunes over three seasons. His 1998 Redbirds qualified for the I-AA playoffs. His fourth and last Illinois State team returned to the playoffs and reached the semifinals, losing to Georgia Southern—coached by Paul Johnson, who left for Navy two years later.

At Berry's introductory media session at West Point, he certainly exuded confidence ("I expect in the near future that we will be 11–0.") and professed to embrace what made Army different from most I-A rebuilding challenges ("I like thinking about the ideals of West Point. I want to be around people that think big, that dream big, that aspire to be all that they can be."). Greenspan lauded the new hire's charismatic personality. Lieutenant General Christman spoke of Berry's absolute love for the academy, adding that the new coach impressed everyone involved in the interview process. That process included a formal dinner at the superintendent's home with the most recent of West Point's three Heisman Trophy recipients, 1958 honoree Pete Dawkins, among the guests. Berry located his assigned seat and spotted a Post-It note affixed to his plate. It read "BEAT NAVY." Berry's hiring certainly didn't surprise Navy's coaching staff. During the season, some of the Middies' assistant coaches received phone calls from members of Berry's Illinois State staff asking what it was like to coach at a military academy.

Early on in Berry's stint at Army, he let it be known the offense would look considerably different; anyone familiar with his teams at Illinois State would have already realized that. His offenses would line up with only one running back behind the quarterback and would pass much more often than Army fans had seen for more than ten years in the option attacks used by Sutton and predecessor Jim Young. It would be possession passing; football's trendy West Coast offense had, at least in some fashion, arrived at West Point. Some Army fans welcomed the transition. While Army had been one of the top rushing teams in Division I-A under Young and Sutton, those overall offenses—running and passing—rarely ranked among the division's best because they were one-dimensional. The exception was the '96 squad that played in the Independence Bowl in Shreveport, Louisiana, ranking 17th in total offense. Such was also typically the case with the other option programs. Navy topped the nation in rushing in 1999 but was 46th in total offense. Some Army fans eagerly anticipated an offense that was more exciting than the one that often plunged into the line looking to gain four yards; one that could produce more winning seasons. Berry also touted a defensive remake, using four linemen and four linebackers that would often stunt and blitz to increase pressure on the opposing quarterback. His remarks came across to at least some as belittling the previous regimes that had produced bowl teams. Greenspan had a remake of his own in the works, a new branding for the athletic program in general. That summer, the academy unveiled a new official nickname; Black Knights would replace Cadets.

With Berry's hiring, Ryan Kent realized his football future at West Point would probably look greatly different. During spring drills at the prep school, he worked with one of the assistant coaches whose background included time at an NCAA Division III program that ran four- and five-receiver sets. Kent left Fort Monmouth confident that he was as prepared as possible for the challenge of fitting into Berry's offensive scheme. The coaching change concerned Jeremy Campbell, who had enjoyed a standout season. That Campbell had even signed with Army had pleasantly surprised Sutton, given the high-profile schools who recruited him. Sutton communicated with Campbell soon after his firing and made sure the linebacker was aware he had football options other than West Point. Campbell got in touch with Rutgers, which had recruited him out of high school, and arranged to transfer there for the 2000–01 academic year. He planned to remain at Fort Monmouth for the balance of the 1999–2000 school year. But after his signing with Rutgers was reported by local media in early February, the situation at the prep school became too awkward for him to stay.

Berry and his staff were just getting settled in at the academy when the defensive line coach who followed him there, Chris Wilson, took a job at Colorado. (Wilson was on the Philadelphia Eagles that won Super Bowl LII in February 2018). To fill the vacancy, Berry contacted the man who'd hired him as an offensive assistant in 1991 at Southeast Missouri State. John Mumford was recently let go following nine years as head coach at "See-Mo," and had decided to leave coaching at least temporarily, taking a job in radio sales right there in the school's hometown of Cape Girardeau. That professional decision afforded Mumford the opportunity to spend more time with wife Leslie and their three daughters following 20 seasons in coaching. In late May 2000, the Mumfords and some friends were days away from taking a 10-hour round trip to the Indianapolis 500 when Leslie marched out of the house and across the backyard to where John was grilling chicken. She shoved the phone toward his chest and quietly but sternly said, "Todd Berry's on the phone." So much for the radio business; the morning after the race, Mumford was off for West Point. Back in 1991, he'd hired Berry as his offensive coordinator at Southeast Missouri to replace future NFL head coach Marty Mornhinweg. Mumford liked Berry's attention to detail, his passion for the game, and his passion for the profession. Berry arrived at Cape Girardeau on a fast track. He worked for Mumford only the one season, entering Division I-A as East Carolina's offensive coordinator the following year.

John and Leslie Mumford met in junior high . . . sort of. He played basketball for Lawrence (Kansas) South Junior High, and she was a cheerleader at West Junior High. He made a mental note to introduce himself once they both reached the same high school. They were married soon after graduating from Pittsburg (Kansas) State, where he lettered three seasons as a tight end. Aside from wanting to get right back into college coaching, Mumford was intrigued by the prospect of working at the academy. He figured he'd be coaching a special type of athlete, highly motivated. The three Mumford girls—high school freshman Jenna, sixth-grader Meghan, and third-grader Lauren—didn't initially share their father's enthusiasm for relocation to West Point and its adjoining small town, Highland Falls. Their on-post residence, while quaint, didn't quite match their house back in Missouri, and prompted one of the girls to blurt out, "That's it?" Mumford continued to sell them on the high quality of individual who would essentially be their neighbors. "They'll be your mentors. They'll be your sports coaches," he said. On one of the family's first trips into Highland Falls for dinner, the quiet of the evening was disrupted by a group of local kids walking down the main drag banging on signs and cussing up a storm. Meghan turned to her father and said, "Four thousand of America's finest, huh, Dad?"

It wasn't long before Berry and some assistants traveled to Fort Monmouth to meet with the prep school players whom they had inherited. In any college athletic program, the athletes should be aware that a new coach won't necessarily embrace them. In such situations, some coaches have bluntly told the player or signee that his or her chances of playing aren't good, that backing out of the commitment and finding another school would be in their best interest. It can be a callous undertaking; a coach going so far as to say the player not only won't get into games but won't even be used in practices. An athletic scholarship is typically thought to extend for an entire college career, but it's really a business arrangement that's subject to annual review and potential renewal. Berry gathered the 1999 Fort Monmouth football players in an auditorium. He told them that he really needed them, that they shouldn't worry about the coaching change. Bo Reynolds looked at a teammate sitting next him and wanted to say, "Wanna bet?"

Chapter Three

"I'D REALLY LIKE TO PLAY ON A NATIONAL STAGE"

Peter Stewart spent his first two football seasons at Nimitz High School, located toward the northern end of Houston's vast school system, on junior varsity playing multiple positions on the offensive line. Stewart was finally situated at left guard as a junior to begin the 1998 season, though he wasn't getting much playing time. He was sent back to the JV team to receive more reps, a demotion that he hardly appreciated. The '98 Nimitz Cougars varsity roared through the regular season with only one loss, winning a district championship for the first time in the school's 20-year history. Nimitz boasted one of the best high school offenses in the area, led by running back Quentin Griffin (who later played at the University of Oklahoma and in the NFL). The Cougars were coached by Burnis Simon, who'd played for Jackie Sherrill at Texas A&M in the early 1980s. Simon employed aspects of Sherrill's coaching philosophy, including a desire for the players to treat each other as family. "You guys can't win until you love each other," Simon recalled Sherrill saying. The Cougars often held team meals and did other activities together. This familial atmosphere sometimes resulted in tough love, which Simon dispensed with the help of a wooden paddle.

Nimitz's dream season in 1998 came to an abrupt end in the first round of the playoffs, losing 35–7 to Humble in a game that followed a bizarre set of circumstances. It rained heavily in Houston that day, so much so that classes at Nimitz were cancelled. Simon wanted to reschedule the game to another day, but his request was denied. Some Nimitz players had difficulty simply reporting to school for the bus trip to the stadium. The convoy left 90 minutes late, the team arrived about 15 minutes before the scheduled kickoff, and the start of the game was pushed back by 30 minutes. By halftime, the Cougars trailed 28–0.

Big things were expected from Nimitz in 1999, when Stewart made the varsity as a senior, though some of the '98 stars were then on college rosters. Instead, the Cougars struggled through a 3–7 campaign that left them far from postseason qualification. Stewart played guard and center and was named to the all-district first team. There was little interest in him among college football programs, probably because he was a 230-pound lineman; the average lineman in the district weighed 260. Stewart checked out some Division II and III programs and took a visit to D-III Trinity University in San Antonio. A private school, Trinity would have been a terrific academic choice. But as a member of Division III, the institution didn't offer athletic scholarships, and the tuition would have likely taxed the budget of the Stewart family; Peter being the third of five children. He'd long been a fan of Texas A&M football and considered walking on with the Aggies. Grades likely weren't an issue; mother Nancy spent her entire working life as an elementary school teacher, and father Pete's time in academia included being principal of a middle school. Stewart entered high school with the goal of earning four years of straight A's and fell short with a B in Chemistry. His senior class rank was fourth among 435. In December 1998, neighbor Gene Green, who happened to be a US Congressman, asked Stewart if he'd be interested in attending one of the military academies; Stewart respectfully said that wasn't for him.

Signing day 2000 came, and only three Cougars signed. Stewart wasn't one of them, continuing to mull his options. The day after he took a school trip to Austin to participate in a youth government activity, a friend told him that an assistant football coach from West Point had visited Nimitz the previous day and asked about him. That was John Bond, Army's newly hired offensive coordinator under Todd Berry. Bond returned to Nimitz the following week and met with multiple Cougars football players, and Stewart agreed to visit West Point. Michael Brewster, a mercurial running back at 5-foot-5, was also invited to consider Army football but declined. Stewart, born and reared in south Texas, was startled by February temperatures at the academy. Still, he was enamored with West Point and with what Berry said about the possibility of playing in an offense that resembled what his Nimitz Cougars ran. While enamored, Stewart wasn't ready to commit to joining the Army football program before he returned to the warmth of Houston.

Stewart was still leaning toward West Point a few weeks later when he and a classmate were headed toward the Astrodome to take in an evening of the Houston Rodeo and Livestock Show, which ran for three weeks. This was a huge date on the Stewart family calendar. They would often attend more than a dozen performances annually, and Pete was a member of the rodeo's organizing committee for years. (The event includes more than ropin' and steer rasslin'. The musical acts that performed in 2000 included Merle Haggard, Willie Nelson, and Rod Stewart.) Peter was driving to the dome when his cellphone showed a call from West Point, and he pulled off the freeway. It was John Bond again. If Bond didn't demand an answer from Stewart right then, he certainly came close to doing so. Stewart provided the response that Bond sought; he'd be a Black Knight—and give his country five years of active-duty military service after graduation. Soon after, like all of the other high school students who earned acceptance to the United States Military Academy at West Point, Stewart was mailed an attractive plaque to commemorate the occasion.

The tuition-free education was the primary motivation for Stewart. Of the five Stewart siblings, it's worth noting that Nos. 4 and 5 were born within a minute of each other under perilous circumstances when Stewart was about three years old. Patrick and Anna arrived three months prematurely, and each was hospitalized for months before coming home. The twins initially had problems with their lungs, and Anna had multiple surgeries on her eyes. Nancy Stewart brought little Peter along to the neo-natal nursery, where he would sit on a stool and look in on his little brother and sister. As Stewart grew up with two older sisters and eventually two younger siblings, he quickly established an ability to attract attention and mark his territory—even if that sometimes antagonized his older sisters. Stewart became extremely active in sports, seemingly always with some kind of ball. And he grew. By the time he entered Nimitz High, he was built to be a lineman, though a relatively small one. Stewart had no real appetite for the military when he committed to West Point, but his younger brother did. Patrick had given up football in the seventh grade after the first practice, was steered toward his school's officer training corps and loved it. Here was a future West Point cadet being schooled in the art of facing movement by a younger sibling.

* * *

Video viewing for young Brian and Scott Hill during the early 1990s in the living room of their home in Port Orange, Florida, wasn't always titles like *Fievel Goes West* or *All Dogs Go to Heaven*. Fourth-grader Brian and third-grader Scott were glued to footage from recent games played by their rival football teams in the pee-wee division of Central Florida's Pop Warner League. Their father, Tom—who played linebacker at Virginia Tech during the early 1970s—showed the boys their opponents' tendencies. Tom served as an assistant coach. Since he was already going to review the tapes in that capacity, he might as well have Brian and Scott watch, too. The Hills weren't the only family on the team to engage in such activity. Teammate Kent Magueri, a year older than Brian, sometimes came over to watch, and some of the film sessions were held at his house.

When Hill entered Spruce Creek High as a freshman in 1996, he joined a football program coming off an 0–10 varsity finish. He helped the freshman team to six consecutive wins and was promoted to the varsity for the last five games of the season. Alas, the varsity Hawks again finished 0–10. Spruce Creek's football fortunes began to improve in 1997 with the hiring of Rocky Yocam as head coach. Yocam was a familiar name amid the high school football community in the Daytona Beach area, having won a state championship during his 13 seasons coaching at Seabreeze High. One of Yocum's first decisions upon his arrival was to develop a better working relationship between football and the school's successful weight-lifting team, which Hill was also a member of. The lifting team was coached by Lane Lowrey, who was also the team's defensive coordinator. During lifting meets, Hill became acquainted with a member of the team at nearby New Smyrna Beach High who was a year ahead of him in school, a heavyweight named Josh Davis.

Yocum adopted the Iowa Hawkeyes' logo, in Spruce Creek's orange and black, and printed team T-shirts that proclaimed, "Things Have Changed." But little or nothing changed in Spruce Creek's 1997 opener, at least according to the scoreboard; crosstown-rival Atlantic won 43–0. But the second week brought to town Orlando Oak Ridge, a playoff team during the previous season. The Hawks fell behind 14–0 before returning a blocked punt for a touchdown and stunned Oak Ridge 22–14 to end the 21-game losing streak. Things *had* changed; Hill and the previously lowly Hawks finished 5–5. They became a playoff team in his junior season, a first for the 23-year-old school, going 8–2 during the regular season with six shutouts. When Hill was a senior, Spruce Creek won its first district championship and took a 9–0 record into its season finale. He missed that game after hurting an ankle the previous week when tackled after he made an interception, and Spruce Creek lost to New Smyrna 14–7.

Those film sessions were still part of the Hill routine when the boys were in high school; the boys' mother, Nancy, did the filming. Brian got to where he'd follow up the screening in the living room by taking the tapes into his bedroom to watch again on his TV and recall what his father had emphasized. The family's pigskin devotion was displayed in the 2000 Spruce Creek yearbook on the page devoted to the Hills' celebration of their new graduate. "First down of your life into the second quarter" was the sendoff message. There was a photo of little Brian posed with "Buzz," the mascot at Georgia Tech. Hill's maternal grandfather, Phil Upchurch, played football for Tech's Yellow Jackets, and the Hills lived in Atlanta until the late '80s.

Hill earned second-team all-area honors and played in the Central Florida All-Star Game that also featured DeLand High quarterback Craig Candeto, who'd committed to play for Navy. Hill wasn't recruited by the state's three most prestigious college football programs—Florida, Florida State, and Miami. Academic performance certainly wasn't an issue given his 3.9 grade point average. Georgia Tech, the program that he idolized since childhood, indicated he wasn't fast enough. He considered walking on at

Virginia Tech, where his father played, and probably could have received a football scholarship following his freshman season. He talked with representatives from the then-burgeoning programs at South Florida and Central Florida about similar arrangements, along with Duke and Wake Forest. Furman and Georgia Southern in Division I-AA made scholarship offers. Then, an Army assistant arrived at Spruce Creek saying he'd heard that the Hawks had a great linebacker. Soon after, Todd Berry became the only college head coach who traveled to Spruce Creek to visit him. Berry made an offer on the spot. The stunned senior said he'd talk it over with his parents.

Among those who weighed in on Hill's West Point opportunity was Lane Lowrey, who considered Hill his defensive captain, a player who seemingly always did the right thing. Lowrey was also proud of Hill's performance with the lifting team. Lowrey told the senior that he'd never heard of anyone who graduated from a service academy and wasn't successful in life. Hill had one more official recruiting visit remaining and traveled to West Point on a military aircraft while his parents followed along commercially. It was Hill's first exposure, literally, to snow and real winter weather; he visited at the same time as Peter Stewart. West Point made its offer, and Brian told his father, "The Furmans and Georgia Southerns are fine. But, Dad, I'd really like to play on a national stage."

"Well, if that's what you want to do," Tom said, "this is a tremendous offer."

Brian didn't reply; the next morning, he told his father, "I'm going to West Point." Hill accepting the chance to play college football fulfilled his dream, as well as dreams for him shared by his father and grandfather. On signing day, he was reminded by a sportswriter from the *Daytona Beach News-Journal* that his old football and lifting opponent at New Smyrna, Josh Davis, had signed with Army the previous year and was spending the 1999–2000 school year at the academy's prep school. Hill traveled to West Point again before the end of his senior year to watch Army's spring game. There he met up with two Spruce Creek alums who were playing football about an hour east of the academy at Western Connecticut State—his former Pop Warner teammate, Kent Magueri, and Tarek Reslan, both older than Hill.

The 1999 prep school players came up from Fort Monmouth for the game, and Hill was reintroduced to Josh Davis.

* * *

The photos taken to celebrate Clint Woody's high school graduation in the western North Carolina hamlet of Hayesville in 2000 included a shot of the proud grad cradling an infant girl. That was Megan, the youngest of Woody's six younger siblings. It's difficult to not imagine "The Waltons" come to life amid the family's vast acreage spread across the Blue Ridge Mountains only a few miles north of the Georgia line. Whether playing outside the five-bedroom home that members of the Woody family built or visiting nearby relatives who owned 80 acres, there was plenty of room to play paintball or hunt ground hogs. The Woodys' mode of transportation was a full-sized van, and Clint's career as an officer unofficially began as a young teen when assigning seats for family trips.

Woody's first athletic love was baseball. He was a catcher while in grade school and, like many boys who grew up within a few hours' drive of Atlanta, idolized the Braves' Dale Murphy. But squatting behind the plate became problematic when he grew to be 6-foot-5 in high school. Conversely, that was a terrific size for a wide receiver on the Hayesville High Yellow Jackets. Hayesville played in the smallest of the state's high school enrollment classifications and wore black-and-gold uniforms that were amazingly similar to those worn then by Army's football team. Woody was serious about school, serious about his job at the local hardware store's lumber yard, and serious about playing sports, participating in one each season. On the sidelines during football games, he often paced by himself with his arms folded, pondering how to capitalize on the Jackets' opportunity at hand. At Doc Sellers' hardware store, Sellers could often depart early and leave the lumber yard under Woody's supervision. Woody was fanatical about daily attendance at school. Such scholastic commitment ran in the family; his father, Denny, didn't miss a day from kindergarten through 12th grade and was rewarded after high school graduation with a new car. Clint's perfect attendance streak ran out around Valentine's Day of his senior year, when he became physically spent during basketball season and had to miss a few days. In the closing seconds of his hardwood finale, he dunked for the first time—possibly coerced by the prospect of a $50 "inducement" from his Aunt Clara, who reportedly took up a collection among family members to see him finally jam one home.

Woody graduated with a 4.0 GPA, was in the school's 1200+ SAT club, and was the male selection for "Ideal Seniors" in the Hayesville yearbook. Earning a college scholarship was his goal from the time that he realized his family could be footing the bill for numerous college tuitions. Woody didn't think he was capable of playing college football until he was encouraged during his junior year by assistant coach Barry Owens, who'd coached a then-active NFL player at the time and told Woody he had the height to play "at the next level." Woody wanted to major in engineering and play football. That made Clemson, located about 80 miles away, naturally attractive. He attended a North Carolina State football camp during the summer before his senior year; the receivers were shown plenty of film of Torry Holt, the former N.C. State star who had recently been drafted by the NFL's St. Louis Rams. One of the State assistants working the camp complimented Woody after making a difficult catch and said, "Maybe we'll see you in the future." That Wolfpack staff was fired at season's end.

Woody was intrigued by the recruiting letter that he received from Army, began researching West Point and talked about the possibility of attending the academy with his family. His parents mentioned the prestige of being a West Point graduate and the career opportunities that would follow the post-graduate active military commitment. And there was the free education. Woody decided to take a recruiting trip to West Point following his last high school football season, accompanied by his father. They flew into Newark, New Jersey, and shared a van to West Point with Peter Stewart. Clint was awestruck by the academy, and Denny was impressed by Todd Berry as the two ate breakfast. Clint applied to only one other school, Clemson, but had his heart set on returning to the banks of the Hudson to spend the next four years. The prospect of military service was tucked far in the back of his mind, as it often is with graduating seniors eyeing an academy appointment in peacetime. At Hayesville High's post-season football banquet, it was announced that Woody would attend Army with the US government covering the entire expense. He received a standing ovation.

Chapter Four

"IT'S RAINING ON YOUR R-DAY"

Monday, June 29, 2000, found 1,200 young men and women gathering in the west stands of Michie Stadium at 6:30 a.m. along with family and friends beneath what slowly developed into brilliant morning sunshine. They hoped to return to the football field in May 2004 to be handed their diplomas, the culmination of 47 months of intense academic instruction plus sophisticated military training. Such daydreaming would have been predictable, but the "new cadets," as they were referred as, would have been better served to simply concentrate on what lay ahead that day. It was Reception Day. R-Day. The first day of West Point's version of summer orientation.

The din of pleasant chatter involving the would-be students and their guests came to an abrupt halt when one of the upperclass West Point cadets who was supervising the day's events announced, "I will now ask parents to prepare their final goodbyes. You will be moving out in 90 seconds." The cadet then looked down at his watch, as if to reinforce what he'd just announced. A progression of handshakes, hugs, tears, and all-out wails soon followed. Nancy Hill's goodbye to Brian was about the hardest thing that she ever had to do. She was intensely devoted to her children. She worked in the front office at Spruce Creek High while her children were there, often wearing her two sons' football jerseys and continued to work there while battling hepatitis. As Brian descended the stadium steps, her eyes were glued to him. He and all of the other newcomers crossed the field single file and eventually were too far away for any of the guests to see any longer. The phrase "final goodbye" applied only to that morning, but Nancy felt like she was saying goodbye to Brian forever. The mother of Thomas Roberts, one of the quarterback recruits, kissed him goodbye and said she would return to West Point for only one reason—his graduation.

The students were loaded onto buses, told to cup their hands and—above all—not to speak unless spoken to. They were taken to Thayer Hall for the beginning of 12 hours that provided a preview of what the next four years would entail—for those who would remain at West Point until May 2004. The cadet hopefuls were run through a series of stations for picking up or dropping off, reporting under the watchful eyes and brusque commands of the cadet cadre—decked out in white shirts and gray pants—to be measured, weighed, and assessed in multiple ways. They picked up their academy-issue shoes, socks, T-shirts, shorts and, where applicable, eyeglasses (Clark Kent style). They were adorned with two cardboard tags—one as a means of identification, the other containing a checklist for the day's many stops. The males dropped off the majority of their hair, courtesy of West Point's efficient barber brigade. Males and females alike dropped off any cash that exceeded $40 with the academy's treasurer office. They were checked for tattoos and body piercings that might be an indication of political leanings that didn't mesh with academy values.

Thayer Hall is one of the primary instruction buildings at West Point, its eastern side towering over the Hudson River. Like the Thayer Award that Douglas MacArthur received in 1962, it was named for Sylvanus Thayer, a brigadier general and the fifth person to hold the office of superintendent as ultimate authority over the academy. Thayer was West Point's "supe" from 1817 to 1833 and is considered the father of the academy; his name also graces the Thayer Hotel, which has stood just inside the academy's main gate since 1926. Of his many accomplishments while serving as superintendent, Thayer is best known for his approach to classroom instruction that has come to be known as the "Thayer method," and his devotion to the academy's strict code of conduct. At the core of the Thayer method is the philosophy that the student is essentially in charge of his or her own learning instead of an instructor lecturing and the student passively absorbing. The philosophy works hand in glove with the development of young leaders and, ultimately, officers. Thayer's commitment to a code of conduct evolved to a formal statement established in 1947 by the academy's superintendent, then General Maxwell Taylor. It states that a cadet will not lie, cheat, or steal—or tolerate those who do. The final portion of the code can be the most vexing for cadets to abide by, essentially agreeing to turn in peers whom they know to have violated West Point rules.

There was one more important piece of business to attend to on R-Day, conducted in the 4,500-seat auditorium within Eisenhower Hall that accommodated them all. Each was handed a copy of the official academy commitment form—the Oath of Allegiance. Lest any of them had second thoughts about their ability to embrace the West Point culture and make it through the next four years, it would have been the time to speak up. The form, a contract, detailed what would be expected of the cadet during his or her West Point stay and for eight years following graduation—five years' active military service plus three more years in the army reserves. The form stated that any unseemly conduct by a cadet, even off the academy grounds, could result in military punishment. The cadet confirmed that he or she is single—no West Point cadet can be married—and didn't have custody of a child. The cadet would uphold the US Constitution and follow the academy's policies and procedures.

The new cadets were then taken to Central Area, a paved square amid the campus where cadets would gather each weekday to begin the day once the school year began. They stood, wearing the curious combination of white T-shirt, black shorts, high black socks, and black shoes. Cory Wallace, a recruited defensive end from Gillette, Wyoming, tried to accept his new environment but considered what he was wearing and thought, "This makes no sense." It was in Central Area where the newcomers became acquainted with the cadet supervisors known as the Cadets in the Red Sash. Much of the rest of the day resembled a high-anxiety game of Simon Says. The upperclassmen shouted various commands and questions. Woe upon the new cadet who was tardy in replying or, worse yet, provided either an inadequate response or nothing at all. "Do *not* move! Do *not* smile! New cadet, step up to my line!

Not *on* my line! Not *over* my line! Not *behind* my line! Step *up* to my line!" Brian Hill quickly understood that the churlish critique, while screamed in his face, shouldn't be taken personally.

Peter Stewart occupied a position in one of the last R-Day groups to run through—literally in some instances—the various stations. His group was so bottlenecked at the rear that he ended the day lacking such cadet candidate essentials as socks, underwear, and the robe that's worn to and from the barrack showers. It took three weeks for Stewart to acquire everything that he was supposed to receive on R-Day. Until then, he resorted to borrowing the far-too-short robe from his summer roommate and fellow football recruit, Adam Rafalski.

Those who arrived on R-Day following a year at Fort Monmouth were typically amused to watch those who came directly from high school be jolted and emotionally jostled by the constant yelling and harping from the cadre and the Cadet in the Red Sash. No one had to instruct the prep schoolers how to salute, left face, right face, and do it again and again and again. And since prep schoolers also had already received the required inoculations, Ryan Kent finished the opening check-in relatively early and enjoyed some downtime in his new barracks room. That actually worked against him when his squad leader lost track of him and forgot to have him report for the closing event of the day, the cadet parade. Kent barely made it to formation in time.

As the cadet candidates hustled to line up for the parade, the morning's sunshine had long given way to an overcast sky and, eventually, rain showers. A member of the cadre felt compelled to say, "New cadets, it's raining on your R-Day. Do you know what that means? Your class is going to war." Within the immediacy of R-Day, it also meant the parade was cancelled. The class crest would feature a storm cloud and a lightning bolt along with the class motto: "For Country and Corps." The class mottos typically rhymed with each class' graduation year.

R-Day was merely the warm-up act for the six-week test of physical and psychological acclimatization that would begin the following day at 5 a.m. Fermented to its simplest form, Beast Barracks separated chaff from wheat, designed to make the newcomers react to extreme and repeated pressures.

For all of the intensity, hazing—once considered an essential element of West Point preparation—had been prohibited three years earlier. During the coming weeks, the new cadets pulled themselves across a one-rope bridge using only a harness attached to the rope. They did orienteering and night patrols, learned first-aid training and how to use a bayonet. They climbed mountains and then repelled back down. They learned marksmanship and land navigation. They were exposed to tear gas. And there was marching. Plenty of marching. Rain, shine, whatever. The first half of Beast included jaunts of 3 miles, then 5, then 10. During the summer session's second half, the marches covered 6 miles, 8 miles, 12 miles, and 15 miles. The amount of marching, walking, and just plain standing on asphalt in the academy-issued leather-bottomed shoes caused Clint Woody's feet to swell and ache.

Another important aspect of West Point culture is that no cadet makes it through alone; a popular academy phrase is "cooperate to graduate." During Beast, new cadets are typically paired to team someone coming straight from high school with a prep school grad. Brian Hill's Beast roommate was Anthony Miller, another football player. While each cadet candidate was issued a book of standard operating procedures that detailed how to best organize his or her room, closet, desktop, etc., Miller wasted little time in tutoring Hill on the basics of military decorum. He showed him how to correctly fold his shirts, how to shine his shoes. Miller explained what rules should definitely be followed and which ones could be skirted. From the Washington, DC, suburb of Temple Hills, Maryland, Miller was a small, quick wide receiver, one of Ryan Kent's favorite targets at Fort Monmouth. He graduated from a private school basketball powerhouse, DeMatha Catholic, arriving there late in his high school experience after his single mother was finally able to fulfill her son's wishes. Miller was far from an elite football prospect, but DeMatha football coach Bill McGregor recognized that Miller was a solid youngster and tried his best to land an athletic scholarship for him. McGregor's rolodex included Army recruiting coordinator John Bonamego, who agreed to visit DeMatha during spring 1999 though the school held no formal spring football practice. Bonamego was impressed when watching Miller during the informal workouts. It appeared Miller was always the first in line, and he stood out performing a four-cone running drill. Bonamego added Miller's name to his list of prospects to receive West Point football mailings. Soon after, he gave the academy's admission director an impassioned recommendation for Miller's acceptance within West Point's minority admissions program since Bonamego didn't have any football slots left: "I like the kid. He can be a leader. He's a hard worker. He's earned the respect of everyone. If he doesn't make it in football, he'll still be a great officer."

Ryan Kent was paired with Zachary Kaye, a placekicker from the University of Alabama's hometown of Tuscaloosa. At 5-foot-4 and about 150 pounds, Kaye was named to the all-state first team as a junior at Tuscaloosa Central High School for Alabama's largest enrollment classification and then broke the state record for point-after kicks as a senior by hitting all 76 of his attempts. Kaye was not only dependably accurate but also a threat from distance, having kicked a 51-yard field goal. His father was from Kansas City, a colonel in special forces when he retired from the US Army. While the Kayes weren't the most zealous of Crimson Tide football fans, Zac and his father attended a couple of home games each fall, and Zac dreamed of running out onto the field at Bryant-Denny Stadium.

Kaye's high school football pedigree was greater than that of fellow kicker Anthony Zurisko, but even he was left to choose among walk-on offers if he wanted to play for a Division I-A program. Kaye had scheduled visits to Alabama, Mississippi, Mississippi State, and South Carolina—all members of the Southeastern Conference (SEC). He planned to kick on Saturdays and enjoy undergrad life much of the rest of the week amid the southeast's near-religious devotion to college football. There was another important reason why attending Alabama was a priority. Kaye was dating a Central High grad two years' his senior, Ann Cox, who was enrolled at Bama. Their relationship was still relatively informal—no engagement—but the plan was certainly to continue seeing each other as they attended the same college. That was before Army assistant coach Dennis Therrell visited Central's campus and asked Kaye if he would take an official visit to West Point. Given Kaye's military lineage, he accepted the invitation. By trip's end, he was enthralled and decided to change his young life's course.

Anthony Miller proved to be engaging to his fellow newcomers in other ways. Sue Petroff, recruited from her Connecticut high school to be an Army diver, struggled at rifle qualification—hitting targets at 300 meters—despite having fired shotguns with her family since she was eight years old. Just about everything at Manchester High School, just east of Hartford, had come easy to Petroff. The suddenly adversarial relationship with a government-issued firearm had her atypically unnerved. Petroff and the rest of her company broke for lunch in a nearby pavilion. She found a cool spot in the shade, sat on the concrete and tried as best she could to put the pending rifle crisis out of her mind at least long enough to somewhat enjoy her pre-packaged, military-style lunch, or MRE (meals ready to eat). Miller recognized that something was bothering Petroff. He sat next to her, told her a few silly jokes to take her mind off her immediate plight, and succeeded in putting her as ease. How much Miller's intercession contributed to Petroff passing rifle qualification will never be known, but she certainly gave him immense credit. She added an ally among her fellow cadet candidates, a valuable asset as the newcomers would need to band together and depend on each other in the wake of the daily challenges that were barked at them by the academy's upperclass cadets.

Making the transition from high school football standout to college rookie is rarely easy, and the degree of difficulty of doing so at Army is compounded by Beast Barracks. Virtually every new cadet will experience significant weight loss during Beast. For a football hopeful, that can make earning a roster spot increasingly difficult. Incoming cadets who were recruited to participate in varsity intercollegiate athletic are excused from Beast Barracks for an hour or two once or twice a week to take part in athletic drills. That isn't well received by the other newcomers; thus often begins a stratification in which "mainstream" cadets bristle at what they perceive to be favored-nation status that's bestowed upon Army athletes. The perception isn't considered unfair by the athletes themselves. Many of them rejoice at the opportunity to return to the "real world"—though it involves strenuous workouts with their teams—rather than devoting all of their summer to marches and an array of military activities.

* * *

Cory Wallace wanted to follow high school graduation by enlisting in the Marines, but was coaxed into applying to West Point by his father. Wallace attended Army football camp the previous summer and was told by Bob Sutton: "You're what we're looking for in a lineman." On the second day of Beast, names of football recruits were read off by the squad leaders. Wallace didn't hear his name and assumed he'd simply missed his being called. He mentioned that to the squad leader who read off the list only to be told his name indeed wasn't on it. "There must be some mistake," he said. The squad leader looked again for Wallace's name. There was no mistake; his name wasn't on the list. Wallace looked into the matter and learned his football status had been changed from recruited football player to walk-on. Being a walk-on at a big-name college meant trying to make the team without an athletic scholarship. While that didn't apply to West Point athletics, Wallace recognized that being a football walk-on meant the new coaching staff wasn't counting on him to be a contributor. He began Beast weighing 275 pounds and finished at 225, losing much of his strength.

Football players were also allotted larger meal portions than the other cadets given the rigors of summer football drills. They didn't participate in the final march back from Lake Frederick, leaving Beast Barracks a week earlier than their peers. They *did* make the long march out to Beast's main location, and were accompanied by Todd Berry and his assistant coaches.

The relationship between academy personnel and the athletic coaching staffs can sometimes be onerous, especially when coaches have no military background. Berry wanted to immerse himself and his staff in the West Point experience as much as possible. Later on, he would travel to Fort Bragg, North Carolina, and jump from an airplane (tethered to a member of the elite Golden Knights parachute team), stand at the demilitarized zone that separated the two Koreas, and visit army bases across the continent. Such ventures served to both send a message to West Point staff and Army football players that he wanted to share their experience as much as possible, and so he could speak to recruits and their families with a greater degree of expertise on what would await a young man who considered playing Army football and committing to future military service.

The letter of the law at the academy allowed for a maximum weight of 212 pounds. If Army sports teams were held to that standard, competing in multiple intercollegiate sports would be unrealistic. Brad Waudby was admitted to West Point officially measured at 6-foot-4 and 296 pounds. Taking the APFT for the first time, his run time was more than nine minutes over what was necessary to pass and so was prohibited from partaking of the football team's increased meal portions, the so-called "heavy tables." Waudby was retested a month later and allowed to have a pace man. He ran the two miles in 16:30 to pass the test.

Berry made significant personnel cuts before summer drills had yet reached the midpoint. His approach to the roster differed significantly from what Bob Sutton employed. Sutton typically retained many more players, up to 200, though relatively few would get into varsity games. Most of those who would never see the field were nonetheless enthusiastic about spending years—if not their entire Army football careers—on the scout team, helping to prepare the varsity. Berry wanted a roster size of 110 to 120 players, akin to what his teams would face in Conference USA. Army's decision for the program to be part of the league beginning with the 1998 season was contentious. Army had previously competed as an independent in football while most of its other intercollegiate teams participated in the Patriot League with other institutions in the northeast that shared similar academic profiles. Conference USA offered nothing of the sort. Few of its members mirrored West Point's classroom expectations. What membership in Conference USA did offer was a better chance to play in a bowl, since most postseason games have become contractually bound to specific leagues, and the increased opportunity for the exposure that comes from regular appearances on a conference's television package. Months before the decision was announced to join Conference USA, West Point's understanding was the 1996 team that took a 9–1 record into the Navy game would need to beat the Midshipmen to earn a bowl invitation.

The six weeks of Beast Barracks ended with the long march back to the academy grounds for the parade across West Point's storied Plain on Acceptance Day. About 10 percent of a given incoming West Point class will be long gone from the banks of the Hudson by the time that Beast ends. The newcomers, exhausted but relieved, faced the rest of the cadets and, upon command, became full-fledged members of the Corps of Cadets and joined their new companies that included members of the other three academy academic classes. Were they at Iowa State or Stanford or Syracuse, they would have been known as freshmen. At West Point, they became plebes—short for plebeian, the moniker for those on the lowest societal rung in ancient Rome. Ahead of them were the yearlings or yuks (sophomores), the cows (juniors), and the firsties (seniors).

Acceptance Day provided friends and relatives their first opportunity since R-Day to see their cadets, though there was occasional phone contact during Beast Barracks. Nancy Hill treasured each chance to talk to Brian while he was going through cadet basic training. She would excuse herself from a night out on the chance that he would call. One night, Tom Hill and their other children just returned from dinner when the phone rang, and Nancy eagerly answered. It was Brian. When Tom and Nancy greeted Brian upon the conclusion of Beast Barracks, Tom saw an entirely different person. He saw the difference in Brian's eyes, even in his step. Tom felt like he'd dropped off a kid on R-Day and, only weeks later, was greeting a man.

Chapter Five

"KEPT FINDING WAYS TO SHOOT OURSELVES IN THE FOOT"

West Point, New York, was significant to the nation's military history before the United States Military Academy was founded on a bluff there in 1802. The zigzag of the Hudson River on its eastern banks yielded topography that General George Washington capitalized on during the Revolutionary War, when the British were transporting troops up the Hudson. The river's undulating path created a narrow channel of only a few hundred yards. With the cooperation of a nearby iron works, the continental army procured a huge chain that was transported to the river bank by oxcart and then floated into place across the Hudson aboard fifteen log rafts that were coated with pitch to prevent them from being waterlogged. The chain linked West Point with Constitution Island, in the middle of the Hudson. For the balance of the war, the massive chain was removed when the river froze during the winter and repositioned each spring. The "great chain," as the structure became known, became an efficacious tool to prevent the Redcoats from sailing north from New York City.

Washington and other commanders proposed the establishment of a military academy from the first days of the war. His chief of artillery, General Henry Knox, contended, "officers can never act with confidence until they are masters of their profession." Reasons that made West Point strategic to the fledgling nation's defense likewise made perfect sense when seeking to identify the location for a national military training institution, and the land was purchased by the US government for $11,085. Students were first informally quartered there in 1794, but it was eight years later that President Thomas Jefferson signed legislation on March 16, 1802, that created the academy. With a faculty of two, a graduating class of like number—Joseph Swift and Simon Levy—became the first to be commissioned as second lieutenants the following September from an initial enrollment of 10.

At the conclusion of Beast Barracks 2000, West Point's incoming cadets were assigned to one of the academy's 32 companies, each one overseen by an adult TAC officer and consisting of equal parts from all four academic classes, about 30 students from each. Plebes abided by a set of rules and constraints befitting their place within the West Point food chain as Cadet Private. When walking outside their barracks rooms, they were prohibited from talking, other than to reply to a statement, command, or query from a cadet of higher stature. They could not so much as look to one side or the other outside of their rooms. They were required to cup their hands. Plebes were assigned the menial tasks such as hauling laundry and delivering mail. Before 1964, plebes weren't permitted to leave the academy for Christmas break.

Much of academy life deals with learning how to react to stressful situations, to prepare for far-more-taxing episodes on a battlefield that could mean life or death. That can be difficult for a plebe to appreciate and accept when an upperclassman calls upon one to spout out mundane facts and phrases that are part of Plebe Knowledge. Such as, how many days are left in the academic year, what will be served for lunch that day at Washington Hall, etc. Each freshman is armed with a small book called "Bugle Notes," the unofficial plebe Bible. It contains items of further memorization, such as the academy alma mater, noted quotations, and speeches throughout academy history, songs, trivia and, of course, the honor code. A freshman can be stopped at any time in any place by an upperclassman and presented with the pseudo-pop quiz that is only pass-fail, the latter typically declared in a loud, unsympathetic tone. The best mindset for a plebe to have is to accept that he or she is going to fail, but the goal should be to limit the failures to minor aspects of West Point life and not to repeat those mistakes. The upperclass-men seek for plebes to develop from their missteps. Those who came to West Point from Fort Monmouth again held an advantage when it came to Plebe Knowledge, having a year's head start on learning the contents of "Bugle Notes."

Another example of stress was being assigned five hours of homework in a day that allowed for three hours of study. Mountain Dew, with its sig-nificant caffeine content, was a popular drink at the academy. One plebe reported getting a combined seven hours' sleep on Wednesday, Thursday, and Friday nights one week. That wasn't considered a noble sacrifice at West Point. The cadet's platoon sergeant learned of the unsavory scenario and required the freshman to report to him each morning how much sleep that he received the previous night. The realistic cadet would learn early on that he or she should plan to add Saturday or Sunday to the homework-study time commitment.

West Point instruction falls into four categories: academic, military, physical, and character development. The academic aspect is meant to develop cadets who can integrate knowledge and skills from multiple dis-ciplines and adapt them to an ever-changing world. The military portion is predictably designed to hone skills for developing superior officers. There's the physical emphasis, which was fused with athletic competition during the academy's earliest days. Those three joined beneath the umbrella of character development, the absence of which would render the other skills wasted.

The cadets' weekday began with a wake-up call at 6:30 a.m.; that was another plebe obligation. They vacated their barracks, some of the plebes dutifully standing at attention in the hallways and yelling out the proper uniform of that day. At 6:55, they were neatly lined up outside the mess hall in breakfast formation no matter the weather. Inside the mess hall, all stood behind chairs at their assigned tables until given the command to take their seats; football players sat together during meals. Plebes again performed a useful service, stating what was about to be served. That could often become a verbal version of hopscotch, with a mistake cited by an upperclassman and the first-year student forced to start over.

Classes were held from 7:30 to 4 p.m. Mathematics and engineering have long been the staples of West Point academia. The first electives were made available in 1960, only after years of administrative wrangling. Once classes were finished for the day, the remainder of the afternoon was set aside for athletics. That's when corps squad cadets practiced with their teams. The remainder of the cadets participated in sports on an intramural level. Plebes were required to take a boxing course and a survival swimming program that some described as "plebe drowning."

It's one thing to learn how to swim; it's another to navigate through the water while wearing a full battle uniform and carrying a rifle. Cows and firsties were allowed to stray from the books during the evening hours if they chose, the juniors with access to the Officers' Club and the seniors the Firstie Club. All cadets had to be in their rooms by 10:30. "Taps" was played at 11:30, and lights were to be out at midnight.

Athletics became an academy priority under the 1903 West Point graduate who returned as superintendent in 1919. Brigadier General Douglas MacArthur perceived a deficiency of physical fitness among army officers during World War I. He concluded that diminished their effectiveness in battle and was determined to eliminate that inadequacy at its root—the United States Military Academy. MacArthur was an overall stellar student at West Point who served as First Captain during his firstie year, but he took tremendous pride in his participation in academy athletics. He was one of the football team's managers and played left field on the baseball team.

"Supe" MacArthur was far from the first academy figure with a driving passion to emphasize physical activity. Herman Koehler is considered the father of physical education at West Point. He arrived at the academy in 1885, and soon after instituted mandatory exercise for the plebes, which was later expanded to all four academic classes by President Theodore Roosevelt. During Koehler's time on the Hudson, Army and Navy met for the first time on the football field. During autumn 1890, cadet Dennis Michie organized West Point's first football team, for accepting a challenge from the Navy squad that was in its 10th season. Michie had acquaintances who played football for Navy and was able to arrange the meeting at West Point in part because he knew people in high places; his father, Peter Michie, was the head of the academy's academic board. Michie both played for the team and coached it. West Point students pitched in 52 cents each to cover the Midshipmen's travel expenses.

Army and Navy met only two days after the Middies played Lehigh and lost for the first time in six outings that fall. About one thousand spectators crowded around the makeshift gridiron that was marked off in the southeast corner of West Point's parade ground. The game's most significant occurrence was Navy's fake punt that was run for a touchdown, which exasperated a fair number of onlookers who assumed it was a brazen breach of the rules. Fair or not, Navy dominated play and returned to Annapolis with a 24–0 victory. West Point played its first actual season—more than one game—in 1891 and evened the score with Navy, winning 32–16 at Annapolis. The Army football stadium that was completed in 1924 was named for Michie, who was killed at San Juan Hill in Cuba during the Spanish-American War in 1898.

The last week of Beast Barracks was spent out in the field, sleeping in a tent. What was viewed as essential, hardline training in the development of a military officer wasn't optimum for producing a football player capable of proving his worth for the team that fall. That was certainly the case for Ryan Kent. During summer football drills, his arm strength was depleted and his accuracy inadequate. He struggled to throw a routine spiral, and many of his passes dove aimlessly into the grass. Kent came to the brutal realization that his performance during preseason camp might not be good enough to merit a starting spot on the Woodbury Thundering Herd. He was pleasantly surprised to emerge from preseason camp listed as Army's third-string varsity quarterback behind junior Chad Jenkins and senior Joe Gerena.

Todd Berry was acquainting himself with the entire West Point roster, most of it having been recruited to plug into Bob Sutton's vastly different system. The result was that many of the incoming 2000 Black Knights freshman football players were cut from the program before the varsity opened the season on Labor Day afternoon at Cincinnati, a member of Conference USA. The Army media guide going into the season didn't account for all of the freshmen in the program, but did list 14 "Plebe Prospects." Brian Hill and Clint Woody made that list, as did Zachary Kaye, who was included as both a kicker and a wide receiver and generously listed at 5-foot-8. Kaye and Anthony Zurisko faced uphill battles to win time in Army's kicking game as freshmen, though the position in many college football programs can be more fluid than those of so-called scrimmage players. Senior Brendan Mullen had handled kickoffs as a junior and was the front-runner to add field goals and PATs to his duties. (When Mullen attended the prep school during the 1996–97 school year, he made his goal to be the first person to touch the football during the 100th Army-Navy game in 1999—and did exactly that by winning the kickoff chores before the season and having Army win the pregame coin toss and elect to defer.)

Josh Davis, Peter Stewart, and Brad Waudby—all offensive linemen—spent the 2000 season working with the scout team and the junior varsity squad, trying to learn from the varsity players. Davis's skills weren't ideally suited to play center in Berry's wide-open attack. In an option offense, Davis would have scrambled side to side whereas Berry wanted his center to be much lighter than Davis and be able to get upfield quickly to block linebackers. But Davis persisted and was rewarded for his hard work during practice by getting to dress for a handful of games. Most important, he earned the right to dress and stand on the sideline for the Army-Navy game.

* * *

Stewart was able to engage in one of his favorite pastimes back in Texas—hunting—with his English teacher. He stopped by the teacher's office seeking help on a paper when he noticed a hunting map on the desk. Stewart's father had been an avid hunter but essentially gave it up as work demands sliced into his free time. Stewart would deer hunt with his sister Amy's husband, Al Hogatt, at the Hogatt family ranch in central Texas, though he never returned with a kill. Stewart asked the teacher about hunting, which led to a series of trips into the woods around West Point that fall. They first scouted an area, then observed from a tree stand, and finally embarked on the actual hunt. With a doe in his sights, Stewart imprudently aimed for the deer's head, struck her in the neck, and she ran off. They tracked the animal for two miles before losing the trail.

Fox Sports scheduled Army's opener at Cincinnati for Labor Day in order to show it to a national audience. The Bearcats' sixth-year coach, Rick Minter, sought to take the sting out of a 3–8 record in 1999 during which his team went winless in league play. The state of Army football entering the 2000 season bore little resemblance to the program that fielded above-average teams for the early part of the twentieth century. When college football's popularity prompted the Associated Press to institute a weekly poll during the 1936 season, Army was ranked third on the strength of wins in its first three games. The program's national profile grew with an annual encounter at Yankee Stadium against Notre Dame that began in 1938, though the Cadets were overmatched in most of the series' early games.

After Army closed the 1940 campaign at 1–7–1 with its second consecutive shutout loss to Navy, the academy turned to "Red" Blaik, a former West Point football player and former Cadets assistant coach. Blaik's first 11 seasons all concluded with winning finishes. His 1944 team was the first of three straight that didn't lose a game, all of them crowned national champions by the AP. When the '44 Cadets snapped a five-year losing streak against Navy to finish 9–0, General Douglas MacArthur distributed the following telegram from his command post overseas: THE GREATEST OF ALL ARMY TEAMS. (stop) WE HAVE STOPPED THE WAR TO CELEBRATE YOUR MAGNIFICENT SUCCESS.

When "Doc" Blanchard won the 1945 Heisman Trophy as a junior, he became the first recipient who wasn't a senior. Blanchard played his first collegiate season at North Carolina, enlisted in the army, then elected to finish his college football career at West Point. When Glenn Davis won the Heisman in 1946, Army became the first school to claim consecutive Heisman Trophies. The only blemish on Army's three-year record of 1944–1946 is considered one of college football's classic games, the 0–0 tie in '46 between No. 1 Army and No. 2 Notre Dame. The scoreless standoff didn't prevent Army from winning its third consecutive national title.

Blaik's final team, the 1958 squad with Heisman winner Pete Dawkins playing end, compiled an 8–0–1 record and finished third in the AP poll; Army hasn't finished in the top 10 since. That team provided an exclamation point to Blaik's legacy with his institution of a unique offensive formation punctuated by a player who never participated in the huddle before each snap. Bill Carpenter was dubbed "the lonely end," and became something of a national sports phenomenon.

That team, like Army's other standout teams to that point, didn't play in a postseason bowl. It was West Point policy that such an endeavor wouldn't be in the best interest of cadets because it would essentially turn their Christmas break into another academy obligation. Army wasn't alone in that stance; Notre Dame, for all of its great teams, declined postseason solicitations from 1924 until accepting an invitation to play in the 1970 Cotton Bowl against top-ranked Texas. As George Vecsey of *The New York Times* reported in 1984, Blaik said his '44 and '45 teams were in line to play in the Rose Bowl before the academy declined the invitations. Dallas' Cotton Bowl was interested in the Cadets twice during the late 1950s. In 1958, officials of the game invited the Cadets in late October as they held a 4–0–1 record and were ranked third in the Associated Press' sportswriters poll. The Dallas group hoped to close the deal when Army traveled to Houston in early November to play Rice only to have the academy's superintendent, Lieutenant General Garrison Davidson (who played for Army during the 1920s and served as head coach during the '30s) decline the invitation. Tom Cahill's 1967 Army team, which took an 8–1 record into the Navy game, was courted by New Orleans' Sugar Bowl, but the Secretary of the Army, Stanley Reasor, wasn't comfortable with the optics of a West Point football team touring the French Quarter while the Vietnam War raged.

Two days before the 2000 opener, Mike Waddell, a member of Army's radio broadcast team, taped a pregame segment at West Point with John Feinstein. The nationally known sports journalist and author was still involved in Army athletics years after writing *A Civil War*, which focused on the 1995 Army-Navy game. After the taping ended, Waddell told Feinstein to make sure not to miss Army's first offensive play in Monday's game. The Bearcats won the toss, elected to receive, but gained only one first down before punting—an 18-yard effort that presented Army with terrific initial field position at its 48-yard line. The offensive unit approached the line of scrimmage under the direction of junior quarterback Chad Jenkins and lined up in . . . an option formation? The formation that had essentially been declared dead and buried from the day that Todd Berry arrived at West Point? The Black Knights quickly shifted out of that, Jenkins took the snap, dropped back, and threw deep for Calvin Smith. The heave fell incomplete, but a message had been sent. Army football under Berry wasn't going to plod downfield; it would go long, be bold.

Army had a tremendous opportunity to break a scoreless tie with a touchdown late in the opening quarter after an interception by senior linebacker Lyle Weaver deep in Cincinnati territory gave the Cadets possession at the Bearcats' 7-yard line. But two short runs and an incompletion left the Black Knights settling for a 26-yard field goal. Berry's offense manufactured two impressive touchdown drives in the second half—15 plays covering 80 yards and 14 plays for 95 yards—that gave Army a surprising 17–13 lead with about 10 minutes to play. But Cincinnati replied immediately with a TD drive of its own and stifled the Black Knights' attack the rest of the way for a 23–17 win.

The *Cincinnati Enquirer*'s John Erardi described the result as "disaster averted" for the Bearcats. The winning head coach's postgame interview session reflected disappointment despite the victory and was actually only one statement; Rick Minter wouldn't take questions. The newly-airborne West Point offense amassed 243 total yards—Sutton's 1999 team averaged 323 yards on the ground alone—and split its mode of operation with 34 runs and 29 passes. "At times, you could tell our guys weren't completely comfortable with everything we were doing," Berry told the media afterward. "I've got bright young men out there, and they're going to get better. I think you could see that they were having fun out there." It appeared junior tight end Clint Dodson enjoyed the proceedings. He finished the afternoon with six catches after having only one during all of the 1999 season. "We lost today, and it hurts," Dodson said. "But once we figure this all out, I think we're going to be a dangerous team." The only West Point freshman to play was Anthony Miller. At 5-foot-8 and 176 pounds, he was impressively aggressive on Army's kickoff team.

Next on Army's schedule was the home opener against Boston College the following Saturday, Berry's first opportunity to present his new team to the Michie Stadium faithful. Tom Hill was able to use his business air miles to attend Army games in 2000 both at West Point and on the road. He would later cut back on road games since they didn't afford the same opportunity to visit with Brian after the game. The Zuriskos and Farringtons made the six-hour drive from Pittsburgh. The Waudbys came up from nearby Oakland. Bill and Dawn Livingston didn't drive up from Woodbury, making the difficult decision to instead attend Bill's class reunion that weekend in Colorado. That would be the only Army game during Ryan Kent's four years at West Point—home or away—that they missed. These parents would settle into a routine of tailgating together over the next four years on the large field that's located just inside the academy's main gate at the south end of West Point. The field was originally used for cadet riding instruction and called the Cavalry Plain. It's now named Buffalo Soldier Field in honor of the African Americans who served in the US Army following Congress' 1866 legislation that allowed for racial integration of the armed forces during peacetime. One of the guests at the multi-family gathering was Brad Waudby's hard-charging freshman coach at Indian Hills, Gene Prebola. Prebola was still visiting after one game, long enough to say hello to his former player. Brad gave him a big hug and said, "Because of you, I'm here today."

Clint Woody's practice performance earned him a spot on the active roster as a third-string receiver for the game against BC, which finished third in the Big East Conference in 1999 and played in a bowl. Denny Woody's excitement over his oldest son's home football debut was enough for him to make the drive of more than 800 miles from Hayesville, along with some other family members to watch the game in person (not wife Leslie; she had to stay home to watch over Clint's six siblings). The Woody party arrived in New York in time for Denny to watch the team's light workout on Friday afternoon before the coaches and players boarded buses for that night's stay-over at a hotel about 30 miles southwest of the academy just over the New Jersey line in Mahwah.

Berry was aware that Woody's father had made the arduous drive to watch the game. Maybe that was why Berry sent the freshman receiver into the game after Boston College, quarterbacked by future NFL player Tim Hasselbeck, pulled away soon after halftime to build a 55–10 lead early in the fourth quarter. Woody was sent into the game with 2:07 to play as one of the Black Knights reserves who played out the game that had long since gotten away. Denny was walking back to his seat and was elated to spot his son in the huddle. The thrill was so great that Denny didn't sit the rest of the game; he watched the ensuing drive, which began at Army's 37-yard line, while standing in the aisle.

West Point's quarterback depth chart for the BC game moved Ryan Kent to No. 4, replaced on the third unit by junior Curtis Zervic. By the time Woody entered the game, starting quarterback Chad Jenkins was out, primary backup Joe Gerena was out, and Zervic was called upon to finish the game. On the drive's first play, Zervic found Anthony Miller for a 16-yard connection to immediately move the Black Knights into BC territory. The intrepid Army fans who declined to get an early start to their postgame tailgating or the drive home watched the subs march downfield, even if only against an equally inexperienced bunch of BC defensive reserves. Zervic connected on five consecutive passes to move West Point to the Eagles' 12 before, on 2nd and 2, a pass intended for senior receiver Bo Clift fell incomplete.

On the way back to the huddle, Zervic lit into young Woody. The freshman had been told to run a 10-yard pattern that would cut across the field. He instead cut off his downfield run after only five yards, which, Zervic bluntly informed him, threw a monkey wrench into the play's overall flow. On the following play, 3rd and 2 at the 12, Woody lined up on the left side of the formation and ran a deep post route for the end zone. He cut right, near the back line of the end zone. Zervic delivered a pass far enough in front of Woody that the gangly receiver had to lunge forward. He made the catch despite tight coverage for the first touchdown of his collegiate football career, not realizing where he was until he noticed the turf below him was black instead of green. On the Fox Sports broadcast, the announcer excitedly proclaimed: "What a nice grab by Brian Bruenton!" With all of those subs playing, it apparently was difficult from the TV booth to distinguish between Woody's uniform No. 93 from Bruenton's No. 82. Denny Woody certainly recognized who caught the last-minute Army touchdown pass and high-fived anyone within high-fiving distance while still standing in the aisle. Woody received a big hug from Zervic and a slap on the back from Berry.

The touchdown made the final score 55–17 and avoided what would have been the most lopsided West Point defeat at home ever; the loss merely matched the margin in the 45–7 thumping at the hands of Pitt in 1980. That didn't matter much afterward to the Woody contingent, which convened for pizza at Schades Restaurant on Main Street in Highland Falls. It was the first Woody father-son visit since R-Day, but the enjoyment was briefly interrupted for Clint when he spotted his squad leader in the restaurant. As a freshman, Woody was required to sign out before leaving campus but hadn't done so. In the din of Schades, he escaped notice by his cadet superior and avoided plebe punishment.

Berry's Black Knights lost their first six games by an average of almost 16 points. Their best opportunity for victory during that stretch came when they led 30–18 at Houston in mid-September with 9:21 left to play after Army linebacker Lyle Weaver returned an interception 54 yards for a touchdown. Unfortunately for the Cadets, there was enough time for the Cougars to rally. UH scored about two minutes later to get within 30–25, and again in the closing minutes to pull out a 31–30 win. During the Black Knights' 42–23 loss at New Mexico State three weeks later, Kent was elevated back to third string when Gerena was unavailable. Jenkins was shaken up early, and Zervic took over. That made Kent next up in the event that anything happened to Zervic. Kent began to wrestle with the possibility that he could soon take over a huddle in a real game for the first time since prep school. Part of him reveled in that prospect; part of him hoped nothing would happen to Zurvic. The coaching staff must have shared such mixed emotions regarding the untested plebe. An assistant coach informed junior defensive back Ben Woodruff, who played quarterback in high school, to be ready to go in if Zervic was injured.

With the falling leaves of late October came the Tulane Green Wave to West Point, carrying a 3–3 record. Zachary Kaye's family and girlfriend traveled in from Alabama. The Kayes treated their son and some of his West Point pals, including Kent, to a picnic along the Hudson. The main course was a southern delicacy straight from the Kaye kitchen—father Stephen's deep-fried chicken, which took multiple nights to prepare. The Kayes also introduced Kent and the others to a commercial treat from

Alabama—Milo's Famous Sweet Tea. It was a sweet day for the Cadets as Army scored a touchdown with 40 seconds to play on an 18-yard pass to cap a 15-play, 80-yard march to edge the Green Wave, 21–17. The Black Knights converted three third downs and a 4th and 11 along the way. Four plebes got into the game—Miller (one catch), Woody (no catches), linebacker Jay Thomas, and running back Larry "D. J." Stancil.

Each of Brian Hill's former high school teammates at Western Connecticut State began their college football careers elsewhere. Tarek Reslan played his first two seasons at Tusculum College in Tennessee. Kent Magueri spent a year at Marist College 90 miles outside New York City. For Hill, the "West Conn" campus became a regular weekend refuge to escape the rigidity of academy existence; to experience "real" college life. And he often brought along his Army teammate from central Florida, Josh Davis.

Autumn also brought the first of two stagings of the APFT, the second to be administered during the spring semester. The largest of Army athletes, including the football team's linemen, qualified for the Selected Athletes Program. That allowed them to substitute the timed two-mile run that concluded the three-part test with a 12-minute ride on a stationary bike. That modification of the test was available to athletes while they had intercollegiate eligibility remaining. Each was aware that any remaining time at the academy after they were done participating in corps squad sports would find them finishing the APFT with the run.

Clint Woody played in only the BC and Tulane games that season but, after missing the season's initial trip to Cincinnati, traveled to the remaining road games as part of the varsity team. That was a huge perk given that first-year cadets were generally prohibited from leaving the academy. Four plebes earned varsity letters during the 2000 season: Miller, Stancil, Thomas, and defensive lineman Odene Brathwaite. Miller played the most, in 10 of Army's 11 games. His special-teams highlight of the season was a fumble recovery for a touchdown on a kickoff against Memphis in September. Miller earned his only start in the season finale against Navy, which was played for the first time at Baltimore's relatively new PSINet Stadium. The game was a quasi-home game for the Midshipmen and practically a home game for Miller, who grew up in Maryland near Washington, DC. The Black Knights brought in a 1–9 record, the four-point win over Tulane all that separated them from the ignominy of West Point's first winless season since 1973. But Navy lost all of its 10 previous outings, leaving the Midshipmen seeking to avoid their first winless campaign since the 0–8–1 finish of 1948. (The tie was huge, 21–21 vs. an Army team that went into the game 8–0 and ranked third in the country.) Navy had not won since beating Army 19–9 in 1999 in Bob Sutton's final appearance as the Cadets' head coach.

Army got off to a promising start on a sunny, breezy day near Baltimore's Inner Harbor. Navy's opening possession ended after only three plays with a fumble that was recovered by Brian Zickefoose at the Cadets' 35-yard line, and West Point running back Michael Wallace raced 65 yards on the ensuing play for a 7–0 lead. But Navy responded with scores on its next four drives to lead 20–7 at halftime. The Midshipmen collected 16 first downs during the first half to Army's six, 282 yards to Army's 130, and held possession for an astounding 23 minutes and 23 seconds. West Point's first four possessions of the third quarter were one punt and three turnovers, one of the latter being a fumble inside its 5 that Navy recovered for a touchdown. The Middies' lead grew to 27–7 before the Black Knights began to scramble back into the game. The score was 30–21 before Miller caught a 21-yard touchdown pass with 2:44 to play.

An onside kick failed because the Cadets were guilty of recovering the ball before it traveled the required 10 yards. Yet Army, trailing 30–28, still had life by holding Navy to a 43-yard field goal attempt with 1:33 to play that, at worst, would leave the Black Knights behind by five points. The kick fell short, but West Point was penalized for roughing the kicker to give the Midshipmen a first down with Army out of timeouts. The penalty was the last of nine that day, heaped upon five turnovers. Navy ran out the clock for its only victory of the season—equaling Army's total in a forlorn season for academy football. (Not to besmirch Air Force's program, which easily claimed the Commander-in-Chief's Trophy and won nine games.) Berry accurately noted afterward that his team "kept finding ways to shoot ourselves in the foot." There naturally was a far different feeling in a one-win season for the Middies, as was expressed by senior safety Chris Lepore: "All I will remember about the year is beating Army."

Spring break meant more to the freshmen than a chance to escape the constraints of academy life. Just before leaving the academy grounds, the Plebe Recognition ceremony was held. In military terms, it meant promotion from Cadet Private to Cadet Private First Class. Pragmatically, it meant the plebes were freed from much of the procedural bondage in which they'd existed since reporting to West Point nine months earlier. Upon completion of the recognition ritual, the frosh were allowed to speak beyond the minimal utterances of "Yes, sir." "Yes, ma'am." "Beat Navy" or "Beat . . . whomever the football team was playing next." No longer were they obligated to cup their hands while walking outside their barracks room. No longer were they required to face directly forward. And, when members of West Point's other three classes addressed them, plebes were referred to by their first names for the first time. The transition was sealed with a handshake and a PFC rank insignia pinned to the uniform collar.

The effervescent Roberts celebrated his regained freedom of expression and promptly mouthed off to an upperclassman. The offended party was white, and Roberts, an African American, assumed the upperclassman thought the incident was racially motivated. The two exchanged a couple of shoves, Roberts feigning to deliver a punch. They went their separate ways, and Roberts assumed nothing more would come of the altercation. Such thinking lasted less than a day. Roberts was summoned to Todd Berry's office and told he was off the team. Roberts suspected there was more behind the punishment, given that Roberts's occasional class-clown persona led him to do impersonations of Berry and some other coaches when they weren't around. Roberts spent the majority of his non-class time during the second semester of his plebe year confined to his barracks room and didn't give up hope of rejoining Army's football team.

About 10 percent of a West Point class is black. Racial desegregation arrived at the academy soon after Robert E. Lee, a West Point graduate and the academy's superintendent from 1852 to 1855, surrendered at the Appomattox Court House to end the Civil War in 1865. The effort was started in 1867 by Massachusetts Congressman Benjamin Butler and resulted in four blacks receiving government appointments for the 1870–71 academic year. Two were denied enrollment for medical reasons, and one failed to pass the entrance exam. The fourth, James Webster Smith of South Carolina, became West Point's first black cadet. The former slave was appointed to West Point by Congressman Solomon Hoge, who had relocated from Ohio following the Civil War after serving as an officer in the Union army. Smith was far from embraced. He was assigned no roommate. Peers overtly conveyed that he wasn't welcome. Smith's response to such hostility was to bow his back and confront it, essentially fighting fire with fire. His grades suffered, he was forced to repeat his first year, and eventually dismissed.

During Smith's last year at West Point, he finally enjoyed the company of a roommate. The second black to attend the academy was Henry Ossian Flipper, a Georgian and another former slave. Flipper was likewise shunned by the majority of academy students and, upon Smith's departure, was left to finish his time at West Point in relative solitude as a solo border. But he dealt with the collective cold shoulder in a fashion far different from Smith. Flipper ignored it as best he could and declined to report any incidents to the academy hierarchy. In his autobiography, *"The Colored Cadet at West Point,"* he wrote, "I refused to obtrude myself upon the white cadets and treated them all with uniform courtesy." In 1877, Flipper became West Point's first black graduate. Fellow grads came to his room afterward and congratulated him. He wrote of his closing days at the academy: "All signs of ostracism were gone. All felt I was worthy of some regard, and did not fail to extend it to me."

* * *

Spring football 2001 began during the final week of March. After taking 180 players into such drills the previous year, 102 players dressed out for the four weeks that culminated in the Black-Gold Game in late April. That included 40 letter winners and 15 returning starters. Thirty-eight players were sophomores, only a handful of whom were listed on Army's three-deep depth chart. That included Anthony Miller and Clint Woody at receiver, Odene Brathwaite at defensive end, and Jay Thomas at one of the outside linebacker positions. But there were opportunities for other sophs to earn playing time that fall, including Brian Hill at inside linebacker and the offensive line trio of Josh Davis, Peter Stewart, and Brad Waudby. And the placekicking position was up for grabs with the graduation of Brendan Mullen, with Zachary Kaye and Anthony Zurisko among those waiting to show their stuff.

One of Thomas Roberts's fellow defensive backs was classmate Russell Burnett of Marietta, Georgia. Burnett was recruited by Georgia Tech and offered an academic scholarship at the school just down the road from his hometown. But he was interested in attending college far from home and was taken by the aura of West Point. Burnett was hampered during the 2000 season in part by a case of turf toe and didn't get into any varsity games. He headed into spring drills determined to what he called "right the ship" and become a valuable contributor. But he was instead told early on that keeping a position on the team wasn't going to happen. Not even just playing special teams, Burnett asked. Not even that, he was told.

Ryan Kent was intent on competing for the starting quarterback position while fully understanding that one of Berry's February high school signees would probably become the favorite for the job. Reggie Nevels was a three-sport star in high school who quarterbacked a combination of pro-style and spread offense. Nevels, son of the county sheriff in Marion, Indiana, was a starting point guard alongside Zach Randolph, who played at Michigan State and became an NBA all-star. Nevels initially planned to play professional baseball following high school but scrapped that plan, at least coming out of high school, after separating a shoulder in a football game during his senior season. He originally committed to play football for Northwestern, with the opportunity to walk on with the Wildcats' baseball team. But Army assistant Tucker Waugh showed up at a Marion High basketball practice and asked Nevels if he'd ever thought about going to college in New York. Nevels didn't even know what the United States Military Academy was then, took his last paid recruiting trip to West Point, and was smitten by history and the Hudson.

One week into spring drills, one of the equipment managers approached Kent in the locker room before a film session and told him that Berry wanted to see him in his office. Kent prepared for the worst—being dropped from the squad—yet also put together his thoughts in making what might be his last pitch to play quarterback. He politely entered and sat in a chair in front of Berry's large desk. The coach said he would support Kent if it was his intention to continue playing quarterback, but . . . "What would you think about playing defense?" Kent immediately understood that his opinion in the matter would definitely be secondary: "What do *you* think about me playing defense?" Kent, like most college football players, had played both offense and defense in high school. Most are standouts on both sides of the ball and then specialize in one position in college based on which position they play better, the needs of the program, or both. Kent was an all-state safety at Woodbury and was recruited by Lehigh to play that position, which wasn't his preference. The scholarship opportunity at Delaware technically classified him as "an athlete"—something of a sports euphemism for a talented player whose position in college is yet to be determined. Kent was determined to address his status at quarterback to Berry one last time: "I've been training and working hard to make a run at quarterback. If you're bringing me in the first week of spring ball and telling me you think I can make more of an impact on defense, I'd rather try it." He added that he did like to hit people. Kent left the meeting and returned to the locker room, traded in his offensive playbook and helmet for defensive versions and sat in on his first meeting with his new unit. He finished spring drills fourth on the depth chart at outside linebacker, or "sniper" in Berry's lexicon.

Anthony Zurisko outkicked the competition and finished spring ball as the No. 1 kicker, becoming the first member of West Point's Class of 2004 to be listed as a first-stringer on the football depth chart. Junior Paul Stelzer was the runner-up and in position to continue to push Zurisko for the kick-off chores. A handful of other sophomores headed to the fall listed on the second team: receiver Anthony Miller, running back Marcellus Chapman, and defensive end Peter Salfeety. On special teams, Miller upgraded from the kickoff and punt coverage teams to the return units. He missed part of spring practice because of prolonged bouts with pneumonia and strep throat.

Cory Wallace was called into Berry's office soon after spring practice ended. The head coach thanked him for his time and told him he was off the team. Though Wallace had struggled through his freshman season, he wasn't prepared to be dropped from the squad. It hung over him like a black cloud for weeks. He'd been recruited out of high school by Air Force, Wyoming, and Colorado State, but he never considered leaving West Point to continue playing college football elsewhere. "I'm not going to quit," he told himself. "I'm going to make them throw me out." Zachary Kaye also made a visit to Berry's office, to tell him that he had chosen to leave the team, as he wanted to increase the amount of time that he devoted to his studies.

With a full academic semester behind them, cadets in the Class of 2004 began to, if not feel comfortable, at least be able to function more efficiently than during the fall semester. One additional learning resource available was the Center for Enhanced Performance. It was started in 1989 for the benefit of corps squad athletes but later made available to all students. The mission of the "CEP," located in Washington Hall, was to help cadets study more efficiently, learn how to take notes in class more efficiently. Center personnel stated a cadet's reading rate could be doubled, from 300 to 600 words a minute, without losing any comprehension. The emphases were divided between two specific programs designed for academic excellence and performance enhancement. The former focused on what could help students retain more information and earn higher grades while the latter was aimed toward improving their ability to lead and to strengthen their character. The staff would later include former Army football captain Joe Ross, who also taught a course in twenty-first century army leaders.

Another of the academy's efforts to provide guidance to corps squad athletes beyond the coaching staff was the mentor program. West Point teachers and staffers volunteered to play a "big brother" role to a handful of athletes. Mentors attended team practices as often as possible, ate with the team on occasion, and invited the cadets over to their residences—some on post, others off—so the young men and women could share their experiences and challenges in an informal atmosphere. The players enjoyed a "regular" family experience and had someplace other than their barracks to watch events like the Super Bowl or the final round of the Masters.

Supervising the football mentors as the officer representative was Colonel Patrick Finnegan, a 1971 West Point graduate and head of the academy's law department. In the case of the football team, mentors typically were assigned three or four cadets who played the same position. Hill and Kent, both linebackers beginning in the spring of 2001, were mentored by husband-and-wife lieutenant colonels who taught systems engineering. Michael and

Brigitte Kwinn both graduated from West Point and had two children, four-teen-year-old Cheryl and twelve-year-old Michael III. "Big Michael" didn't specifically ask to mentor linebackers but preferred to avoid entertaining linemen, who might eat the Kwinns out of house and home. The cadets were free to bring along a friend or two, and Tom Farrington was often among those who joined in. The Kwinns lived about 15 miles from West Point in the town of Monroe. Soon after the Kwinns joined the mentor program, they bought a sectional sofa and a big-screen television, the latter equipped with one of the new technological marvels of the day—TiVo. If TV viewing ever led to boredom, a pool and a hot tub in the backyard were inviting alterna-tives during suitable weather.

Thomas Roberts, no longer on the football team, wasn't terribly engaged with his assigned mentor but gravitated toward his geography professor. Colonel Gene Palka was head of the department and a 1978 academy grad who played football and baseball. Roberts reminded Palka of himself during his own cadet days—possessing a burning desire to succeed but a little rough around the edges. Palka's body language as a cadet often got him in trouble, and West Point helped him conquer that issue. Palka struggled academically while playing multiple sports; Roberts's quandary had been trying to succeed in football, which threatened to consume him. Palka tried to convince Roberts to stop focusing on long-term goals every day and instead simply make it to Thanksgiving break, then to Christmas break, then to spring break.

Palka's house on the academy grounds was only a few doors down from the head football coach's quarters. Palka got to know Todd Berry, as he did Bob Sutton, and considered him a friend. Palka recommended Berry become involved in his players' lives beyond the football complex. He suggested he watch their parades, check out cadet basic training, and take in special functions such as Branch Night and Post Night, when the seniors learned what they would do and where they would initially be stationed following graduation.

Chapter Six

"DUDE, HAVE YOU BEEN
WATCHING TV?"

West Point made an administrative change during the summer of 2001. Lieutenant General William Lennox Jr. became the academy's 56th superintendent, succeeding Daniel Christman. A 1971 West Point graduate, Lennox grew up in Yonkers, New York, and played football for Cardinal Hays High in the Bronx. When he wore his cadet uniform on trips into New York City, he discovered first-hand the public loathing for the Vietnam War—some called him a baby-killer; others spat at him.

Eight weeks of summer training in 2001 for the Class of '04 began about eight miles from the academy grounds at Camp Buckner. Not as grueling as Beast Barracks but far from summer vacation, "Buckner" has long been sarcastically referred to by those who have experienced it as "the best summer of our lives." It focused on close ground fighting, other physical challenges, and the further honing of leadership skills. That included the "Slide for Life"—riding a pulley 100 feet in the air over Lake Popolopen before dropping into the chilly water. That proved unnerving for many a cadet. For Tom Farrington, whose right hand wasn't fully healed from the incident that took place during his senior year at Shaler Area High, it was a dreaded assignment. The slide itself wasn't as foreboding to Farrington as was the preceding climb up the tall tower to simply reach the pulley. The metal bars

67

were unusually slippery, and the distance between the rungs made the climb like doing pullups. When Farrington reached the top, he actually was excited about getting to the slide portion of the task. He struggled to hang on with both hands but was confident that, if his right hand proved inadequate, he could hang on with only his left. That wasn't necessary. He reached the drop area just fine and let go. The impact didn't harm Farrington in any way. It did cost him his wristwatch, which came loose during impact and was subsequently the object of a scuba search.

The closing weeks of summer training took place at Fort Knox, Kentucky, where the cadets participated in something of an informal job fair staged by the US Army. They were introduced to all of the army branches. As seniors, they would apply to enter a particular branch—aviation, field artillery, armor, infantry, etc. At Fort Knox, Clint Woody played the role of tank commander with two fellow cadets under his watch. They were females—Sue Petroff, the diver from Connecticut who made it through rifle qualification during Beast Barracks with the assistance of Anthony Miller, and Abby Racster from Woodbridge, Virginia. Racster and Petroff quickly became friends during Buckner, often sharing downtime by sitting by the lake at sunset, drinking Powerade, and eating plums.

The Class of 2004 initially included 195 females. The academy's first co-educational class, which set foot at West Point on July 7, 1976, featured 119 likely trepidatious young women. The previous autumn, President Gerald Ford signed Public Law 94–106 that opened all service academies to females as a response to years of lagging numbers of applications to West Point, Annapolis, and Colorado Springs. Seventeen of those ladies decided either during or after Beast Barracks '76 that academy life wasn't for them. That was 14 percent of the females who bid *adieu* compared to 10 percent of their male counterparts. Not all of the female plebes came straight from high school. Colleen Brennan, twenty-one, had already graduated from East Stroudsburg State in Pennsylvania.

One of the 102 who stayed was Carol Barkalow, whose experiences at the academy form the bulk of her 1990 book *In the Men's House*. Those experiences predated her enrollment at West Point. Barkalow was finishing lunch on a campus visit as a high school senior when a male cadet at the table asked why she wanted to attend West Point. "Because I want to become the best army officer I can be," she said. "That's fine," the young man replied, "but couldn't you do it someplace else?" The 102 women who began the 1976–77 academic year as plebes became 86 by the second year, 79 for the third year, and 62 who walked on graduation day 1980—including Barkalow. Andrea Hollen of Altoona, Pennsylvania, was the first female to be handed a West Point diploma, by Secretary of Defense Harold Brown. Barkalow recalled male cadets remarking during her firstie year: "My God! You're still here!" She retired as a lieutenant colonel following 26 years of military service.

It didn't take Sue Petroff long into her West Point career to recognize that not all of the upperclassmen who supervised Beast Barracks 2000 were enthusiastic about young women being admitted to West Point. Following an eight-mile road march, the cadet candidates were ordered to run from their barracks basement up the six flights of stairs to the top floor—while still wearing the weighty ruck sack that felt heavier by the mile during their march. The entire platoon hit the stairs on a dead run. Along the way, Petroff was running alongside one of her female peers. Suddenly, one of the male cadre members shoved the woman into the wall and yelled, "Get out of my army!"

One of Petroff's primary motivations for attending West Point was altered only a few weeks after she took her seat in the stands on R-Day. Diving coach Brad Szurgot left for the University of Arkansas because his coaching duties at West Point didn't constitute a full-time position. And once the academic year began, that first semester's course work proved to be more difficult than Petroff had anticipated. A few weeks in, she feared failing almost all of her courses. On a phone call home, she unloaded on her mother that the intense structure of the academy and the military aspects of daily life left her feeling insignificant: "I'm just an ant marching in line with the other ants! I don't know if it's for me!" In fending off the temptation to bid an early farewell to West Point, Petroff at least experienced relative escape as a member of the swimming and diving team. For example, upperclassmen would include the often-beleaguered plebes in dinner outings. Such privileges rankled the non-athlete students, though in the case of a typical member of the swim team, they slept about only five hours because of five hours' practice divided into two sessions with one practice taking place well before most cadets were up and about.

But within the ecosystem of the swimming and diving team, the swimmers didn't hold the divers in high esteem. Divers were to the swim team much as placekickers often are to a football team. Divers didn't undergo the same strenuous training, lap after lap of practice. Their value to the team was considered much more of a skill than a result of training and endurance. Hence, the divers usually hung out among themselves when the team traveled to competitions away from West Point. All of the road meets were within driving distance, and the divers sat together on the bus. They sat together when the team ate on the road. The divers were sometimes tempted to chow down as much as the swimmers, though the latter were burning off more calories in their practices and competitive meets.

As a freshman, Petroff scored victories on the three-meter board in meets against Bucknell and Penn while her highest finish of the season on the one-meter board was a second vs. Siena. The annual meet against Navy was held at West Point the day before the academies' football teams met in Baltimore. Army's hope was that Petroff could finish first or second that day. She finished third, and Army lost the meet 151–149. The team's head coach, Ray Bosse, expressed his disappointment to Petroff; if she had done better, they could have beaten Navy.

* * *

Abby Racster grew up near Washington, DC, with an older sister and a younger brother. Her motivation for enrolling at West Point following a year at the prep school was somewhat a combination of personal ambition and devotion to family. In high school, Racster liked fantasy books like *The Lord of the Rings* but fought being perceived as a nerd. She quit the high school band after her sophomore year, was on the swim team for a couple of years, and participated on the crew team for one. Taking advantage of the school's proximity to the nation's capital, she attended page school at the House of Representatives. Her father, Larry Racster, participated in ROTC in college and wanted to fly helicopters in Vietnam but was prevented from becoming a pilot because he was color blind. A girlfriend took him to a Bible study

meeting that changed his life's direction, though still with a military emphasis. He attended seminary, became a pastor, and then an army chaplain. He
worked his way up to a position at the Pentagon as a colonel by the time
Racster, his middle child, was in high school. Her interest in West Point in
some way was connected to the combat dream that her father was never able
to fulfill.

It was during Buckner's "job fair" that Petroff first became enamored
with aviation as her future in the army. Most of the academy's aviation graduates move on to helicopters while a select few will specialize in fixed-wing
aircraft. Helicopters were brought in and set up, with the cadets allowed to
climb and also talk to the aviators. One caveat of going toward aviation was a
post-graduate active-duty commitment that amounted to seven years instead
of five—six years active duty after taking a year after graduation to attend
flight school. But the reward of flying for those years was worth it.

At Fort Knox, Petroff found it easy to take orders from Woody, the
laid-back Carolinian, and the two struck up a relationship that continued
informally the following fall back at West Point. But with Woody's time
obligations for football heaped upon the already-onerous schedule for any
cadet, the rapport never really progressed beyond simple hellos when passing
each other during the course of a West Point day. At Army football games,
she kept an eye on Woody when the Black Knights' offense was on the field
and often fumed when perceiving that he was open downfield while the play
went elsewhere.

That summer, Brian Hill chose to be part of the cadre that drilled the
new cadet candidates during Beast Barracks rather than attend further
instruction at Camp Buckner. Among his reasons was at least one that was
pragmatic; going to Beast allowed Hill more time to work out. The TAC
NCO in his cadet company paved the way for serving as a company training
officer in exchange for some Army football tickets for the coming season.
That company conveniently contained most of the football hopefuls in the
Class of 2005.

For the Class of 2004, the beginning of the 2001–02 academic year in
July meant they'd advanced from plebes to yearlings, or yuks. It also meant
a reorganization of their companies, called scrambling or shuffling. The

sophomores would remain in their new companies for the remainder of their West Point experience. Brian Hill chose to room with Mark Patzkowski, and they landed in B3—the Bandits. Patzkowski was from northern New Jersey, an honorable-mention all-league football player from DePaul High School. For a Floridian like Hill, having a roommate whose home was within an easy drive was a pragmatic plus. It meant an occasional home-cooked meal that was otherwise unavailable, even better than dining out on the trips to "West Conn" with Josh Davis. Peter Stewart and Thomas Roberts roomed together amid the C2 Circus. Ryan Kent and Zachary Kaye, Beast buddies, were reunited as roomies with the E2 Brew Dawgs.

Clint Woody moved to the E1 Vikings. The company motto, which would be inscribed in the members' senior class rings, was *Illegitimus non Carborundum* (Don't let the bastards get you down). Woody became reacquainted with Abby Racster in E1. Another of the new Vikings was Grace Chung, who grew up only 25 miles south of the academy in the town of Conyers. Chung didn't enroll at the academy because she was gung ho about the military or because it offered the best chance to compete in major-college athletics. She wasn't terribly sure what she wanted to do with her life. At worst, West Point would serve as a weigh station—one with free tuition—until she better determined her future. Another company member was Michael Cerrone, a military brat born in Tennessee who took a certain pride in successful procrastination: "If you wait to the last minute, it will only take a minute." Woody's new roommate was Skyler Munekata, from Honolulu. Woody frankly didn't know all that many fellow cadets beyond his football teammates. In Munekata, he was paired with one very social academy animal. Munekata came from Honolulu's prestigious Punahoa School, which would later become known for the high school graduation of President Barack Obama. In high school, Munekata realized that, with an older brother attending private Baylor University in Texas, it would be difficult for his parents to additionally fund his college career. That's why he began to explore the military academies. Munekata applied to West Point, the Naval Academy, VMI, and The Citadel. Luck would have it that he had a class cancelled and free time on his hands when a West Point recruiter dropped in at Punahoa. At West Point, Munekata appealed to Woody's more devilish side. It's doubtful that Woody would have thought of keeping an orange construction cone in their room, so they could "reserve" parking spaces when needed most. It was Munekata's idea to have Woody's father send them a couple of his old Pepsi delivery uniforms. No one suspected the two "deliverymen" were actually cadets as they left the academy grounds.

The football team reported for fall drills in advance of the 2001 season opener, when the Cincinnati Bearcats would return the favor from the previous campaign and play at Michie Stadium. Odene Brathwaite, one of the four 2000 frosh to earn a varsity letter, skipped football that semester to concentrate on academics. Anthony Zurisko reported after doing no kicking over the summer while immersed in military training. On the first day of practice, he pulled a hip flexor and was sidelined for three weeks, almost until the season began. In his stead, freshman Derek Jacobs was chosen for point-after attempts and field goals while junior Paul Stelzer was tabbed for kickoffs. Brad Waudby's football status was also hampered by "the best summer of his life," even more directly. During the summer session's final days, Waudby fell during a team-building activity and injured his left shoulder. He missed all of preseason practice and only played in three varsity games as a reserve all season. Thomas Roberts was reinstated to the football roster. He started out with a jersey with no number during preseason practice and sat with the new plebes during squad meetings. Marcellus Chapman suffered a wrist injury that fall and missed the entire season.

* * *

Todd Berry's second season on the Hudson began with Army dropping its opener for the fifth consecutive year. At first, it appeared the Black Knights had pulled out an unlikely victory over Cincinnati when they took a 21–17 lead. With only 1:16 remaining in the game, senior Omari Thompson ran for a 39-yard touchdown run on a play that resembled something out of the *Little Rascals*. Senior quarterback Chad Jenkins slipped the ball to Thompson between his legs and ran right, with most of Cincinnati's defense in pursuit, while Thompson ran essentially alone to the left for the score. But the Bearcats, beginning their subsequent possession 70 yards from the end zone, moved downfield with urgency and reached Army's 12 with 10 seconds left, using their final timeout of the game to stop the clock. A pass from Gino Guidugli (a freshman who'd replaced UC injured starter Adam Hoover during the first quarter) to Tye Keith completed the comeback, and Cincinnati led 24–21 with seven seconds remaining. On the ensuing kickoff, Army repeated the typically unsuccessful attempt at replicating the California Golden Bears' astounding touchdown to end their 1982 game against Stanford, seven laterals that resulted in college football's most unlikely touchdown (*"The band is on the field!"*). Thompson took the kickoff and reached Army's 40-yard line before whipping the ball back to Roberts. He lateralled back to Thompson, who lateralled to Aris Comeaux, who fumbled the ball over to Cincinnati to end the game.

* * *

The Black Knights were scheduled to host Buffalo the following Saturday, September 15. That Tuesday morning, Peter Stewart walked across the pedestrian bridge to Thayer Hall when Josh Davis passed in the opposite direction and blurted, "Dude, have you been watching TV? We're under attack!" The disbelieving Stewart replied, "OK. Yeah. Sure. Whatever." Ryan Kent prepared to leave his dorm room to attend his next class when he watched live television reports on his computer about the events taking place in lower Manhattan. In his next class, and in every classroom across the academy, instructors and cadets put aside the lessons of the day to watch the continuing TV coverage of the 9/11 terrorist attacks from New York City, Washington, DC, and rural Pennsylvania. Some cadets wondered why helicopters were flying over West Point that day; they were removing special forces personnel. Another sophomore in E1, Erik Wright, lived near Washington, DC, and his father was a colonel who worked at the Pentagon. For hours, Wright heard nothing either from his father or about him. Only after an agonizingly long period did Wright learn that his father was unharmed.

Larry Racster's office in the Pentagon was on the building's southwest side, near where American Airlines Flight 77 struck it at 9:38 a.m. Eastern time, resulting in the deaths of 125 people who were in the building and all 64 aboard the aircraft. Abby Racster recalled her father having a meeting scheduled there that morning. During lunch in the mess hall, a West Point captain asked her if her father was OK. She awkwardly said she had nothing to report. It turned out Larry Racster wasn't in the Pentagon that morning. Abby's younger brother had a date in traffic court that morning, having been involved in multiple accidents during his first months with a driver's license. Larry drove his son to that court appearance. Once done with that obligation, learning what had happened at the Pentagon, he drove there as soon as he could. As the officer in charge of the chaplains, he was responsible for making sure any survivors or relatives of the deceased had someone to talk to. He slept in his conversion van there for the next two nights.

Around 6 a.m. Pacific time that same day, Bradford Waudby's first cousin once removed, Al Breen, awoke in his hotel room near Los Angeles International Airport. Breen, Naval Academy Class of 1963, lived next door to Waudby's hometown of Oakland, in Franklin Lakes, and was a long-time pilot for United Airlines. He was up early that Tuesday to get back out to LAX for a flight to Newark that would complete a four-flight circuit— Newark to San Francisco, to Boston, to LAX, and back home. Breen didn't typically turn on a hotel TV as part of his early morning routine when flying out of LAX, but he did that day. He saw two news anchors in front of a live shot of the smoldering World Trade Center's north tower. One of the announcers said something about the possibility of a small aircraft striking the tower, and it didn't take much of a look for Breen to discount that. It wasn't long before Breen, like millions of other Americans, was horrified to watch a second plane strike the south tower.

Breen's disbelief was connected to how close he'd come to being personally involved. United Flight 175 from Boston to Los Angeles, which was flown into the north tower, was his route the previous day. United Flight 93 from Newark to San Francisco, which crashed in a field in Somerset County, Pennsylvania, southeast of Pittsburgh after passengers overpowered the hijackers, was the route that he'd flown two days earlier. Breen's wife, Katherine, couldn't recall where her husband was flying that day and naturally became frantic. She was straightening out their shore home and tried to reach him on his cellphone with no luck. All she heard was static and could only envision the phone laying out in a field. Since she couldn't call him and wasn't receiving any calls from him, she drove up the Garden State Parkway toward Bergen County. Access to the southbound Parkway, much of which would have come from New York City, was blocked off, and few people were headed north. She spent much of the two-hour drive as the only car that she could see on the highway. It reminded her of a scene from a science-fiction movie. "I'm here," she thought, trying to compose herself. "I'm OK." Then she began to cry. The Breens finally connected by phone hours later, long after he'd begun making his way to LAX only to be told by airline personnel that wouldn't be necessary. Breen was told to return to his hotel and, with national air travel suspended later that day, remained in Los Angeles for a week before being cleared to return home to New Jersey.

Later that week, every West Point cadet walked out to the darkened Plain in silence to participate in a midnight vigil to remember those lost in the terrorist attacks. The 20-minute ceremony included a 21-gun salute, a bugler playing "Taps," a bagpiper playing "Amazing Grace," and the cadets signing the alma mater. The academy broke with policy in allowing the event to be recorded by television cameras. Abby Racster was among those who were conflicted by the approval of that decision. A solemn gathering, meant to be held in darkness, was intruded upon by the presence of TV lights. In New Smyrna Beach, Mike Davis was certain he saw Josh in the footage that he watched the following day.

Within the next few days, all college football games that were scheduled for the upcoming weekend were either postponed or cancelled, given the overall state of tension and the uncertain status of air travel across the country. (Army's game against Buffalo was rescheduled for November 10.) Their next game would instead be a trip to Birmingham, Alabama, to face Alabama-Birmingham on September 22. At Legion Field, an assemblage of FBI agents, city police officers, and bomb-sniffing dogs combed through every inch of the stadium a day before kickoff to ensure the safety of all who would attend Saturday afternoon's game. Officials contended the security measures weren't much different from what was executed when Legion Field hosted soccer games as part of Atlanta's 1996 Summer Olympics.

With an Army game only one state away, Josh Davis's parents had previously made plans to attend the UAB game. Many others at Legion Field would watch West Point's football team for the first time as a gesture of patriotism. Doug Segrest, a sports columnist for the *Birmingham News*, urged local fans of the Alabama Crimson Tide and Auburn Tigers to set aside their zealous allegiances for a day and instead attend the Army-UAB game: "Pick your team and root throughout the game. But when Army takes the field, and when Army exits for the dressing room, stand up and cheer. Cheer not for a football team but for the future military leaders who will be on the front line as their declared war is fought. Your voices will be heard in Birmingham. Your support will reverberate throughout the nation."

UAB's kicker was a senior named Rhett Gallegos from Hueytown, a small town just outside Birmingham. Going into the 2001 season, Gallegos was listed among the early nominees for the Lou Groza Award that's given to the nation's top kicker. He walked on at UAB and earned a scholarship beginning in his sophomore year after being recruited by both Army and Navy. Both of his grandfathers were military men, and his parents were enthused about the possibility of their son attending West Point. On his recruiting trip to the Hudson, he learned of the challenging daily schedule that the typical Army football player/academy student must endure. He was also told about the post-graduate military commitment, though it was peacetime back then. It was more than an eighteen-year-old was prepared to shoulder. At that point, playing college football was central to his thoughts.

On the morning of 9/11, Gallegos was driving range balls with the instructor of a UAB golf class when someone came by and mentioned the attack on the Pentagon. He tried to work his way through a crowd of people that gathered in front of a small TV at the range's shop but couldn't really tell what was on the screen. He later learned at home the scope of the American tragedy. It was an hour or two later, while watching CNN, that he made the connection of the now-real prospect of US military action and how close he'd come to probably being a participant in that. It washed over him again and again as he watched the replays of the towers falling.

Game day for the Black Knights was atypical even before arriving at Legion Field. A fire alarm at the Sheraton Birmingham sent the football party and the hotel's other patrons outside before it was ruled a false alarm. Team buses were closely checked before leaving the hotel parking lot. A moment of silence was held before the Blazers' marching band played the national anthem, during which the Army team broke with tradition and saluted the stars and stripes waving high above the south end zone. UAB went into the game favored by 16.5 points; those who arrived at the stadium known locally as "The Gray Lady on Graymont Avenue" to root on America's future military officers found little to cheer for. A first-quarter field goal by Jacobs was all that West Point's offense had to show for its day's efforts. Six turnovers plus a blocked punt helped do in the Black Knights, who trailed by 31 points at halftime and lost 55–3—their worst football defeat in 19 years. With the verdict decided early in the third quarter, Berry sent in players who'd seen little or no playing time to that season. Josh Davis took the field as a varsity Black Knight for the first time, at center.

As players from both teams gathered on the field afterward to exchange greetings, their social interaction lacked the usual animation. "There wasn't a lot we could say," UAB defensive back Avery Warner said, according to the *Atlanta Journal-Constitution*. Nor was there much that Todd Berry could say afterward. He called the game an "embarrassment." The Black Knights were outrushed 239 yards to 46 and, while committing six turnovers, didn't claim one from the Blazers. "If we played them 10 times, I don't know if we could have beaten them," Berry told reporters, "but I know we're a better football team than we showed."

Army's record fell to 0–3 two weeks later with a 31–10 loss at Boston College, during which Anthony Miller forced two fumbles. Houston traveled to Michie Stadium with an identical record to face the Black Knights on a windy, chilly first Saturday of October for the first football game played at West Point following the terrorist attacks. West Point started two sophomores that day—linebacker Ryan Kent and running back C. J. Young. Miller and Young contributed as the Cadets scored a touchdown on the game's first drive. That launched a see-saw battle before Army shut out Houston during the second half and notched its first win of the 2001 season, 28–14. (The Cougars finished 0–11 that season.)

Kent, in addition to his increasing solid play at sniper, provided a flashback to his ball-carrying days at Woodbury High midway through the third quarter. The Black Knights, leading 21–14, lined up to punt on 4th and 4 at the 50-yard line. Kent stood in his usual position as the "up man," standing a few feet in front of punter Dan MacElroy to call out the signals and provide a last block if necessary. But Kent wasn't there to block. He recognized a flaw in the Cougars' alignment and called for a fake—a run—with him receiving the snap instead of MacElroy. And run he did, for 39 yards, down to Houston's 11 to the delight of the Michie Stadium crowd.

The 2001 Black Knights clinched a season that would outdo their 1–10 finish of the previous year when they beat Tulane, 42–35, at Michie Stadium in late October for their second victory of the season. Young's 192 rushing yards that day trumped the 384 Green Wave passing yards from future NFL quarterback J. P. Losman. Young ran for four touchdowns, the last one breaking a 35–35 tie with 2:26 to play. Tulane then advanced to midfield only to have Kent and junior linebacker Jason Frazier tackle receiver Carl Davis short of a first down to end the visitors' final possession.

If the following week's 34–24 defeat at Air Force was considered a morale victory of any ilk—it was the Cadets' best showing against the Falcons in five seasons—the subsequent 26–19 loss at home to Buffalo in the game that had been rescheduled in the aftermath of 9/11 was not. Buffalo was in only its third season of Division I-A play; this was a program that was shelved for much of the 1970s because the students refused to fund it. Yet here were the Bulls, hanging on to defeat the Black Knights when an Army pass into the end zone on the game's final play was batted down. Injury was added to insult; quarterback Chad Jenkins hurt a knee, left the game, and was feared lost for the season.

A 42–10 loss at Memphis left Army dragging a 2–8 record into the season finale against Navy in Philadelphia. Yet the Cadets program appeared to be in comparative stellar condition when compared to that of the Midshipmen. Navy was 0–10 and had dispensed with head coach Charlie Weatherbie seven games in, handing the team over to assistant coach Rick Lantz to close the season. The teams' combined 2–18 record failed to dim the nation's interest in the first Army-Navy game to be played following 9/11. Attendees at Veterans Stadium included President George W. Bush and the military hero of his father's Gulf War victory, retired General Norman Schwarzkopf. The commander in chief's previous appearance on a national sporting stage in the aftermath of the attacks was judged to be a command performance, when he threw out the first pitch of Game Three of the 2001 World Series between the Arizona Diamondbacks and New York Yankees—the first game of that series to be played in New York, in the virtual shadow of the fallen twin towers. Moments earlier, Yankees star Derek Jeter jokingly warned "W" that fans would boo him if he bounced the ball up to the plate. Bush was no rookie at the assignment, playing baseball in high school and given his years as an executive with the Texas Rangers major-league ballclub before becoming the governor of Texas. He stood on the pitching rubber (not all dignitaries throw from the full sixty feet, six inches to the plate) and lofted a pitch that his receiver, Yankees bullpen catcher Todd Greene, barely shifted his glove to grab.

Bush participated in the coin toss, but not all of his pregame activities were performed in full view of the almost 70,000 fans at Veterans Stadium, the largest gathering in the venue's 30-year history. He visited both of the locker rooms. In the Black Knights' quarters, he addressed the then-embryonic war on terrorism: "It's a just cause, and we will win because we are America." Schwarzkopf accompanied the president into the Army locker room and added: "We beat them in the Gulf War, and we'll beat them in Afghanistan. They don't know who they are messing with." (Over in the opposing locker room, Bush was joined by the Navy alum and former Vietnam prisoner of war, Arizona Senator John McCain.)

The Cadets were in no mood to be messed with that afternoon. They hit on big plays early—a 60-yard touchdown run around left end by freshman running back Ardell Daniels and a 42-yard scoring pass; while enjoying the rare challenge of trying to hold a lead. Brian Bruenton caught the pass from Chad Jenkins, whose mere presence in the huddle was inspirational to the rest of the Army roster. Jenkins wasn't about to be a spectator for his final Army football game. West Point fans cared little that Jenkins threw four interceptions that day since Navy converted the miscues into only three points. A third big play by Army—a 96-yard kickoff return by Thompson to open the second half—gave the Black Knights a 20-point lead. The score was 23–9 late in the third quarter when Bush and his traveling party left, after which stadium security people breathed a collective sigh of relief. The final score was 26–17, giving Todd Berry his first win over an academy opponent in four tries.

Brad Waudby saw action against Navy on special teams and on a few offensive plays. The noise at Veterans Stadium made it difficult for him to hear the holder calling out the signals preceding the snap of the ball. Anthony Miller, crestfallen a year earlier when Army lost to Navy near his hometown, was naturally elated and proud to have contributed to the victory in making his second start of the season. He caught two passes and blocked a punt that led to a Black Knights field goal. Miller finished the season with 16 receptions for 217 yards. A story published the following Monday in Navy's hometown newspaper, *The Capital*, compared the state of the two academy football programs—the Midshipmen without a win that season and without a coach that day—and cited Miller as one of the young Army talents whom Navy would have to contend with for another two seasons. Reggie Nevels got into a few games at quarterback. His primary contribution as a freshman was on special teams. Josh Davis played once more after the UAB game. Clint Woody appeared in all 11 games, on special teams and as a backup receiver, and didn't catch a pass all season.

During the academy's Christmas break, Waudby and some of his Oakland friends went on a bar-hopping run that wound its way into Manhattan early the following morning. Some ironworkers seated nearby struck up a conversation with the girls in the group, who mentioned that Waudby was a West Point cadet. One of the workers said, "Come with us." They walked about 10 blocks through the cold and wind to Ground Zero. The workers took the visitors to the family observation deck, guiding their guests through multiple police checkpoints. A New York City police officer must have overheard some conversation and asked Waudby if he was the cadet. The officer handed Waudby a hard hat and drove him on a four-wheel vehicle down into the pit of ruins.

More than three months after the attacks, the smell of jet fuel and burning bodies still dominated the immediate area; Waudby, given his family history with crematories, was certainly familiar with the latter. After the pair rejoined the rest of the group, one of the ironworkers motioned toward the wreckage and said to Waudby, "Look what those assholes did. You have to go get 'em." The man then walked a short distance to his car and returned with a piece of an I-beam from one of the towers that had been formed into a miniature version of the towers. "Here. I want you to have this," he told Waudby.

The revelers of only a few hours earlier returned to New Jersey in near silence. The sun was peaking over the horizon when Waudby was dropped off at home, where his father was anxiously waiting. Brad Jr. walked in the house with the mass of dark steel, to which his father asked, "What the hell is that thing?" There was plenty for Brad Jr. to explain about the trip to Manhattan.

Just before the cadets left for Christmas break, Thomas Roberts was involved in another contentious incident, this time in the mess hall. A freshman football player at his table pulled a stunt that offended a female cadet who was dating a senior football player seated at another table. Roberts essentially told her to relax, that the table's horseplay wasn't any of her business. That didn't sit well with her; the young lady told her boyfriend, who reported the episode to Todd Berry and Roberts was dismissed from the team for the second time. He left the athletic offices, walked down to the Michie Stadium field, kissed the logo at midfield, and cried. Roberts walked back to his barracks and pondered whether there was a future for him at West Point.

Early in West Point's second semester, Roberts was willing to try anything to regain a spot on the team. That's why he was eager to participate in flag football games involving varsity players at Michie Stadium during the offseason. His hope was to show his former teammates that his skills merited having him as a teammate again. One such game was held on the Thursday afternoon just before the yuks celebrated the Yearling Winter Weekend during the first weekend of February, with a banquet at the academy followed for most by a weekend on the town in Manhattan. Minutes after the game ended, Roberts sat in the locker room with one of the other participants that day. Anthony Miller said he was tired and was going to take a shower. Soon after, Miller suffered through a bout of vomiting and was admitted to Keller Army Community Hospital there on the academy grounds. His condition worsened by Friday. Miller suffered a heart attack and was revived before dying that evening at the age of twenty. He was later diagnosed with immune deficiency that left him vulnerable to a virus that attacked his system quickly and enlarged his heart.

The joy of the Yearling Winter Weekend abruptly evaporated when word spread of Miller's death. A memorial vigil was held at the academy at midnight Monday, with Miller's name hauntingly called out with no reply. The entire football team boarded buses the following day—Roberts was allowed to ride—and traveled to Maryland for Miller's funeral. It was a "homegoing service," as stated in the printed program, which contained first-person comments from the deceased: "I lived an abundant life on earth and, in my mind, I made it to the NFL. . . . 'Notorious for Life' eternal in the Heavens." The West Point contingent included Daniel Christman, who was the academy superintendent when Miller arrived on the Hudson. One display of flowers near the open casket consisted of gold mums arranged in an Army "A." Miller was dressed in his full dress-gray academy uniform, holding tickets from an Army-Navy football game.

Roberts soon considered an exit from West Point, prepared to pack his belongings, but agreed to meet one more time with his chosen mentor. Colonel Gene Palka told him, "West Point needs you. The army and the country need you. They need talent like yours and people like you to lead our soldiers." Roberts returned to his room and wrestled with his decision. He fell asleep amid tears, awoke the next morning, headed to class, and never again pondered resignation from West Point.

* * *

In March 2002, Michael and Brigitte Kwinn's thirteen-year-old son, Michael III, began suffering persistent migraine headaches. A CAT scan revealed a brain-stem tumor. It was inoperable. The Kwinns were told their son had six months to live. They held out hope of at least extending Michael's life through surgeries, the first of which took place soon after the diagnosis, plus radiation and chemotherapy. The treatments confined to bed the once-active youngster who played football and loved Harry Potter books and the Miami Dolphins. The Kwinns' daughter, Cheryl, refused to accept her brother's plight, relying on the family's strong Catholic faith that God wouldn't allow Michael to be taken at such a young age. Friends reached out to the Kwinn family offering gifts, like tickets to a New York Yankees game. Young Michael appreciated such generosity but told his parents that, while his situation appeared dire, they should focus on doing something to help other youngsters who shared his plight. They raised $15,000 in only two weeks for the Brain Tumor Society and personally handed over the check at the Race for Hope in Washington, DC.

More football-playing members of the Class of 2004 left either the program or the academy. Among them was D. J. Stancil, who established himself as a valuable member of Army's rotation of running backs in 2001, withdrawing from West Point during spring 2002. Adam Rafalski, the former quarterback-turned-wide receiver, left the football program that same spring. But two members of the class came out of spring practice having earned starting positions for the coming season—Ryan Kent and running back Marcellus Chapman.

The first West Point graduation ceremony following 9/11 featured the commander in chief as the commencement speaker for the first time since President Bill Clinton in 1997. The address was written by Michael Gerson, Bush's chief speechwriter (now a columnist for the *Washington Post*). Bush and Gerson saw the presentation at West Point as, in addition to congratulating the graduates, continuing the president's public identification of the "Axis of Evil" that he'd referenced during his State of the Union speech in January. At Michie Stadium, Bush would focus on preemption being America's best way of dealing with those countries who threatened the nation rather than deterrence or containment. "The war on terror will not be won on the defensive," Bush said from a stage in the stadium's south end zone. "We must take the battle to the enemy, disrupt his plans and confront the worst threats before they emerge." The speech took 30 minutes and 20 seconds. The president never said the word Iraq.

Chapter Seven

"I'M EXACTLY WHERE I WANT TO BE"

Most of the football-playing members of the Class of 2004 spent the summer of 2002 doing their CTLT—cadet troop leadership training—while the others honed their officer skills supervising at either Beast Barracks or Camp Buckner. If part of the Buckner summer was something of a job fair to expose the cadets to the army's various branches, CTLT was a progression in the process that would hopefully help the participants decide which branch to pursue when they became seniors.

Josh Davis did his CTLT at Fort Sill, getting a taste of the field artillery's big guns, part of the base's "Big Red One." Tom Farrington, Ryan Kent, Peter Stewart, and Anthony Zurisko completed theirs at Fort Hood with the 4th Infantry Division under the ultimate authority of General Ray Odierno. The general seemed to always take a liking to Army football players. He played tight end for the Cadets during the 1972–73 seasons, acknowledging years later that his primary motivation for enrolling at the academy was to play football. One of their more hands-on mentors was Brody Howatt, a former Army hockey player whose father (Garry) played with the Stanley Cup champion New York Islanders.

During CTLT, football players were permitted to eat as much as they wanted in the chow hall and provided with plenty of time to work out. The players became acquainted with the abundant nightlife in Austin, located about an hour's drive south of Fort Hood, and Stewart was able to make a couple of visits home to Houston. In addition, they participated in the various games held as part of the post's "Ironhorse" competition. Zurisko proved to represent something of a ringer in Fort Hood's version of the NFL's long-time Punt, Pass, and Kick competition for youngsters; he finished first across the entire base. After completing CTLT, the players moved on to PIAD before the summer came to an end; that was a course in "physical individual athletic development" that was often offered to corps squad athletes beginning with their third West Point academic year (but not limited to them).

Brian Hill, Brad Waudby, and Clint Woody deferred their CTLT to 2003 and spent the summer giving orders to the incoming plebe hopefuls or rising sophomores. Juniors-to-be served as squad leaders, platoon sergeants, or 1st sergeants for Beast or Buckner. Seniors-to-be were the platoon leaders, company commanders, executive officers, and brigade commanders. Cadets in both classes submitted requests online listing their preferences. Both Beast and Buckner were broken into halves with the supervising cadets switched out at "halftime." Woody, who worked Beast, enjoyed having a captive audience that hung on his every word and that most of them absorbed his commands and took their first baby steps toward becoming cadets. He didn't enjoy dispensing discipline to those who didn't immediately catch on.

The West Point-to-Danbury runs for Hill and Davis continued late in the summer of 2002, when Tarek Reslan subleased an off-campus room in a house that was rented out by a local woman named Misa Froehlich. She was a 1997 graduate of nearby Brookfield High, the daughter of a former Boston College football player, and a three-sport athlete herself (soccer, volleyball, and softball). When her father helped coach Brookfield High's football team, she begged him to be the "water girl" and eventually became a cheerleader.

The relationship between Froehlich and Reslan was essentially sister-brother, and he pretty much advised visitors like the two Army football players that she was untouchable. As Hill and Davis were leaving for the academy following one weekend, Davis asked if he could call her. Davis and Froehlich struck up a conversation soon after a barbeque held elsewhere in Danbury.

Their first date was the following weekend at a restaurant named Amberjax, and the relationship blossomed quickly.

* * *

In West Point vernacular, the Class of 2004 cadets became *cows* in August 2002 with the beginning of the academic year. And just why cows? The academy offers no official explanation. One popular version dates to the earliest days of the institution and offers that cadets would finally be able to travel back home to see their families for the first time during the school year at the Christmas break of their third academic year, not "until the cows come home."

On the Sunday night before the 2002–03 academic year began, West Point's pending third-year students gathered inside Robinson Auditorium in Thayer Hall for the Affirmation Oath ceremony. It was a continuation of the Oath of Allegiance that the "new cadets" committed to during the first hours of R-Day two years earlier. For any member of the Class of 2004 who was unnerved by the prospect of deployment into a war zone in the aftermath of 9/11, this was the final opportunity to walk away from West Point with no strings attached. From that day forward, any cadet from that class who wished to leave the academy would still owe the government military service—as a soldier instead of as an officer. Also, they would be obligated to pay substantial restitution to the government—estimated at $125,000 and increasing incrementally from then on—for partaking of two years or more of academy education. The 30-minute event came complete with a speaker, General David Petraeus. The cadets stood, raised their right hands, and repeated the oath. The TAC officers then distributed commemorative coins.

The decision was routine for most but high drama for some. Abby Racster was unsure of her intention. She'd failed two classes during her sophomore year. In some cases, cadets who were reluctant to make the commitment sidestepped the indignity of quitting by no longer qualifying academically. Racster knew she shouldn't have failed those classes. She knew she didn't want to deploy to a war zone. But peers talked her into staying. Her parents drove from Virginia to West Point and stood in the back of the auditorium as the cows raised their right hands. The deed done, Racster felt no better. She left Thayer Hall with a sinking feeling. Upon reporting to her first class the following morning, her instructor said, "Oh. You decided to stay."

Mike and Cheryl Davis drove Josh back to West Point for the beginning of the school year, taking daughter Nicole along with them. As the four of them stood on the academy grounds, Mike verbalized the thought that hung heavily in the air: "Are you sure you want to do this?" Josh appeared taken aback that the question was even asked. "I'm exactly where I want to be," he said confidently. His parents felt both comfort in his resolve and apprehension for what could lay ahead for their son. Soon after Josh said goodbye to his parents and sister, Mike pulled Cheryl aside and said, "He's a grown man. He's going to make his own decisions whether we like it or not."

Grace Chung had no doubts about remaining though she somewhat muddled through her first two years at the academy. Toward the end of her yuk year, Chung decided she needed to get serious about some aspect of West Point life. Her TAC officer suggested applying for the academy's special leadership program, which would provide opportunities for service to the corps in something of an extracurricular fashion. She was accepted and, beginning with her junior year, assumed the rank of battalion command sergeant major.

In early August 2002, President Bush arranged to meet with his national security council by video conference. The virtual get-together was arranged to give his secretary of state, Colin Powell, the opportunity to present his stance that the United States' next major move in the war against terrorism wasn't to send American troops back into Iraq but to instead have the US commander in chief seek a solution through the United Nations. When Bush asked for reaction to Powell's proposal, no one spoke up in opposition. The president met with media later that day and stated that Saddam Hussein "desires weapons of mass destruction." Bush later conveyed to speechwriter Michael Gerson that his talk to the UN should indicate the body would deem itself irrelevant if it didn't act to subdue the Iraq threat. Four days later, Bob Woodward of the *Washington Post* interviewed Bush to follow up on the prospect of an invasion of Iraq. "As we think through Iraq, we may or may not attack," the president said. "I have no idea yet." There was no reference to weapons of mass destruction. The following day, Bush described himself as a patient man when it came to dealing with Hussein.

On August 27, 2002, Vice President Dick Cheney was the featured speaker at the 103rd convention of the Veterans of Foreign Wars in Nashville, Tennessee. His message was that Hussein didn't seek weapons of mass destruction; the vice president stated that the Iraqi dictator already possessed them: "There is no doubt that Saddam Hussein now has weapons of mass destruction. There is no doubt that he is amassing them to use against our friends, against our allies and against us." When President Bush spoke in Cincinnati, Ohio, a few weeks later, he stated the Iraqi regime "possesses and produces biological and chemical weapons." Such pronouncements from the two highest voices of American government prompted the compilation of a National Intelligence Estimate of Iraq's arsenal, which concluded, "Baghdad has chemical and biological weapons. . . . Although we have little specific information on Iraq's CW stockpile, Saddam probably has stocked at least 100 metric tons and possibly as much as 500 metric tons of CW agents—much of it added in the last year." Woodard of the *Post* wrote in *Plan of Attack* that those in the administration who rejected that stance didn't say so publicly, "because so much intelligence would have to be discounted. The real and best answer was that he *probably* had WMD, but that there was no proof and the case was circumstantial."

* * *

Sue Petroff ended her two-year stint with Army's swimming and diving team before the 2002–03 season began. Unfortunately for her, she never developed a bond with either of West Point's diving coaches during the two previous seasons like the one that she had formed with Brad Szurgot during the recruiting process. She apparently wasn't the only diver who had such issues. Petroff and some teammates went to head coach John O'Neill, who succeeded the retiring Ray Bosse in 2001, following the 2001–02 season and said they wouldn't return in '02–03 if the rest of the staff remained intact. When there wasn't any personnel adjustment, she didn't report to the team at the beginning of preseason practices.

Thomas Roberts prepared for his first academic year without football since before high school. He managed to remain close to the program, literally and figuratively. Roberts joined the cheerleading Rabble Rousers and became the "mike man" on the sidelines during games. Most Army fans likely hoped the victory over Navy that concluded the three-win season of 2001 would carry over momentum into the season of 2002, which happened to be the academy's bicentennial year. Todd Berry must have thought so during the team's preseason media day, when he said, "I expect to win every ballgame, go to a bowl game and win that. . . . I don't let myself even think about anything else." Numbers like 27 of Army's 119 players being sophomores or freshmen—26 of those listed among the 44 starters or primary backups on offense and defense—might have indicated that would be a tall task. Before the Black Knights reported for the beginning of fall drills in August, twenty players were subtracted from the roster for various reasons. One was the late Anthony Miller. The group included three starters—senior cornerback Emiko Terry, junior running back C. J. Young, and sophomore kicker Derek Jacobs, all lost to academic issues as reported by the nearby newspaper that provided daily coverage of Army athletics, the *Times Herald-Record* of Middletown, New York. Terry and Young would concentrate on their academy classes that semester in the hope of regaining their athletic eligibility. In the case of Jacobs, it was reported he chose to leave West Point to pursue a line of study that wasn't available there (polymer sciences). His unexpected departure left the kicking duties up for grabs again. Paul Stelzer, who handled kickoffs in 2001, added placements duties as a senior.

Returning to active football duty was defensive end Odene Brathwaite, who sat out the '01 season to regain his academic eligibility. He was reclassified as a sophomore for football (as far as the NCAA was concerned), like a player who had red-shirted and figured to make the starting unit. Marcellus Chapman returned after missing the 2001 campaign because of a wrist injury and figured to be one of Army's primary running backs along with senior Josh Holden, who also played on Army's baseball team, and freshman Carlton Jones. Plus, another member of the Class of 2004 joined the varsity football roster for the first time. George Feagins, from Birmingham, Alabama, spent his first two academic years at West Point playing quarterback for the academy's sprint football team. The sprint team played helmets-and-pads football just like the varsity, likewise facing competition from other schools, including Navy. Feagins was "imported" to the varsity, as stated in Army's football media guide, to play wide receiver and was listed on the second team.

A bowl trip for the 2002 Army team, as stated by Berry, would have marked the program's first in six seasons and only the fifth in the long history of West Point football given the academy's once long-standing policy. Jim Young, who became Army's football coach in 1983, succeeded in qualifying the Cadets for the program's first bowl. Young arrived at West Point following successful stints at Arizona and Purdue, but he didn't experience immediate success at the academy. Army lost its '83 opener at home to lightly regarded Colgate and stumbled to a 2–9 finish that included a similar defeat to Lehigh. Young then replaced his pro-style offense with the triple option in an effort to better play to the strengths of his roster, and his 1984 team finished the season 7–3–1. That included a head-turning 24–24 tie at Tennessee early in the season, and Army ended a six-year winless streak against Navy. When Army was invited to play in the inaugural Cherry Bowl in suburban Detroit, the academy accepted. And the Cadets beat the quasi-host school, Michigan State, 10–6. Army earned another bowl bid the following season, to Atlanta's Peach Bowl, and went to the Sun Bowl in El Paso, Texas in 1988.

The change in offensive formations was certainly the primary catalyst. Senior Nate Sassaman was the top rushing quarterback in major college football in 1984, while completing only 24 passes. In the '83 win that clinched the Cherry Bowl bid—45–31 over Montana, a game played in Tokyo— Army became the first college football team to have four players rush for 100 or more yards in the same game. The ground attack was led by junior Doug Black, who made the team in '84 after twice being rejected in tryouts, breaking Army's season-rushing record that year.

But Young also increased his team's chances to win by convincing academy officials to provide football players certain allowances beyond limits that were placed on other cadets. Some of those had been debated since the mercurial one-year stay of Lou Saban in 1979. The well-known pro coach of the 1960s and '70s railed on his way out the door (stating upon his hiring that he'd stay at West Point "until they put me out to pasture") that the academy restrictions prevented Army from fielding a successful football program. Young began the practice of heavy tables during Beast Barracks. Players were provided with supplementary vitamins and night-time snacks and given more access to the trainers' facilities. In 1984, senior linebacker Jim Gentile told *The New York Times*' Vecsey that, as a cadre officer overseeing Beast, he saw plebes who actually gained weight by the end of the summer session. Players were no longer scheduled for afternoon classes that resulted in them heading directly from the lecture hall to the practice field or to fulfill routine cadet duties scheduled for late Friday nights or Saturday mornings. While West Point football players still faced academic challenges beyond those experienced by most other young men playing major college football, their academy lives shifted at least slightly toward that of a big-time collegiate football player.

Young retired following the 1990 season at age fifty-five, having guided the Cadets to six winning finishes in eight seasons. Bob Sutton, whom Young brought to West Point on his initial staff, ascended to the head coaching position. Sutton's nine seasons as Army head coach rank second only to Earl Blaik. The high point was the 1996 team that finished 9–2, with a fifth consecutive win over Navy, and played in the Independence Bowl in Shreveport, Louisiana. As was the case with Young's best squads, the '96 Cadets were led by an undersized option quarterback who seemingly refused to be tackled. Ronnie McAda Jr. grew up in the blue-collar Dallas suburb of Mesquite. He was recruited by Notre Dame, USC, and Texas early in his high school career, but that interest diminished after he suffered a knee injury as a junior. Against Navy that year, McAda led a 99-yard touchdown drive—kept alive by a scrambling completion on 4th and 24 at the Middies' 29-yard line—that produced the winning touchdown with 1:03 to play. As memorable as that finish was, McAda and the '96 Cadets might be best remembered for their bowl loss to Auburn. Army trailed 32–7 going into the fourth quarter, then proceeded to construct a comeback for the ages. The Cadets scored three fourth-quarter touchdowns to pull within 32–29 with 1:27 to play and appeared poised to send the game into overtime, lining up for a 27-yard field-goal attempt in the closing seconds. But senior kicker J. Parker's right foot grazed the ground before striking the ball, and the kick sliced to the right of the goalposts.

There was certainly enough optimism to think the 2002 Black Knights could at least win their opening game for the first time since that 1996 season. Their initial foe would be Holy Cross, Army's first NCAA Division I-AA opponent since 1997, and the game would be played at Michie Stadium. The Black Knights' depth chart going into the game featured 12 senior starters and only two juniors—Kent and Chapman. Only one junior was listed on Army's second team—right tackle Adam Wojcik. Josh Davis, Brian Hill, and Brad Waudby were third-teamers, while Anthony Zurisko was the second-string kicker. Peter Stewart was finally healthy for an entire season and was moved to tackle despite being at a greater weight disadvantage against defensive linemen than he faced at guard. He dressed for every home game and made the Navy trip with the team for the first time but, three years into his time at West Point, had yet to take the field.

Army and Holy Cross were tied 14–14 in the second quarter, the Cadets having lost two fumbles, when starting quarterback Reggie Nevels tore a hamstring, knocking him out for the game and, most likely, a large chunk of the season.

Enter freshman Zac Dahman, a quiet, lean redhead from Texas whose appearance and demeanor earned him the nickname "Opie" for his resemblance to Ron Howard's character on the early 1960s *Andy Griffith Show*. A two-year high school starter at Fossil Ridge High in the Fort Worth suburb of Keller, Dahman had been contacted by Notre Dame, Clemson, and Colorado only to learn that he apparently stood no better than second on those schools' lists of quarterback prospects. Army was the lone Division I-A program that sustained interest in Dahman, and his decision came down to West Point and two regional I-AA schools—Central Arkansas and McNeese State in Louisiana. He took his paid visit to the academy with his parents and indicated to his father, Fletcher, that he wanted to fulfill his promises to the staffs at McNeese and Central Arkansas to visit their campuses. Fletcher said if Todd Berry offered the chance to play for the Black Knights before their visit ended, he'd play the bad cop and fend off Berry. They sat down together a few minutes later, and Berry wasted no time going to his hard sell: "We need you here, Zac. You may even end up playing your freshman year.

We really want you here." To which Dahman replied, "I'm ready to sign right now," much to his father's surprise.

Misfortune had only just begun for the Cadets with two lost fumbles and one lost quarterback. They lost three more fumbles during the second half and also allowed a 95-yard kickoff return for a touchdown. The Crusaders returned home to Worcester, Massachusetts, with a 31–21 win. Dahman completed 19 of 34 passes, threw no interceptions, but averaged fewer than 10 yards per completion and lost a fumble at the Crusaders' 6-yard line. Afterward, Berry said that day's Army team was his best-prepared in 20 years of college coaching.

On the anniversary of 9/11, Bradford Waudby Sr. was among the Bergen County residents who were interviewed by the *Record* for their thoughts and feelings. He participated in a memorial held in Veterans Park, just across Ramapo Valley Road from his funeral home. As part of the ceremony, he presented Oakland mayor Robert Piccoli with the steel remembrance of the towers that an ironworker had given to young Brad at Ground Zero after the previous Christmas. "It's just something that I think should be here today," he said.

Nevels's injury required more than a month to heal. Dahman's start in the next game, at Rutgers, was the first by a West Point plebe quarterback in 15 years; freshmen have been eligible to compete in NCAA varsity competition since the 1972–73 academic year. Rutgers was likewise off to an awful start in head coach Greg Schiano's second season. The Scarlet Knights (not to be confused with the Black Knights) also lost their opener to a Division I-AA opponent, Villanova, and followed that with a second home loss, to Buffalo. One national ranking service placed Rutgers at the very bottom of Division I-A after two weeks. But all of that was forgotten on one picturesque Sunday evening in Piscataway, New Jersey. Dahman threw three interceptions, Rutgers devoured 390 yards against the West Point defense, and the Scarlet Knights cruised to an easy 44–0 victory. The margin of the Cadets' 17th consecutive loss in a "pure" road game (not counting neutral-site meetings like Army-Navy) marked the program's most lopsided shutout defeat since 1981. Ken McMillan declared in the following day's *Times Herald-Record* that Army football had "officially hit rock bottom."

West Point's subsequent 45–14 home loss to Louisville at least featured an 88-yard fumble recovery for a touchdown early in the third quarter by Ryan Kent. Unfortunately for the Black Knights and their fans, that was Army's first score of the day after the Cardinals had already put 31 points on the board. Afterward, Louisville coach John L. Smith might have thought he was being polite when he stated his team "didn't play particularly well." That only placed the Army program and Berry in a less favorable light.

Kevin Gleason's column in the Sunday *Times Herald-Record* ran beneath the headline "Army out of its league in C-USA." Gleason wrote: "Army can't win weekly battles in a high-caliber league with sketchy academic standards." He considered Louisville, which graduated about 20 percent of its football players according to NCAA data, a perfect example of the apples-oranges dilemma that Army football faced in the conference. Only one quarter of the way through the Black Knights' schedule, Gleason didn't see any cavalry coming over the horizon for the balance of the season: "An 0–12 record is a distinct possibility."

Halfway through the season, Josh Davis was injured during a run-through before starting seven-on-seven drills when he was playing the role of a defensive lineman. Peter Stewart was also portraying a defender—a linebacker—and collided with Davis. It's possible that Stewart was pushed into Davis by another player. The end result was Stewart went right through the back of one of Davis's knees, causing his to suffer a severe sprain. Davis missed most of the balance of the season, returning in time for the Navy game. Senior kicker Paul Stelzer was also lost to injury with four games remaining. His replacement wasn't junior Anthony Zurisko, but freshman Joe Riley.

The Army losing streak reached nine games in mid-November with a 49–30 defeat at home to Air Force that also set a Michie Stadium mark for consecutive defeats at seven. During the streak, Tom Farrington recovered one fumble each against Southern Mississippi and East Carolina. The Black Knights' defense then played its best game in years in a 14–10 win at Tulane. During the losing streak, West Point allowed an average of 42.8 points and 399 yards per game. In New Orleans' Superdome, Army held

Tulane's pass-oriented offense to 198 total yards, only 26 rushing on 28 carries. Reggie Nevels, who'd returned to the starting lineup the previous week, threw for one touchdown and scored what proved to be the game winner on the ground, barely stretching the ball into the end zone after being hit short of the goal line. The Black Knights won despite losing four fumbles. In 32 games as Army's head coach to that point, Todd Berry was 3–0 vs. Tulane and 2–27 against all other opponents.

The Cadets lost once more, 38–10 at Memphis, before facing Navy. The game completed a two-year run outside of its traditional home in Philadelphia, the 2000 game in Baltimore essentially serving as a Navy home game and the 2002 meeting at Giants Stadium in New Jersey providing the same for Army. It appeared to be an even matchup if not a quality one, each team arriving at the Meadowlands with a 1–10 record. History backed up such an assumption; seven of the previous 10 games in the series were decided by five points or fewer. Before the game, Berry was asked about his preseason expectation to go undefeated: "I thought it was possible. But deep down, I knew this season could go either way."

West Point's Class of '04 was barely represented on the three-deep depth chart going into the game. The only junior starter was Ryan Kent. His standout season resulted in being one of the game captains who were added each year before the Navy game to the season-long captains who were chosen before the opening kickoff. Receiver Clint Woody and left guard Adam Wojcik were listed on the second team, left tackle Brad Waudby and inside linebacker Tom Farrington on the third team. With the game played about 20 minutes from Waudby's hometown of Oakland, a substantial contingent of relatives and friends made the short drive to East Rutherford. Waudby was the subject of a story in that morning's *Record*. It focused on both his 50-or-so relatives and friends who would cheer him on in person that day and the fact that, only a few miles east of the stadium, the New York skyline was eerily devoid of the Twin Towers that were taken down 15 months earlier. "It's something that I saw every day when I woke up and went to high school," he told the newspaper. He'd dressed every game that season and saw regular duty on field-goal and extra-point units.

The even matchup that was envisioned never materialized. Navy set series records for the most points and the largest winning margin with a 58–12 rout, its option offense rumbling for 508 yards—a staggering 6.95 per snap. Navy's hero was Craig Candeto, the junior quarterback from central Florida. He ran for six touchdowns and passed for one more—playing only three quarters. Candeto said afterward: "It felt a lot like a dream out there." It was no dream for Berry and his team: "I don't think any of us could have dreamed that the game could have gone in that direction." George Feagins touched the ball for the first time all season in making his fourth appearance in a game; a first-down end-around run during the fourth quarter didn't fool the Middies' defense, losing 19 yards. Another dismal season capped by another lopsided loss to Navy left the Army coaching staff fearing the worst. The assistants left that weekend for recruiting, unsure if they would still be West Point coaches for the 2003 season. John Mumford said goodbye to wife Leslie and told her to be prepared: "Something could happen this week."

"Supe" William Lennox indeed considered making a coaching change. He inherited Berry and his staff in 2001 and was naturally encouraged by Army's win that year over Navy to close an otherwise disheartening 3–8 campaign. Lennox believed the triumph was the sign of a program on the rise. He witnessed no such rise with the 1–10 finish of 2002. Lennox struggled with what to do about the football leadership for days before ultimately deciding to retain Berry, who had two years remaining on his contract.

Reggie Nevels, expected to be Army's starting quarterback for another two seasons, left the football team in February. He was quoted in an athletic department news release saying, "There are several areas in my personal life that I need to focus on at this time. These issues continue to pull me away from baseball and football. I feel it is in the best interests of everyone involved that I take some time away in order to concentrate on those areas." Nevels left the team but not the academy, and he confided to those closest to him that he was trying to cope with multiple deaths in his family plus the murder of a close friend back home in Indiana. Nevels was back on the squad in April following the conclusion of spring practice and technically listed at the bottom of the depth chart behind junior Matt Silva and sophomores Dahman, Laron Bybee, and Connor Crehan.

* * *

In February 2003, Josh Davis took Misa Froehlich back to the Connecticut restaurant where the couple had gone on their first date eight months earlier. He'd already asked her father, Craig, for his permission to marry Misa following his graduation from West Point in May 2004. The reply from his prospective father-in-law was not only a hearty yes but the suggestion that, in the event she said no, to keep asking. She said yes on the first try.

* * *

One of West Point's forms of punishment could be found in progress most Saturday mornings in Central Area, where the cadets begin each weekday with morning formation. It's called marching the hours, and that's exactly what it is. Certain infractions of academy rules carried with them a certain number of hours of punitive marching. In many cases, the number of hours couldn't be marched off all at once. There typically was more than one miscreant doing the marching, and no talking was allowed. That led to creative methods for multiple cadets to add something of even minimal interest to break the monotony, such as kicking a pebble back and forth to each other or signaling discreetly to any amused observers who peered down from their barracks windows.

Sue Petroff was hit with a prohibitive number of hours for an incident that took place during her sophomore year. She and a handful of her female friends were relaxing one Thursday night in her barracks room when two of her buddies brought a bottle of tequila to the room. One of the young ladies consumed more than she should have, returned to her room for "Taps" and then became sick. A senior girl on the hall had witnessed the sequence of events and came over to Petroff's room and asked if she could be of any help. No, Petroff replied, all was well. The senior then headed straight to the company commander and reported the incident.

The following morning, the cadet who'd imbibed too much stopped at Petroff's room on the way to her first class and tearfully confessed that she had to turn in Petroff for her role in the misadventure. Her penalty was assessed at 80 hours of marching. The time frame for completing the punishment coincided with a planned trip by her parents, who held a strong aversion to drinking at that age. Petroff dodged them as best she could. She then underestimated her mother's time spent on social media and posted on her AOL instant messenger account that she had to march the hours. Rita Petroff, who *never* looked at AOL on weekends, did so that weekend and was stunned. If Petroff's parents learned why she had to march, she feared they might withdraw her from the academy and place her in alcohol rehab. She fudged and said the penalty was for burning a candle in her room.

* * *

Michael Kwinn III, given six months to live in March 2002, presented a check for more than $50,000 at the 2003 Race for Hope in the nation's capital 14 months after the diagnosis of an inoperable brain-stem tumor. From the time that Army cadets learned what the Kwinns faced, they rallied around the family. Brian Hill and Ryan Kent visited with Michael when his father brought him to football practices. They signed footballs for him. The Kwinns began a foundation, Friends4Michael, to increase awareness of brain cancer in children and to help support their families. That included annual participation in the Washington race and starting a fundraising golf tournament in Monroe. When the tournament was scheduled to take place on the day before Army football's annual tournament, many returning Black Knights played in both events.

Young Michael endured nine brain surgeries, two other related operations, and 50 rounds of radiation. That left him with scars all over his head and in constant pain from the tumor that pressed on his skull. Radiation made his hair fall out and then grow back in misshapen patterns. He was given various types of steroids that bloated and deformed his face. The former starting center on the school basketball team used a walker to navigate the halls each day, and some of his fellow students couldn't help but react awkwardly.

He eventually couldn't close one eye, became deaf in one ear and could barely speak. The night before West Point's 2003 graduation ceremony in late May, young Michael—unable to move anything below his neck at that point—was rushed from the Kwinns' home to Keller Army Community Hospital. Just before his eyes closed for the last time the following morning, he smiled and mouthed to his father, "Dad, I love you." Michael Kwinn III died only hours before the graduates filled the floor of Michie Stadium and listened to the remarks of Vice President Dick Cheney, at age fourteen.

Chapter Eight

"WE BELIEVE WE'RE GOING TO WIN"

Brian Hill's CTLT during the summer of 2003 took place at Fort Sill, Oklahoma. The instillation was founded in 1869 by Major General Philip Sheridan and named to honor a West Point classmate who was killed during the Civil War, Joshua Sill. The fort is located about an hour's drive north of the Oklahoma-Texas border, around 85 miles southwest of Oklahoma City and 191 miles northwest of Dallas-Fort Worth. Both of those metropolitan areas were popular destinations for soldiers and cadets. Hill arranged an Independence Day trip to Fort Worth—to the famed Billy Bob's Texas honky-tonk—through Michael Lennox, a Class of 2002 West Point graduate and football player from Fort Worth's Boswell High School. Lennox helped arrange to hang out with some young ladies, including an '02 Boswell graduate who'd just finished her first year at the University of Texas at Austin.

Morgan Hesse was the oldest child of Lennox's high school football coach, Charlie Hesse. Morgan liked to describe growing up in a football coaching family thusly: "We interrupt this marriage to bring you the football season." Charlie and wife Mindy grew up in Arkansas; he played football for Ouachita Baptist, and she was a cheerleader. Morgan's dream while growing up was to cheer for her father's team on Friday nights, which she did. Hill and Hesse would keep in touch during the coming school year through long emails and instant messages since he spent so much time on computers while working academy projects. If Hill's plans came to fruition, he would branch field artillery following graduation, come through Fort Sill again for his officer basic course early in 2005, and then be assigned to Fort Hood, Texas. It was the largest active-duty armored post in the country's armed services, home to the 1st Cavalry and the 3rd Armored Cavalry Regiments among other entities. The post was named for John Bell Hood, a general in the Confederate army. If nothing came of Hill's long-distance relationship with Hesse, he at least had a contact for making further social connections in Austin.

Brad Waudby's assignment for CTLT didn't resemble Fort Sill; he was dispatched to Hawaii. Waudby roomed with a fellow New Jersey native, Dennis Zilinski II, at Schofield Barracks while stationed with the D Company of the 725th Main Support Battalion. The cadets lined for physical training at 5 a.m. and were done with their day's assignments by mid-afternoon. From there it was only a short drive to the beach, be it the relative quiet of the North Shore or the bustling social life of Waikiki. Waudby and Zilinski were quartered at a five-star hotel and enjoyed their downtime together in Honolulu. They sometimes caught each other's eye during PT and seemed to say to each other, "How lucky are we?"

Zilinski was a member of the Army swimming and diving team, specializing in the butterfly stroke and freestyle. He was far from the most talented member of the team but was chosen to captain the men's squad for the upcoming 2003–04 school year. Swimming didn't start out as Zilinski's sport of choice. Like most of the other young boys growing up in the central Jersey town of Holmdel, he wanted to play baseball. But he was chubby, began wearing glasses at a young age, and never developed the kind of hand-eye coordination necessary to excel at and enjoy baseball. He then tried soccer but wasn't really a good enough runner for that. His mother, Marion, placed him and younger brother Matthew in a summer camp that gave them regular access to a swimming pool. There, Zilinski embraced an activity that he enjoyed. Matthew was initially the better swimmer. But while Dennis didn't have natural athletic skills, he did possess an intense focus. He channeled that into swimming and was good enough to land a berth on the Red Bank YMCA squad. Marion and "Big Dennis," a state trooper and Vietnam veteran, were happy to drive the fourth of their five children all over New Jersey for swim meets.

Swimming was the primary reason why Zilinski, when graduating from the eighth grade, begged his parents to send him to nearby Christian Brothers Academy, a high school swimming powerhouse. CBA was an all-male Catholic high school, and Marion somewhat bemusedly reminded her son, "We're not Catholic." But Dennis wasn't convinced that was a deal-breaker and coerced his mother to take him to an open house at the school. She was certain they'd be turned away and Dennis would be crestfallen. Instead, a school official told them, "We teach all religions." CBA taught all religions, but that didn't excuse a non-Catholic like Dennis from attending Mass at the school each Friday. Church and community involvement were important aspects of Zilinski's young life. He delivered food baskets to the poor as a young boy. As a teen, he urged the worship committee at Middletown Reformed Church, where his family worshiped, to reinstate its Sunday sunrise service—and promised that his parents would prepare breakfast each week. And he made Christian Brothers' swim team. As a senior, he was chosen as team captain, though he didn't win many races.

With the same drive that led Zilinski to attend CBA, he made West Point the object of his collegiate affection during his sophomore year. He often finished high enough to earn points toward his team's total, but his times didn't attract the attention of Army coach Ray Bosse. That prompted Zilinski's exasperated YMCA coach to implore Bosse to sign him, saying that Zilinski would contribute to the team by scoring points even if he didn't win races. Still, the Zilinskis didn't hear anything back from West Point, and Dennis wasn't interested in the Naval Academy. The swim coach at the Coast Guard Academy *was* interested, and that appeared to be Zilinski's best option. That is, until he took a preliminary physical that revealed he was colorblind, which prohibited him from becoming an officer at sea. Zilinski's persistence with West Point paid off, and he was admitted to the academy directly from high school and brought onto Army's swim team. He quickly disproved his YMCA coach's claim that he wouldn't win any races, finishing first in the 200-yard butterfly in a dual meet against Dartmouth, and compiled three top-five finishes during his plebe season. Because Zilinski's home was a short drive from West Point, caravans carrying more than a dozen Army swimmers and divers often made the trip to Holmdel. The tab for feeding the gleeful escapees from academy rule often went into four figures. But when they left for the Hudson early Sunday, it was difficult to recognize that any wayfarers had spent the weekend there.

Zilinski concentrated primarily on the butterfly, notched three wins, and was selected as the most improved sophomore or junior on the team. In the days that immediately followed 9/11 the previous fall, his mother implored him to resign from the academy: "You're getting out of West Point!" Zilinski was as adamant in his disagreement: "You don't quit West Point." He considered leaving the academy—to enlist and immediately join the war effort. Zilinski distilled his viewpoint to the following: "Mom, why would I leave now when my country needs me most?" Marion argued no further and simply prayed for the best.

Waudby, Zilinski, and the other cadets who spent that summer in Hawaii participated in the 25th Infantry Division Light Air Assault obstacle course, part of the DISCOM Lightning Leaders Challenge at Schofield Barracks. Two teams competed in various physical challenges—similar to a field day at an elementary school—featuring academy cadets plus junior officers and non-commissioned officers. That included a softball game, tug-o'-war, a Humvee pull, and swim races. That led to the unlikely aquatic encounter between Zilinski, the upcoming Army swim team captain, and Waudby. As they stood in the starting blocks, Waudby looked over at his competition and said, "I know you're going to kick my ass in this. But next is the truck pull, and I'll smoke you in that." Zilinski looked back and calmly said, "I know." Zilinski predictably reached the far end of the pool while Waudby still had a fair amount of doggy paddling ahead of him.

Tom Farrington and Peter Stewart took their turns at commanding rising sophomores that summer at Camp Buckner. Farrington served as an executive officer while Stewart ranked a rung below as a commanding officer. Farrington proved to be a huge help to Stewart. After Buckner ended, Farrington met up with Hill and younger football teammates Matt Silva and Greg Washington at Fort Benning, Georgia, to take a course in army combatives. They received instruction in hand-to-hand combat. As stated in the course description, it "enhances unit combat readiness by building sol-diers' personal courage, confidence, and resiliency as well as their situational responsiveness to close-quarters threats in the operational environment." They all passed, were certified as combative trainers—even Farrington, hand issue and all—and had a blast doing so.

Sue Petroff also worked at Camp Buckner, her duties performed with a carryover of the punishment from the previous school year. She was demoted one rank for the summer and forced to wear a uniform that featured her before and after positions on her shoulders. It was personally embarrassing for Petroff, like wearing the Scarlet Letter. For her charges, it proved to be confusing. One cadet reported to her, spotted the incongruous look of her uniform, and smarmily replied, "Yes, sergeant. Or corporal. Or whatever you are." By then, Petroff's circle of friends included Grace Chung. And, with the beginning of the class's firstie year, Chung became the cadets' deputy brigade commander—essentially the vice president of the 4,000 or so cadets.

* * *

For the *Times Herald-Record*'s 2003 preseason preview of Army football, writer Justin Rodriguez asked three starters—senior Ryan Kent, junior receiver Greg Washington, and junior guard Andy Dytrych—to identify the easiest opponent on the Black Knights' upcoming schedule. "I wouldn't necessarily say easiest," Washington initially replied. He paused, then added, "Starting out with Connecticut and Rutgers, those would be our easiest." Those choices, the first two teams on Army's schedule, certainly made sense. UConn was a relative newcomer to major college football while long among the elite in basketball. Rutgers was coming off a 1–11 season. Dytrych said, "Can't really say because they're all going to be tough, but I think Connecticut and Rutgers are going to be the easiest to start off with." Kent was typically in no mood to play games with such a question: "I don't think we have one." At a subsequent preseason gathering at the ornate West Point Club, Kent had luncheon guests near tears with an emotional speech that conveyed not the slighted doubt in his teammates. He spoke boldly in a voice that bordered on breaking but, like a ball carrier shaking off a tackler, proceeded directly toward his goal. "A lot of people don't believe we can win, but *we* believe we're going to win."

Changes to Todd Berry's staff for the 2003 season included the addition of a director of football operations. Major Bill Lynch was no stranger to West Point or the football program. The Massachusetts native played for Army during the late 1980s and, after graduation, served as both a company tactical officer within the Corps of Cadets and with the football team as an operations officer before graduating from the army's Command and General Staff College at Fort Leavenworth, Kansas. Lynch was intimately familiar with the workings of both the football program and the larger academy and how they both meshed and conflicted. He became the first active-duty army officer to serve on Army's football staff since 1994.

Lynch helped Berry execute some of the suggestions mentioned by people like Gene Palka to familiarize himself with the culture and mission of West Point and the "big army." Lynch accompanied Berry on offseason trips that included making the tandem ski-dive jump at Fort Bragg and peering into the eyes of a North Korean officer from the underground bunker within the demilitarized zone shared with South Korea. The North Korean officer appeared confused by Berry's garb—a custom-made, black battle-dress uniform that featured the coach's name on the patch that typically read "US Army." Lynch didn't want Berry roaming in such high-intensity military locales looking like a tourist in casual clothes. In visits to bases in Washington state and Alaska, Lynch arranged for Berry's lunches to include former Army football players so they could learn first-hand what was new at West Point. Back at the academy, Berry also tried to walk in the cadets' shoes—almost literally. The entire football staff would make the same long march from the academy grounds out to Lake Frederick that the plebes did during Beast Barracks. The staffers wore backpacks, though not weighed down as heavily as the froshes' ruck sacks, and wore regular athletic shoes instead of combat boots. Similarly, the coaches executed the "Slide for Life" zip-line drill during Camp Buckner and learned how to qualify on a rifle and fire a 105-milimeter Howitzer.

Friday, August 29, 2003, was uncomfortably humid in the Hudson Valley. It was no weather for formal attire, but members of the Class of 2004 gladly donned their "India white" uniforms to abide by the dress code and headed to the amphitheater at Trophy Point for one of the most anticipated moments of their academy experience—Ring Weekend. The practice of producing senior-class rings that's observed at colleges across the country was started at the United States Military Academy during the 1830s. The class ring awarded to each senior featured the letters "USMA," an eagle, an officer's saber, arrows and leaves from the national emblem, and the class motto. More than 900 seniors stood at attention before family and friends, sang the alma mater, and waited for an academy representation to declare: "Don your rings."

The firsties then walked back to Central Area on the way to their respective barracks to change clothes for that night's celebratory ball. In Central Area, plebes descended upon the newly bejeweled like the flying monkeys did upon Dorothy and her four curious companions on their way to Oz—except the firsties were aware of the plebes' impending oral ambush. The frosh broke into a chorus that, like Plebe Knowledge, they'd long prepared to deliver. Their recitation is commonly called "Ring Poop." Depending on the freshman, it included at least some of the following: "Oh, my God! What a beautiful ring! What a crass mass of brass and glass! What a mold of rolled gold! What a cool jewel you got from your school! See how it sparkles and shines? It must have cost a fortune! May I touch it? Can I touch it?"

To determine where Army's football team stood going into the 2003 season, there likely wasn't a better source than the preseason ratings that appeared in *USA TODAY* (and do to this day). They've been compiled by a 1970 MIT grad named Jeff Sagarin since 1985. So highly has Sagarin's work been regarded that his ratings for major college football were part of the calculations that determined the Bowl Championship Series' two championship finalists and his similar rankings of all Division I basketball teams have been employed when the NCAA's selection committee chooses the at-large teams for the annual tournament that has become known as "March Madness."

Sagarin's computerized prognostication listed the Black Knights 116th among the nation's 117 teams in Division I-A going into the 2003 season, ahead of only the Buffalo Bulls. That was one step below where Sagarin placed West Point at the end of the 2002 season. He ranked Army behind 39

Division I-AA teams. Army was predictably the consensus selection to repeat as the last-place team in Conference USA, which grew to eleven football programs with the addition of South Florida.

But the Black Knights wouldn't finish last in CUSA much longer, no matter the state of the team. That summer, West Point leadership decided to pull Army out of the league following the 2004 season. It was obvious to academy administrators that, week in and week out each fall, their football team faced conference opponents equipped with better athletes who most likely didn't rise to the same academic standards. The decision followed a study of academy football conducted by a committee that included Bill Parcells, then head coach of the Dallas Cowboys, and Tom Osborne, who coached the Nebraska Cornhuskers to three national titles during the 1990s. In making the announcement, athletic director Rick Greenspan assured the departure from a Division I-A football conference didn't also mean abandoning major college football overall. Army, Greenspan said, would return to competing as a football independent with the balance of its athletic teams still in the Patriot League. Lieutenant General William Lennox had been lobbied by some academy alums to consider making Army an Ivy League athletic program, at least informally through scheduling if not through outright membership in that Division I-AA conference, since West Point's academics were long considered the equal of those eight storied institutions. Lennox appreciated that line of thinking but countered that the more germane comparison for Army was Navy and Air Force. As long as the Midshipmen and Falcons competed in Division I-A football, so, too, would the Black Knights.

Kent was joined by Hill on the starting defense with Farrington listed as a third-team inside linebacker. The offense's preseason depth chart showed two members of the Class of 2004 on the first team: Waudby at right tackle and Clint Woody at one of the three receiver positions. Josh Davis and Stewart were on the third team, at center and left guard, respectively. The names of Marcellus Chapman and George Feagins from that class no longer appeared on Army's varsity football roster. Both remained at the academy, Feagins returning to the sprint team. The running game would be led by sophomore Carlton Jones, who topped the team rushing in 2002 averaging 50.9 yards per game. And Anthony Zurisko took over the placement duties from sophomore Joe Riley while the kickoff chores went to plebe Austin Miller. The 2003 season would mark the first time that Damian Zurisko would be able to attend each of his son's games at West Point instead of only an occasional autumn trip. Previously, younger son Jeff was playing for the Springdale Dynamos on Friday nights or Damian was officiating games himself. In such cases, one of Anthony's uncles often attended in his father's stead.

Army tradition called for a senior defensive player to carry the football team's own flag—black with a white skull and crossbones—as they ran onto the field before each game. Hill earned that honor. In the aftermath of 9/11, a senior offensive lineman carried the American flag. Waudby, the only one of the three senior O-linemen listed as a starter going into the season, was the logical choice to do so.

While the players went through pre-practice stretching one day in August, assistant coach John Bond sauntered amid them, stopped near Clint Woody, and said, "How does it feel to be a team captain?" Woody couldn't really provide a worthy reply because he didn't know how it felt given that he wasn't aware that he'd been chosen as one by his teammates. Ryan Kent was also chosen, not terribly surprising given his performance during the previous season.

Army's schedule began with four consecutive home games. Brian Hill was among the eight Black Knights who made their first start on offense or defense in the season opener against the Connecticut Huskies on Saturday afternoon, September 6. UConn's football program moved from Division I-AA to I-A in 2000, finishing its brief term as an independent in 2003 before enjoying full Big East football membership beginning the following season. College football's *nouveau riche* would meet old money at Michie Stadium. UConn had already played a game, christening its gleaming new home stadium with a 34–10 win over Indiana. The offensive star was sophomore running back Terry Caulley, all of 5-foot-7 and 185 pounds. After averaging 124.7 rushing yards per game as a freshman in 2002, Caulley opened the '03 campaign going for 166 on 22 carries. While 6-foot-5 junior quarterback Dan Orlovsky was certainly a capable passer, the Army coaching staff decided to focus its defense on stopping Caulley.

The Cadets' initial possession served as a microcosm of what would be the day's travails for the home team; junior quarterback Reggie Nevels threw an incomplete pass, lost one yard on a keeper, then threw another incompletion. The Huskies finished the first half with more touchdowns than Army had first downs (five to four—the first Black Knights first down came on a 13-yard connection from Nevels to Woody). The halftime score was 34–0, and Lou Saban might have jumped in Lusk Reservoir right then.

For the second consecutive season opener, Nevels was lost to injury. He hurt a knee late in the first half and was replaced again by Zac Dahman. The sophomore's first drive resulted in a touchdown, followed by Zurisko's successful point-after kick on his first varsity attempt. The Michie Stadium crowd erupted, wondering if it was witnessing an entirely different West Point team during the second half. Berry, still staring at an imposing deficit minutes into the third quarter, rolled the dice with an onside kick. He sent in Riley, the most likely among Army's kicking corps to succeed at the tricky assignment. His dribbler was recovered by Army, and the stadium roared again. Army walked a relative tightrope, converting three third downs, and Dahman threw a 14-yard touchdown pass to Aaron Alexander to make the score 34–14. An offense that gained only 76 yards during the first half gobbled up 114 on its first two possessions following intermission.

Army surely wouldn't try another onside kick. That's what the Huskies must have thought, particularly when Zurisko headed out onto the field for his first kickoff of the game. But it *was* another onside kick, though it bounded a little too far and was recovered by UConn. Army allowed only one first down before forcing a punt, but Dahman and the West Point offense couldn't put another point on the board. The Black Knights' only further scoring came on a punt return in the closing minutes.

UConn, relative newcomers to big-time football, boarded its buses for the drive home carrying a convincing 48–21 victory over one of the most tradition-laden programs in the country. Orlovsky set a school record with five touchdown passes, and Caulley ran for 102 yards on 18 carries. Army lost its opening game for the seventh straight season, though maybe not as humbling as the 2002 defeat against Division I-AA Holy Cross, and lost a record eighth straight at Michie Stadium. Speaking afterward, Berry didn't spare the rod when commenting on the Black Knights' offense: "We had no clue what we were doing." While a huge disappointment for Army football, the day was a milestone for Peter Stewart. It was his first varsity playing time as an Army Black Knight.

Next came a visit from Rutgers, struggling along in the third year of the rebuild under coach Greg Schiano. The Scarlet Knights, whose only win in 2002 was the 44–0 victory over Army, won their opener at home over Buffalo and then lost at Michigan State 44–28. Fears of an Army hangover from the demoralizing loss to UConn were stoked on West Point's opening possession, which began at its 6-yard line. On 3rd and 13 at their own 13, Dahman lined up in the shotgun, was sandwiched between two untouched Rutgers edge rushers, and fumbled. In what resembled pursuit of a greased pig, the ensuing scramble for the loose football ended with one of the Rutgers linemen who had caused the fumble, Brian Bender, clutching the ball in the end zone for a touchdown. On the play, Army's starting right guard, junior Jake Holly, hobbled off the field with an injured left knee and was lost for the season. On came Stewart as Holly's replacement.

Army's offense played no better during the first half than it did against UConn. The Black Knights didn't record a first down until early in the second quarter and finally made it past midfield for the first time late in the half. Zurisko trotted on for his first varsity field-goal attempt, from 44 yards, with 2:54 remaining before intermission. The snap from Justin Troy looked good. The hold by Wesley Willard looked good. But the kick hooked to the left of the goalposts.

It appeared that Kent, Hill, and the Black Knights defense could limit Rutgers to one first-half touchdown, but the Scarlet Knights followed Zurisko's miss by driving 74 yards in 10 plays to find the end zone with only 39 seconds left before halftime. The deficit was 13–0, Army having been held to 81 yards of total offense and four first downs.

Rutgers led 20–0 before Army converted a fumble recovery late in the third quarter into a touchdown. The offensive inefficiency led Clint Woody to stomp multiple times on the sideline, a rare public display of frustration from him. The Scarlet Knights led 29–7 with about six minutes to play before Army scored, pulled off another onside kick by Riley—Ryan Kent smothering it at the 50-yard line—and scored four plays later to pull within 29–21—but with only 28 seconds remaining. Riley's next onside effort was pounced on by Rutgers, leading to the day's final touchdown and a final score of 36–21. Rutgers owned a winning record through the first three games of a season for the first time since 1994.

As the final seconds ticked off, one of ESPN's cameras focused on the west sideline and Todd Berry. Play-by-play announcer Bob Stevens noted that West Point's head coach would have to explain another loss—the ninth straight at home, an ignominious school record—to "disgruntled alumni." During the post-game interview session with the assembled media, Berry offered both valiant public optimism ("I think we can run and catch and block and do all those things we need to do with anybody.") and distain for what he had seen of his 2003 team to date ("We were pathetic on offense two weeks in a row.").

Stewart played until the game's final minutes, when the bulk of West Point's regulars were replaced. He returned to his room convinced he'd played terribly and feared he'd squandered the best opportunity of his Army football career to play regularly—if not start given Holly's status. Seeking help for the cerebral portion of his game, Stewart began to attend multiple sessions each week at the academy's Center for Enhanced Performance.

For game three of the opening homestand against Tulane, sophomore Pete Bier was Army's starting right guard instead of Stewart. Army scored four touchdowns but committed eight turnovers in a 50–33 loss. It was a dreadful day for Dahman, who threw five interceptions and lost two fumbles. One of the other fumbles was by Woody on what was statistically the best day of his Army football career—seven catches for 94 yards. Zurisko kicked a pair of field goals. Oddly, the Black Knights never punted. Afterward, Berry attributed some of the turnovers to Army's desperate efforts to try to get back into the game: "I'm not going to apologize for that. We're going to do everything that we can to win."

The last of the four consecutive home games to begin West Point's season brought South Florida to Michie Stadium. It also brought ESPN's *College GameDay*, the popular pregame production that began 1987. It was *GameDay*'s first visit to the banks of the Hudson since the show began doing live broadcasts from college campuses in 1993. The host was Chris Fowler, a staple among ESPN on-air talent who began his work at the all-sports cable network in the mid-1980s. His colleagues were Kirk Herbstreit, an Ohio State quarterback during the early '90s, former college and pro football coach Lee Corso, plus Raghib "Rocket" Ismail, a former football player most known for his days as a returner at Notre Dame.

Why choose the campus of a winless football team to host *GameDay*? It was a good week on the schedule to highlight a different side of the college football experience, one that came with mandatory military training and a post-graduate itinerary that didn't include Radio City in New York for the NFL Draft. ESPN elected to spotlight West Point football players for what they were asked to do well beyond the three hours of competition on autumn Saturdays. The show's planners decided to follow one Black Knight through his typical daily routine during a game week. That was Brian Hill, identified as being from Daytona Beach (close enough). The cameras began rolling at 6:47 a.m., when Hill and roommate Mark Patzkowski made their way to the barracks showers. The piece included Hill answering a question in his history class, enjoying pizza along with Tom Farrington and the other linebackers after practice, and complying with "lights out" at 11:30 following hours of study. The latter was actually staged earlier, the crew asking Hill to set his clock ahead.

The show's opening showed cadets marching amid torrential rain that morning. "Rain or shine," Fowler noted from the weather-protected set, "the spirit of West Point endures." The theme of the presentation's early minutes focused on how that spirit had been badly tested in recent years—one winning football season in the last nine, Todd Berry going 5–32 with a spread offense that critics considered a bad fit for the kind of personnel Army could reasonably recruit. "Yes, there is a higher mission here," Fowler said, "but don't think the present situation sits well with anyone." Herbstreit followed Fowler's lead: "Todd Berry has legitimate pressure to win and win now. You don't patronize Army football by patting 'em on the head and saying, 'Keep giving that great effort, guys!' and take a loss."

A pre-taped sit-down with Berry addressed the conflict of preparing a young man for a career as a military officer and building a successful FBS football program: "We can't ever step over that higher mission and wouldn't want to because, otherwise, those young people that are over in Iraq right now, they're not as prepared as they need to be. And we're never going to compromise that." Hill did a good job expressing confidence in his team during another pre-taped presentation: "We've got players that can make some plays. We've just all got to believe that together we can beat anybody out there on our schedule. We've got to go out there and not beat ourselves and, when something goes bad, believe that we can fight through it and still win the game."

South Florida, like Connecticut, was a newcomer to major-college football. But while UConn represented a university founded in 1881, the University of South Florida was founded in 1956. The school started its football program in 1997 in Division I-AA, moved up to I-A in 2001, and was playing as a Conference USA member for the first time; Fowler noted USF was about to play its 69th football game, Army its 1,070th.

The party that was *GameDay* in the southwest corner of The Plain didn't last long. When the steady rain was accompanied by lightning, ESPN ordered its personnel to abandon the on-site set after about 30 minutes. The rest of the pregame show was done from the network's Connecticut studios. There actually was a semblance of a blue sky by the time the game kicked off just past one o'clock. And Army fans might have thought that relatively clear skies were just ahead for their winless football team when Zac Dahman directed the Black Knights' first possession just beyond midfield, to the Bulls' 45-yard line. Berry certainly exuded optimism in an interview that was taped before the game and shown early in the telecast, noting the team had what he considered the best week of practice during his tenure: "I'm excited about the direction we're headed. Am I excited about our win-loss record? No." But on 3rd and 8, Dahman sidestepped the rush to the left of the pocket, was hit as he threw downfield, and the underthrown pass was intercepted. West Point suffered another turnover on its next possession, but the quarter, which ended scoreless, represented something of a milepost for Army's 2003 team. For the first time during the young season, the Black Knights didn't trail after the opening quarter.

But with the beginning of the second period, Army's offense began to experience the same malaise that troubled the unit during the season's three previous losses. The offensive line failed to open holes for the running game. Dahman was constantly under pressure. When he did get the ball downfield, he sometimes couldn't get it to his target.

South Florida scored two field goals and a touchdown to lead 13–0 at halftime. The Bulls added two more touchdowns in the second half, one on yet another interception—that one thrown by reserve Matt Silva—to win 28–0. Many in the crowd sensed another showing of what they'd witnessed in previous weeks and left Michie Stadium during the third quarter. Sideline TV reporter Kevin Connor did his best to offer some levity to the broadcast during a break in second-half play, interviewing the cadet who supervised the two academy mascot mules who spent the game just beyond the stadium's north end zone. When neither of the animals replied to a question, Connor noted to play-by-play announcer Bob Stevens: "Speechless down here, Bob." To which Stevens bluntly replied, "I can understand that, the way the Army offense has been."

Army averaged only 2.2 yards per offensive snap. Black Knights quarterbacks connected on only 21 of 51 passes. The rushing game produced 17 yards. Turnovers were again costly—six, though converted into only 10 points. It certainly didn't help that two of Army's best "hands" players as returners and receivers, William White and Lamar Mason, were injured during the first half and didn't return. Army suffered its first home shutout since 1981, and the Black Knights' losing streak reached a school-record 11 games.

Of Army's remaining nine games on the schedule, six would be played as the road team—plus the Navy game in Philadelphia. That was noted in the pregame coverage of Keith Goldberg in the *Times Herald-Record* as he considered the South Florida game equal to a bowl game in importance to the Black Knights program: "An 0–4 record? It could quickly become 0–8. Or 0–12." After the game, Woody bemoaned that Army's solid first-quarter performance on offense went to waste: "It would have made a difference. We needed that momentum."

The Black Knights' first road game of the year came against an opponent superior to any of the four that defeated them at Michie Stadium. TCU, located in Fort Worth, Texas, appeared to be the class of Conference

USA. The Horned Frogs had won the league's 2002 title in only their second season in the league. They were ranked 25th in the Associated Press' 2003 preseason poll and had run off four wins, rising to No. 20. While West Point players were answering questions week after week about not being able to beat anyone, TCU players were having to respond to critics who saw an inability to put away inferior opponents. "We've got to start setting the tempo and not letting up," offensive tackle Anthony Alabi told reporters during the week. The Frogs' last three wins came after losing starting quarterback Tye Gunn to injury.

On the Wednesday before the game, the *Times Herald-Record* reported that a lopsided loss at TCU could be Berry's last game as West Point coach. Lieutenant General William Lennox was considering doing what the academy had never previously done—dismiss a head football coach during a season, possibly before its midpoint. But a personal tragedy, the death of Lennox's father, took him away from West Point and caused him to mentally table any thoughts of a midseason firing. When Berry was asked by the *Times Herald-Record*'s Justin Rodriguez about the paper's report, his response might have struck some as surprisingly restrained: "College coaches do get let go during the season more than they used to." Ryan Kent was asked his thoughts on that possibility: "I don't think it should happen. I like Coach Berry. I trust Coach Berry. I think he's a good coach."

Peter Stewart and Zac Dahman were among 29 Texans among the Black Knights, 13 who made the trip to Fort Worth. The Horned Frogs got off to another slow start, with two first-half field goals to lead 6–0 at intermission. Kent helped keep TCU's scoring down by forcing a fumble at the Black Knights' 36-yard line in the second quarter. The Frogs scored a touchdown on their first possession of the second half to move ahead 13–0, added another TD on a fumble recovery later in the quarter, and eased to a 27–0 win. Army football had not been shut out twice in a season since Bob Sutton's final season of 1999. It hadn't happened in consecutive games since Lou Saban's 2–8–1 campaign. Army was outgained 447 yards to 204, managing only 28 net rushing yards on 33 carries as it lost 41 yards on six sacks. The Black Knights advanced inside TCU's 20 just once. One of the fewest offensive high points of the day was a 62-yard catch by Clint Woody. At

Todd Berry's media get-together three days later, before the Black Knights' trip to Louisville, he said he wouldn't discuss his job situation. Lieutenant General Lennox made the trip to Texas for the TCU game. What he saw convinced him of what had to be done. And soon.

Army played relatively even with Louisville for a half at Papa John's Cardinal Stadium the following Saturday in mid-October but succumbed to its familiar combination of maladies afterward and lost 34–10. If Berry wasn't concerned about his employment status, the game's opening play provided evidence to the contrary; West Point's Austin Murphy dribbled an onside kick, only to have Louisville claim possession. The Cadets' only touchdown came on Brian Hill's first West Point interception. The pass from Cardinals quarterback Stefan LeFors hit him between the "4" and the "0" on his jersey, and he bounded 33 yards for the score. With the Black Knights on defense, Anthony Zurisko wasn't prepared to trot onto the field to kick an extra point—he wasn't sure where his helmet was. At almost the last second before the staff would have had to send on another kicker, a teammate raced up to Zurisko and handed him his helmet. Army's other score was a 22-yard Zurisko field goal after Hill forced a fumble near midfield. That was the first of two Louisville fumbles that Hill forced. The Black Knights might have been tied at intermission, which would have been their best showing for a half all season, but a 52-yard march in the closing minutes came to a deflating halt one yard shy of the end zone. Louisville's 619 total yards fell 24 short of the most ever allowed by a West Point football team. Afterward, Berry said he was encouraged in many ways.

Berry's dismissal, with a season and a half remaining on his contract, was announced the following Monday, six days before the 0–6 Black Knights would host 0–6 East Carolina. The final numbers on Berry were damning—five wins in 35 games (3–1 vs. Tulane!), not even one lead at any point through six games that season, and a school-record 11-game home losing streak in progress at the time of his leaving. Lennox delivered the news to Berry that morning, though the deposed coach represented Army on Conference USA's weekly media teleconference that afternoon. Lennox determined the players would have sunken into despair to continue through what had been a winless season with the same head coach.

The players were summoned to a meeting room in the Kimsey Center athletic complex about two hours before hitting the practice field, where Lennox broke the news. He promised he'd get them a fine coach. Berry later met with his former charges, giving each a handshake and a hug. Lennox soon after sent word to firstie captains Kent and Woody to report to his office. Woody had no idea what the superintendent wanted and was apprehensive about the meeting. Any fears were unfounded; the "supe" simply wanted to ask what they thought Black Knights football needed going forward. Lennox referenced the challenge facing Kent, Woody, and the other Army football seniors for the balance of the season—keeping that team together, keeping that team focused—as the greatest test of their leadership skills before they were commissioned as army officers. Woody told him Berry tried to make football work within the confines of the academy's military framework and should have instead focused on winning games.

In the case of most mid-season football coaching changes, one of the two team coordinators is chosen to assume command for the rest of the year. Rick Greenspan instead wanted John Bond to continue overseeing the offense and Dennis Therrell the defense. To fill the role of interim head coach, Greenspan chose defensive line coach John Mumford, given his 10 years' head coaching experience at Southeast Missouri State before accepting Berry's invitation to rejoin him at West Point. Mumford accepted only after an emotional consultation with Berry. He ran practice that Monday and faced the media for the first time on Tuesday. "I'm somewhat bewildered by the whole thing, but we have to press on," he said.

On the Saturday afternoon in which Army welcomed arguably the weakest opponent on its 2003 schedule to Michie Stadium in the beleaguered East Carolina Pirates, a sign was raised atop the east stands: "Thank you Lt. Gen. Lennox." With only 59 points to their credit through six games, the Pirates were the lowest scoring team in NCAA Division I-A that season. To East Carolina's credit, its four non-conference games were all played against teams from power conferences—West Virginia and Miami of the Big East, plus Wake Forest and North Carolina of the Athletic Coast Conference.

Mumford, the defensive specialist, took a very offensive approach to his first game-day decision as Black Knights head coach. When Army won the toss, he chose to receive instead of the popular practice of deferring. The decision appeared to be genius within mere seconds. William White fielded the opening kickoff, broke left, and hugged the sideline for the better part of 67 yards to the Pirates' 28-yard line. On first down, Zac Dahman faked a handoff, faked an end around, and lofted what amounted to a jump ball in the end zone between 6-foot-6 Army receiver Aaron Alexander and 5-foot-10 freshman defensive back Erode Jean. Alexander grabbed the ball just above Jean's helmet and held on as he tumbled in the end zone. All of 17 seconds in, the Cadets scored to take a lead for the first time all season. The faithful at Michie Stadium almost didn't know how to react—except for the cadets on the home sideline, who dutifully dropped for celebratory pushups. Thomas Roberts pumped up the student section more as the "mike man."

Late in the opening quarter, a 29-yard connection between Dahman and Alexander put the Black Knights at East Carolina's 15. A 14-point lead was definitely within grasp. Coming against a winless opponent that had struggled to score all season even more than Army, sweet victory wasn't too much to visualize even that early in the game. But on 3rd and 6 at the Pirates' 11, Dahman looked for Alexander on the right side. Instead of Dahman firing the ball right at Alexander, who was facing him, the ball sailed to Alexander's right—and into the waiting hands of none other than Jean, two yards from the end zone. One of Army's best scoring opportunities of the season was wasted.

As the teams changed ends going into the fourth quarter, with East Carolina leading 31–14, sideline reporter Kevin Connor entertained viewers with another of his offbeat features. Connor trudged off to the far side of Lusk Reservoir to visit with the cadet in charge of the cannon that was fired after Army scoring plays and following the end of each quarter. That was firstie Michael Cerrone, the E1 Viking, who detailed the history of the cannon for the audience: "These were made in 1944. They were used through World War II, Korea, and Vietnam before they were retired to West Point."

East Carolina scored touchdowns on three consecutive possessions—exceeding the Pirates' output for any full game to date that year—and turned a 21–14 halftime lead into a 38–14 advantage early in the fourth quarter, stealing any hope held by Army fans. On one of East Carolina's touchdowns, punt returner Terrance Copper fumbled in his own end zone with Ryan

Kent, Brian Hill, and Tom Farrington among the players from both teams scrambling for the elusive football. Copper beat them all to it for a touchback.

Down by 24 points, Mumford's team didn't go quietly. The Black Knights scored on their final three possessions to pull within 38–32 with 2:45 to play. One of the touchdowns was set up by an interception by inside linebacker Greg Washington. As he was about to be tackled near East Carolina's 35-yard line, Washington executed a rugby-like maneuver and lateraled the ball to the teammate running alongside him on his left. That was Kent, who carried another 20 yards to the Pirates' 12.

It was time to bring on Joe Riley, the onside specialist. His kick simply rolled to the Pirates' Richard Horrigan, a sure-handed receiver. East Carolina gained one first down, ran out the clock after Army used its only remaining timeout, and gleefully celebrated what would be its only victory of the season. The Cadets' record home losing streak reached twelve games. ECU outgained Army by only 44 yards but won the turnover battle with only one to West Point's three. While Army's defense struggled, Brian Hill followed his stellar performance at Louisville by recording a staggering 18 tackles. During the postgame news conference, Mumford blamed himself for the loss, for not having multiple timeouts left in the closing minutes. He said he had talked with Berry a few times that week and would do so again for an assessment of what Mumford could have done better during the game: "He's totally selfless and has been a huge help to me."

Army then hit the road for three straight games—Cincinnati, UAB, and the first half of the Black Knights' battles for the Commander-in-Chief's Trophy, Air Force. The Bearcats were picked to finish third in Conference USA but were muddling along at 3–3 overall and 1–2 in the league, beating only the previously winless East Carolina. They boasted one of the nation's leading rushers in junior Richard Hall, who was averaging 109 ground yards per game, and were coming off a bye week. Cincy chose Army to be its homecoming opponent.

David Kent traveled to the game, checked into the Marriott where the Army traveling party stayed, then circumvented team rules the night before the game. He was determined to deliver some of the famed ribs cooked up at the Montgomery Inn just north of Cincinnati—the restaurant's walls filled with photos showing celebrity patrons ranging from American presidents to Pete Rose chowing down there—to Ryan and a handful of teammates. David bought five racks and called Ryan's cell phone: "Just open the door." The illicit drop-off was made, feeding possibly half of the Black Knights' defense.

Brian Hill sat out the game with a leg injury, which would account for his only missed outing of the season. Beneath a gloomy gray sky, Cincinnati led 7–0 after running only two offensive plays. West Point gained all of six rushing yards the entire game, contributing to a total offense of 138 yards that would be the unit's lowest output of the season. Yet the Black Knights hung on in a back-and-forth affair thanks in part to an interception by linebacker Matt Maimone, who replaced Hill, which set up a short Army touchdown drive. The Cadets also blocked a punt and recovered a bobbled Cincinnati punt snap to lead 29–26 with less than two minutes remaining in the game. That was the first time all season that Army led during the final quarter.

Cincinnati responded with an 80-yard drive featuring three third-down conversions, culminating in a touchdown with about nine minutes left. The Bearcats led 33–29, and the Black Knights' offense stalled during its three subsequent possessions; one Army possession began at West Point's 1 after Kent stuffed Hall for no gain on 4th and goal. The offense's day ended with the last of Zac Dahman's three interceptions. The four-point loss was the closest to date for the 0–8 squad. The six rushing yards represented the fewest for an Army team since 1976.

The subsequent defeats at UAB and Air Force didn't advance the Army cause in any fashion. West Point was again a homecoming foe in Birmingham, where home fans had enthusiastically cheered for the Black Knights two years earlier in the aftermath of 9/11. The host Blazers came in at 3–5, had nearly won at fourth-ranked Georgia the previous week, and desperately needed a victory over Army to remain in contention for a bowl bid. UAB would play with backup quarterback Chris Williams, as sophomore starter Darrell Hackney was sidelined with a thumb injury. Army quarterback Reggie Nevels dressed for the first time since being sidelined with a leg injury in the season opener but wasn't listed among the team's top two on the depth chart.

The Black Knights began in what had become, unfortunately for them, typical team fashion. Their first possession ended at UAB's 25 with a lost fumble. When Army got the ball back following a Blazers punt, Zac Dahman was replaced at quarterback—but not by Nevels. Sophomore Laron Bybee came on and briefly gave Army an option look. If the desired effect was a spark, there was no such luck—three and out.

Following a scoreless first quarter, UAB took command thanks to a 91-yard touchdown pass and a blocked West Point punt deep in Army territory—the second of the game for the Blazers' Jhun Cook—that was recovered in the end zone for a TD. UAB did its best to allow the Black Knights back into the game, losing three fumbles. The results of those turnovers were two Anthony Zurisko field-goal attempts, a miss from 42 yards and one down the middle from 36. UAB added another touchdown after West Point committed a pass interference penalty on third down, and the Black Knights scored a late touchdown on a drive aided by a 10-yard Clint Woody reception on 3rd and 8. Army's losing streak reached 11 games, dating back two games into the 2002 season, with the 24–9 loss.

On the first Friday of November, the Army football team traveled to Colorado, where it played Air Force in odd-numbered years beginning in 1971. Through the years, the Black Knights rarely returned home from Falcon Stadium with a victory. Army football teams had lost 12 straight in Colorado Springs beginning with that infamous 1979 campaign under Lou Saban. Then again, Army had also struggled at home against the Falcons in recent seasons. West Point's overall losing streak in the series was six, the most recent win a 23–7 triumph during their Independence Bowl season of 1996.

Air Force was far from being the third wheel in the world of academy football despite being the youngest of the three institutions, founded in 1955. The Falcons claimed the Commander-in-Chief's Trophy in each of the previous six seasons to extend their lead in the three-headed competition that began in 1972. Air Force had won the trophy 16 times, and did so within only the previous 21 years. Air Force's series lead over Army going into the 2003 game was 24–12–1.

Army coaches, as was their custom during weeks in which the upcoming opponent was one of the other service academies, wore battle fatigues. The Falcons, at 6–3, ranked third in Division I-AA in rushing. Navy was first. Army, averaging 59 ground yards per game, was 117th. The *Times Herald-Record* took the opportunity of Army facing an opponent that was recording winning seasons year in and year out with an option offense to question Army's decision to stray from that. Air Force's starting quarterback, senior Chance Harridge, was willing to support the newspaper's skepticism of West Point's abandonment of the option in an interview: "The spread offense [Army] brought in is a great idea, but you can't get the blue-chip recruits to make it go around. You have to know who you are." Air Force's option offense led to an alteration in Army's defensive alignment. An additional linebacker was employed. That gave Tom Farrington his first varsity starting assignment with the Black Knights.

For all the losing that Army football teams experienced during the early 2000s, it seemed unlikely for the Cadets to uncover new pathways to the same inevitability. Yet their game at Colorado Springs on the second Saturday of November provided just that in the form of a senior Air Force linebacker. Marchello Graddy incredibly recovered fumbles on three consecutive West Point possessions during the first half—all in Air Force territory. The trio of miscues was converted into only 10 points, but it was still a deflating sequence of events. The last of those lost fumbles came from Reggie Nevels, who saw his first playing time since the season opener, when the Black Knights sought a change of pace from Zac Dahman. Nevels carried one other time later in the game and fumbled again, that time recovering the ball.

Air Force led 16–0 at halftime and cruised to a 31–3 win, Anthony Zurisko providing the Cadets' only points with a 22-yard field goal in the third quarter; that was an inadequate consolation prize after Army owned 1st and goal at the Falcons' 3-yard line. It was West Point's seventh consecutive loss to the Falcons; the average margin during the streak was more than three touchdowns. Afterward, winning coach Fisher DeBerry sounded crestfallen in remarks about the defeated visitors: "We want better for them. There's something special between the schools because we're always going to be hinged and hooked together. That's why it bothers me. I'd like to see them win eight or nine games a year. I've got a deep place in my heart for them." The Black Knights were 0–10. Only one other Army football team owned an 0–10 record, the 1967 squad that lost all of its games. "We got ourselves to where we are 0–10," John Mumford told the gathered postgame media. "Now we have to work out of it." Ahead on the schedule lay Houston (5–4) in the Michie Stadium finale, Hawaii (6–3) on the road, and Navy (6–4) in Philadelphia.

* * *

As the football season drew nearer to a close, firsties across West Point received a clearer picture of where their lives following graduation would take them. Branch Night played a major role in that. The mid-November event took place in Eisenhower Hall's auditorium. Each cadet had previously made his or her first, second, and third choices of which army branch would be their preferred assignment as a 2nd lieutenant. Assignments were made according to class rank and placed in envelopes for the cadets to open like youngsters tearing open packages on Christmas morning. Clint Woody was confident that his rank was good enough to land his first option in the coveted aviation branch. And a class assignment had him in Arizona on Branch Night, so Skyler Munekata played proxy and did the honors for him. Cody Wallace decided to branch armor for the simple reason that he liked tanks. Peter Stewart listed armor first, too, though he would have preferred to join Woody in aviation but had eyesight issues that he saw as a deal breaker. Plus, Stewart wasn't sure an aviation slot would be left when his name came up. The other six seniors who would play in the 2003 Navy game all sought assignments in field artillery. That only validated a long-standing West Point joke about F.A. actually standing for "football alumni." Indeed, all six of them received field artillery while Stewart went armor and Woody was chosen for aviation. Sue Petroff also landed aviation.

* * *

On the day before West Point's final home game of the 2003 season, the *Times Herald-Record* published a question-and-answer session conducted by sports reporter Justin Rodriguez with the three seniors who started on offense and defense. Among the questions was: Army has lost a school-record 12 games in a row at home; what's your take on that? Hill and Woody tried their best to placate the writer.

Hill: "It's been tough, but I think we have things going in the right direction. We're going to get this thing turned around."

Woody: "It's been a tough season all around. We've let ourselves down. It's a tough question."

Kent, as had been the case in previous interview sessions during his Army career, wasn't interested in providing a polite reply related to the team's plight: "I really don't have anything to say about that." Mumford was quizzed similarly by Rodriguez, asked what he would take away from his time as the Black Knights' interim head coach: "I had been a head coach for 10 years before coming here, and I was really enjoying the role of an assistant, particularly from a players' standpoint. You really get in tight with your players."

Mumford faced a vexing question that week: Who should he start at quarterback? Reggie Nevels had returned two games earlier but was left in a reserve role behind Zac Dahman. In the losses at UAB and Air Force, Dahman at least had steered clear of the interception bug that previously plagued him, though he did fumble twice at Air Force. Also worth considering was Dahman's performance in 2002 against Houston as a freshman; he passed for 353 yards and four touchdowns in the Black Knights' 56–42 road loss. Mumford let the two figuratively slug it out during the week's practices and awarded Nevels his first start since the season opener.

Senior Day was chilly but delightfully sunny for late November on the Hudson. Most of the honorees posed individually for pictures with Pete Dawkins, the 1958 Heisman Trophy winner. Dawkins approached Denny Woody and congratulated him on his son's West Point career. They also posed together along with senior Mark Conliffe, who played in one game as a sophomore and wasn't dressed; holder Wesley Willard, a senior that fall after starting at West Point in 1999; and senior team manager Chris Klich.

Of the fourth-year firsties recognized that day, Woody was the only one who had appeared in an Army varsity football game as a fuzzy-cheeked plebe three years earlier. The student who nearly got through 13 years of Hayesville schooling without missing a day came close to making it through four seasons of West Point football without so much as missing a single practice. When the streak did end, it wasn't because of a physical issue. Woody had hustled back to the academy after spending time at Fort Carson in Colorado working on a project that was part of his program as a major in mechanical engineering, but he didn't make it in time for the start of that day's drills. He was told not to bother dressing.

Houston came north with a 5–4 record under first-year head coach Art Briles, trying to shake loose of a three-game losing streak. Briles had installed a spread offense, similar to the one that he previously ran as offensive coordinator at Texas Tech under Mike Leach. It resembled the attack that Briles used as a high school coach in Texas, winning multiple state championships at Stephenville High School before going to Tech. The Cougars were quarterbacked by true freshman Kevin Kolb who'd likewise played for Briles at Stephenville as a freshman. UH averaged 29.4 points with 15 touchdown drives that required fewer than two minutes. Conversely, the defense allowed 34 points per game.

Army surprisingly recorded the first electric offensive play of the day when William White turned a third-down slant pattern over the middle into a 60-yard touchdown. But the Cougars predictably required little time to tie the score, covering 73 yards in only 2:50. The 7–7 score held up going into the second quarter, though Brian Hill nearly gave the Black Knights a tremendous scoring opportunity late in the first. Kolb was running left in UH territory, peering downfield for a receiver, when the ball suddenly slipped from his right hand. It bounced toward the hard charging Hill. He tried to fall on it, but the ball squirted out and Kolb made the recovery.

Houston took command in the second quarter. From the early 7–7 tie, the Cougars scored on five of eight possessions during the second and third quarters and took a 34–7 lead into the fourth. The three touchdowns and two field goals each followed a three-and-out possession by the Army offense. The Black Knights added a fourth-quarter touchdown and lost 34–14. Houston ran 98 offensive plays to Army's 57, causing the Cadets' defense to labor much of the afternoon. Nevels struggled in his return to the starting lineup, completing only two of eight passes while being constantly hounded by the Cougars' rush. Army's ground game was minimal; sophomores Carlton Jones and Recardo Evans combined for 24 yards on 10 carries. Tom Farrington received considerable playing time at linebacker during the fourth quarter while the right side of West Point's offensive line for much of the period featured Josh Davis at center, Peter Stewart at right guard, and Brad Waudby at right tackle. With the game's outcome decided relatively early, the television coverage turned toward the season finale against Navy. Pre-taped interviews with Woody, Kent, and Hill about the upcoming game against the Middies were aired consecutively. Said Woody: "We've been gunnin' for Navy since the game last year, and we've got something for 'em. If you look at the years past, the more desperate team is usually the one that wins."

The Conference USA game at Hawaii was what allowed Army to schedule beyond the standard limit of 12 regular-season games. The school moved into NCAA Division I-A in 1974 and had difficulty filling its schedule given the logistical issues with opponents located thousands of miles away. Therefore, the NCAA allowed what became known as the "Hawaii Exemption" for scheduling. A team that had already filled a future schedule could add a game played at Hawaii.

The Warriors went into the Army game averaging 30.8 points per game, having won 6 of 10 games. The Black Knights defense would again be challenged by a frenetic offense, this one amid the run-and-shoot attack of head coach June Jones. The Warriors' most consistent running back was Michael Brewster, Peter Stewart's Nimitz High teammate back in Houston. As a walk-on at Tennessee in 2000, Brewster got into only four games and decided to transfer. He chose Hawaii and earned a starting position as a junior during the '03 season. Hawaii was unbeaten in four home games, with representatives of the Hawaii Bowl—played right there in the stadium in which the Warriors played their home games—prepared to extend an invitation following an anticipated win over West Point. Jones became the latest opposing coach to speak of the winless Army team in glowing terms: "The reason they're at Army is they're special." Dave Reardon of the *Honolulu Star-Bulletin* was far from complimentary, writing before the game: "The score could get uglier than a plebe's haircut."

John Mumford had made a Hawaii game trip before going to West Point and recognized the difficulties experienced by a visiting team. Major Bill

Lynch faced the challenge of not only making arrangements that would allow the Black Knights to play their best but also accommodate a higher West Point mission. That would include practicing at Schofield Barracks, home of the 25th Infantry Division, and a trip to the *USS Arizona* Memorial at Pearl Harbor. The Wednesday before the game back at West Point, the team practiced immediately following breakfast and then began its airborne odyssey. The traveling party took off from Stewart Airport in nearby Newburgh by charter late that morning, refueled in San Francisco, and touched down at Hickam Air Force Base at 8 p.m. local time—about 15 hours after boarding buses at West Point. The team headed directly to Aloha Stadium for a brief workout before arriving at the Waikiki Beach Marriott at 11, sitting down for a team dinner soon after, with lights out at 1 a.m.

Thursday's drills at Schofield Barracks were watched by about 100 fans, Dawn and Bill Livingston among them. On Friday morning, the football party bused to Pearl Harbor for a private visit to the memorial; that included Ryan Kent and Clint Woody laying a wreath. The team shifted lodging the night before the game, somewhat similar to heading off to Mahwah on the nights before home games and checked in at Turtle Bay on Oahu's north shore.

The assemblage that Saturday night included about 5,000 Army fans and soldiers among the announced gathering of about 35,000. On the fifth play from scrimmage, Warriors quarterback Timmy Chang overthrew his receiver on a post route. The ball sailed right to Kent, who made the interception at Army's 33-yard line. Nothing came of the Black Knights' first possession, Hawaii scored 10 points on its first two possessions and added a second touchdown on an interception of Zac Dahman.

Little went Army's way that night. The Cadets trailed 31–0 in the closing seconds of the half when Brian Hill intercepted a swing pass, stepping in front of a Warriors running back and returning it 79 yards for a touchdown—his second of the season. In winning 59–28, Hawaii fell three points short of the most ever allowed by an Army football team. Hawaii's 741 yards broke records for both the Warriors' offense and the Black Knights' defense. Chang took a seat midway through the third quarter thanks to a 38–7 lead. Hawaii never punted. The Black Knights had lost six games under John

Mumford after they'd lost six under Todd Berry. The 0–12 mark equaled that of Colorado State in 1981 and Hawaii in 1998, in those cases the season being completed. Afterward, Mumford said, "These kids are not losers. You have to take the positives back on the plane. You have to refocus on Navy."

The Navy game is, in many ways, the focus for Army's football team every day every year.

Clint Woody and Brian Hill in 2001 at Camp Buckner, the sarcastically-named "best summer" of a West Point cadet's life. *(Photo courtesy of Woody family)*

Some proud Army football dads tailgate at Buffalo Solider Field during the 2001 season. From left: Bradford Waudby Sr., Eric Salfeety (son Peter played 2000-01), Damian Zurisko, and Tom Farrington Sr. *(Photo courtesy of Waudby family)*

President George W. Bush addresses Army players, as he did the Navy players, before their 2001 meeting, which was the first following 9/11. Army head football coach Todd Berry is in the white shirt, West Point superintendent Lieutenant General William Lennox in full dress uniform. *(Army West Point athletics)*

Army coach Todd Berry stands amid players from both teams while Navy players sing their alma mater first after the 2001 game, won by the Black Knights 26-17. *(Dominick Fiorille, Times Herald-Record of Middletown, New York)*

An iron sculpture formed in the image of the World Trade Center from the ruins of the twin towers was given to Brad Waudby by a worker in the Ground Zero pit during Christmas break 2001. *(Jeff Miller)*

Ryan Kent returns a fumble 88 yards for a touchdown against Louisville in 2002. *(Army West Point athletics)*

Todd Berry at the demilitarized zone that separates South and North Korea. *(Army West Point athletics)*

Anthony Zurisko (No. 22) celebrates his first successful point-after kick for Army's varsity, against Connecticut in the 2003 opener at Michie Stadium. Among his teammates on the PAT team are Josh Davis (No. 54) and Peter Stewart (No. 64) *(Army West Point athletics)*

Clint Woody (No. 81) and Ryan Kent, Army's full-season captains during the 2003 season, walk to midfield for a pregame coin toss. *(Army West Point athletics)*

As the Army Black Knights run onto the field for a home game during the 2003 season, Brian Hill (No. 40) carries the team's official flag while Brad Waudby (No. 66) carries the Stars and Stripes. *(Army West Point athletics)*

This postgame gathering includes Brad Waudby (lower center), Ryan Kent (white Abercrombie t-shirt), plus Tom Farrington (back row wearing "P" Pittsburgh Pirates visor) and his father, Tom Sr. (back row center). *(Photo courtesy of Waudby family)*

Peter Stewart poses with 1958 Heisman Trophy winner Pete Dawkins before Army's 2003 Senior Day game against Houston. *(Army West Point athletics)*

Anthony Zurisko poses with his parents, Nancy and Damian Zurisko, before Army's 2003 Senior Day game against Houston. *(Army West Point athletics)*

The eight fourth-year firsties who played Army football during the 2003 season pose before their final game at Michie Stadium along with Chris Klich (a senior team manager: far left), Wesley Willard (Class of '03 who graduated that December: standing between No. 22 Anthony Zurisko and No. 49 Tom Farrington) and Mark Conliffe (played one game, as a sophomore, and left the academy before graduation: far right). *(Army West Point athletics)*

Brian Hill plays in Army's 2003 game at Hawaii. Hill finished the season with 77 tackling assists, the most on the team, to go along with 44 solo stops. He had two interceptions, both returned for touchdowns. *(Army West Point athletics)*

Seniors Brian Hill (No. 40), Clint Woody (No. 81), and Ryan Kent (No. 4) comply with a request for a novel pose late in the 2003 season. *(Jeff Goulding, Times Herald-Record of Middletown, New York)*

While full-season Army captains Ryan Kent and Clint Woody participate in the coin toss at the center of the field before the 2003 Army-Navy game, the remaining seniors plus two of the other special game captains walk out onto the field and hold hands. From left: fifth-year senior Wesley Willard (No. 15), Anthony Zurisko (No. 22), Tom Farrington (No. 49), Josh Davis (No. 54), junior Greg Washington (No. 16), Brian Hill (No. 40), junior Aaron Alexander (No. 19), Brad Waudby (No. 66), and Peter Stewart (No. 64). *(Photo courtesy of Waudby family)*

John Mumford, Army's interim head football coach for the final seven games of the 2003 season, sings the academy's alma mater after the Black Knights' season-ending loss to Navy. Close by are Anthony Zurisko (far left), West Point superintendent Lieutenant General William Lennox (in front of Mumford), and Peter Stewart (No. 64). *(Army West Point athletics)*

The six football seniors who were commissioned following graduation day 2004 pose afterward in the Kimsey Center along with a senior who was a team manager. Front from left: Tom Farrington, Brian Hill, Ryan Kent, manager Chris Klich, and Anthony Zurisko. Back from left: Clint Woody and Peter Stewart *(Photo courtesy of Woody family)*

Clint Woody and Sue Petroff after being commissioned on graduation day 2004. *(Photo courtesy of Woody family)*

Josh Davis receives his United States Military Academy diploma from West Point superintendent Lieutenant General William Lennox in the Thayer Award Room 11 days after the Class of 2004's graduation ceremony. *(Photo courtesy of Davis family)*

Tom Farrington and Ryan Kent take a break amid hot, humid field duty during their officer basic course at Fort Sill, Oklahoma in June 2005. *(Jeff Miller)*

Brian Hill and Anthony Zurisko are able to enjoy some downtime at Fort Sill during OBC during the summer of 2005 in a cooler location. *(Jeff Miller)*

In Anthony Zurisko's hometown of Springdale, Pennsylvania, he delivers the town's 2007 Memorial Day speech after leading the annual parade. *(Mike Werries)*

Peter Stewart just before his move in 2007 from Iraq's FOB Normandy to FOB Warhorse, where he served as a brigade executive officer. *(Photo courtesy of Stewart family)*

Clint and Sue Woody pose in their headquarters trailer in Balad just before Christmas 2007. *(Photo courtesy of Woody family)*

Josh Davis (no sunglasses) poses with members of his military transition team (MITT) in Mosul in 2009. *(Photo courtesy of Davis family)*

Brian Hill poses with Tom Farrington after coming within a foot (or a shoe) of shooting a hole-in-one at The Club at Mansion Ridge in Monroe, New York, during the annual fund-raising tournament for the Friends4Michael Foundation in August 2011. *(Photo courtesy of Hill family)*

Clint Woody is amid the military personnel who gather for a speech given by President Barack Obama during the commander in chief's surprise visit to Afghanistan in May 2012. *(AP Images)*

Ryan Kent prepares to gather his Mizzen + Main teammates for the closing ceremonies of the Carry the Load event at Dallas' Reverchon Park on Memorial Day 2017. *(Jeff Miller)*

Chapter Nine

"I WOULD GO INTO BATTLE WITH ANY ONE OF THEM"

The off week between the loss at Hawaii and the December 6 date in Philadelphia against the Naval Academy provided for speculation regarding Army's head coaching vacancy. Maryland offensive coordinator Charlie Taaffe, a West Point assistant and coordinator during the 1980s, publicly expressed interest in the position. The off week also meant promotional appearances in Philadelphia for the upcoming game, one of the high points of the city's sporting year. Hence the marketing slogan "Philly Loves Army-Navy." The game was first played there in 1899, at Franklin Field on the UPenn campus, and has primarily been played in the city ever since. Ryan Kent and Clint Woody accompanied John Mumford to a luncheon and media session. Among the Navy players in attendance was senior linebacker Eddie Carthan. He admitted to hoping to make sure Army completed a winless season. Carthen knew the feeling since he was a sophomore on the 2001 Navy team that lost to Army 26–17 to finish 0–10. Another Midshipman on hand was quarterback Craig Candeto, who said, "If you don't feel for them, you're not human." Midshipmen coach Paul Johnson abided by a time-honored tradition and said of his winless foe: "They scare the fool out of me." Mumford assured there was no "give-up" in his team. At a subsequent media event, he was asked if his players were thinking about the prospect of finishing 0–13. He said they "are doing it internally because the guys are being bombarded."

On the Tuesday before the game, another West Point tradition in advance of the Navy game was upheld. Special game captains were named and added to the season-long selections of Kent and Woody. They were Brian Hill, Aaron Alexander, and Greg Washington. The five captains joined their Navy counterparts for a lunch that week at the Pentagon.

Gene Palka Jr.—a 2002 West Point graduate, a former Army offensive lineman, and son of the football mentor—sent a hand-written letter of encouragement from his deployment in Iraq addressed to the football staff. The note cited how he benefitted as an officer from playing Army football and closed: "Please tell them that we believe in them and they are playing for so much more than themselves or the corps." The letter was posted outside the team's locker room.

With one game left to play in his final West Point season, Woody had caught more than three passes in a game only once that year. He had all of 24 receptions to show for the season. Nothing on the weekly stat sheet accounted for all the blocks he'd thrown game after game. The four years of Army football had resulted in five victories and 41 defeats. At the annual West Point bonfire before the Navy game, one of Woody's instructors approached him. "Sorry that the season didn't work out better," the lieutenant colonel said. "Back when you made that catch against BC, it looked like big things might happen."

Another name entered the Army coaching search during the off weekend. Frank Solich, successor to Nebraska Cornhuskers icon Tom Osborne, was fired one day after his team won to finish the regular season at 9–3. The Huskers began the season unranked, won their first five games to reach No. 10, but then went 4–3 the rest of the way to fall out of contention for a major bowl, which many amid the Big Red must have considered essential for Solich to remain employed in Lincoln. His six-year record at Nebraska was 58–19. To count back the previous 58 wins for the Army football program, one would go back to 1991. Three of Solich's Huskers teams finished in the Associated Press Top 10. Only two years earlier, his squad played for the national championship. No matter—NU athletic director Steve Pederson indicated he saw the program slipping.

Contact between Army and Solich reached the stage that the academy had a private aircraft in Lincoln at midweek, ready and waiting to bring him to West Point. The *Times Herald-Record* reported Solich was "Army's man." The football team was boarding buses on Friday morning for the ride to Philadelphia when Mumford spotted what appeared to be a shaken Rick Greenspan. The coach asked his boss if everything was OK. Greenspan replied, "He didn't get on the plane." Solich subsequently said the process was moving too fast for him. (He indeed remained out of the coaching for the 2004 season, took the job at Ohio University the following year, and has produced nine bowl teams in 13 seasons.)

Army headed to Philadelphia leading Division I-A with 42 turnovers. Its penalty yardage of 570 was almost twice that of its opponents. The Black Knights owned the least effective running game in I-A, averaging only 61.9 rushing yards per game and 1.98 per carry. Wayne Coffey, a talented writer for New York's *Daily News*, traveled to West Point earlier that week for a wide ranging piece that captured the angst and frustration that coursed through the academy's beleaguered program. The *Daily News* is known for headlines that often can hit below the belt. The copy editor's headline on Coffey's piece contained a smidgen of zing, turning around a familiar Army promotional phrase at the time against its own: "An Army of none: Cadets look to salvage winless season." Coffey quoted 1946 Heisman winner Glenn Davis saying, "The season has been a disaster. . . . I don't understand why Annapolis and Air Force can produce teams that win games and Army can't." Coffey interviewed West Point's two season-long captains. Woody admitted thinking months earlier that the Black Knights could compete for a bowl berth. Kent verbalized how a team that appeared prepared on the practice field week after week couldn't translate that into competition during the 12 games to date: "Sometimes we'd go ahead, and other times we'd look like the worst team in America."

Bill Lyon, a long-time sports columnist for the *Philadelphia Inquirer* and veteran of many an Army-Navy game, collectively characterized the state of Black Knights football a few days before the game:

"No Division I team has ever lost 13 times in one season. Army goes into this game 0–12. You might think by now that they would be numb and couldn't feel the losing.

"You would be wrong.

"You might think that all the losing makes them losers.

"You would be grievously wrong."

Lyon stated that 44 of the Army football players who would take the field that Saturday afternoon at Lincoln Financial Field could have withdrawn from West Point between 9/11 and the beginning of the 2002–03 academic year. They didn't.

One of those was Kent, who'd led Woodbury's Thundering Herd to glory just across the Delaware River. So many of his relatives and friends would attend the game, his family rented a suite. The Navy game would mark his 34th career start and 27th straight. That surpassed the total of all other seniors on the team—receiver Clint Woody (14), linebacker Brian Hill (11, starting with the first game of the 2003 season), and Tom Farrington (1, in that year's Air Force game). The linebacker incredibly ranked eighth in West Point rushing for the season going into the game on the strength of his two runs on fake punts. Lyon's piece in the *Inquirer* included Kent's admission: "I cry after every game. I don't wish that feeling on anyone."

The two teams made drives from different directions into Philadelphia that Friday amid a ferocious snowstorm that dropped about a dozen inches in the city and packed winds that reached 25 miles per hour. About 20 inches fell in the Hudson Valley. The afternoon's Army team walkthrough, typically held where the game was to be played the following day, was moved indoors. The game would now be played at the 15th and newest site of the rivalry, successor to Veterans Stadium in housing the NFL's Philadelphia Eagles. Navy brought a record of 7–4 (the Midshipmen's first winning finish since 1997) and an invitation to play in the Houston Bowl (their first postseason game since '96). Army held a slim 49–47–7 edge in a series. Since Navy had beaten Air Force in early October, the Midshipmen would be playing to claim the Commander-in-Chief's Trophy for the first time since 1981.

Navy, with its option offense, led Division I-A in rushing, averaging 323.1 yards per game. The Middies' primary ground weapon was junior fullback Kyle Eckel with 1,026 rushing yards. Of Eckel's 193 carries going into the game, all of three were stopped for losses. Averaging 5.3 yards per carry,

Eckel routinely kept Navy in short-yardage situations, the Midshipmen grinding their way toward the opposing goal line, first down after first down. He'd done this while dealing with an injured shoulder since late September. Like Kent, Eckel was a local kid, growing up in south Philadelphia. Asked before the game by reporters how many times he had watched *Rocky*, Eckel couldn't guess, beyond the dozen or so times that he'd done so just that fall.

The Army team hunkered down on that snowy Friday night about 15 miles north of the city at the Eagle Lodge conference center. There, the players could both relax—it featured a game room, jogging path, indoor pool, and fitness room—and get in their final pregame preparations with a minimum of distraction. The weather proved to be more of an obstacle to Pete and Nancy Stewart, who'd attended few Army games through the years while teaching and rearing their younger twins. Peter had played little following his extended duty in the Rutgers game, battling the shoulder and knee issues that seemingly never abated. The Stewarts didn't want to miss their son's final college football game, even if he only saw playing time on the extra-point team. They traveled by air from Houston to Washington for a connecting flight to Philadelphia, only to have that final leg cancelled. In the tradition of John Candy and the Kenosha Kickers in *Home Alone*, a fellow passenger on their Houston flight who was trying to reach Philadelphia told them he was going to rent a car and they were welcome to ride along. The Stewarts gratefully climbed aboard. Nancy tried to catch some sleep in the back seat as late night became early morning. That proved to be difficult as their benevolent driver negotiated the icy roads between DC and Philadelphia at a disquieting-if-effective rate of speed. The weary travelers reached downtown at about 4 a.m., safe and somewhat sound.

The snow that began falling across metropolitan Philadelphia early Friday finally stopped on Saturday morning, but not before leaving a white blanket that measured at least six inches in the area surrounding Lincoln Financial Field. The winds had also mercifully lessened. The field was covered by the stadium grounds crew well before the storm hit. By the time the teams jogged out for pregame warmups, the playing surface was in acceptable condition—it helped that the new facility featured underground heating—with mounds of hard-packed, plowed snow pushed up against the stadium walls. But even without the harsh gusts, the wind chill just before game time was 18 degrees. An overcast sky blocked out the sun for most of that afternoon. And with the game scheduled to begin at 4:20 p.m. to accommodate the CBS broadcast, daylight wouldn't be a factor for long, anyway. Just before Betson's rendition, West Point chaplain Father Edson Wood walked out to the yard-line numbers closest to the home team's side of the field, Army's sideline that day, to deliver the pregame invocation. Father Wood wore a sturdy overcoat and a black, wooly cap that allowed a tuft of gray hair to wiggle out the front. His message began with words that connected the day's events to the greater mission of the dozens of football players who either eagerly or anxiously awaited the kickoff, plus the thousands of young men and women adorned in either the navy-blue overcoats and white hats in the northeast corner of the stadium's lower bowl or those occupying the opposite corner of stands dressed in gray topcoats and hats: "Eternal God, source of life, as our nation struggles near and far to defeat those who would destroy our way of life, Army and Navy meet once again on a field of friendly strife."

The 2003 Army-Navy game was the eighth consecutive installment of the 104-year-old series to be televised live by CBS. In the play-by-play announcer's opening remarks, Ian Eagle proclaimed Army-Navy football as "the purest rivalry in all of sports." Ryan Kent and Clint Woody represented the Black Knights for the coin toss at midfield, and all of the other Army seniors left the sideline and stood on the numbers near midfield. Navy quarterback Craig Candeto and linebacker Eddie Carthan, as captains of that year's designated visiting team, were given the honor of calling the coin toss. Candeto called tails—it was—and Navy deferred, a common preference to receive the kickoff for the second half. Every cadet and midshipman stood as Navy's Geoff Blumenfeld kicked off to begin the game. The kick was relatively short, coming down at Army's 14-yard line, and Chuck Wilke's 27-yard return gave the Black Knights excellent starting position at their 41. Zac Dahman, wearing a gray glove on his non-passing hand and a pouch outside his jersey to occasionally protect his passing hand, trotted out. His throwing hand was tested on the first play, with receiver Aaron Alexander racing down the right sideline. Alexander turned back to his left, deep in Navy territory, only to see the ball come down behind him. He waved futilely. The

Cadets gained a net of only one yard on their next two plays and were forced to punt (Tom Farrington was among those on the coverage team) with the Midshipmen taking over at their 26-yard line.

Navy proceeded to show off the offense that led major college football in rushing that season. Eckel was predictably the main weapon, primarily pounding the middle of West Point's defensive line. The Midshipmen drove 74 yards on 14 plays for the game's first touchdown without throwing a single pass. Candeto dropped back once, searching for an open receiver downfield with Navy at midfield. He instead took off and ran for 11 yards. While the margin was only seven points, CBS color analyst "Boomer" Esiason wasn't optimistic about the Black Knights' chances for giving the Middies a run based on one possession per team: "It couldn't be worse for Army."

Army's second possession also went nowhere, but the Cadets caught a break when Navy subsequently faked a punt at midfield only to have punter John Skaggs's pass to a wide-open receiver at Army's 33 fall inches short. The Black Knights methodically moved toward the Midshipmen's goal line as the game advanced into the second quarter, Dahman connecting with Alexander on a key third-down pass to reach Navy's 1. Army lined up in an option formation, and Dahman pitched to sophomore running back Carlton Jones for the touchdown. Anthony Zurisko came on to attempt a point-after kick to tie the score, with Peter Stewart, Josh Davis, and Brad Waudby among his protectors on the offensive line. But holder Wesley Willard didn't adequately handle the snap from Justin Troy and was left trying to run for two points. Zurisko approached the ball, only to see his holder fleeing like a fugitive, and vainly tried to block for his partner. With 13:24 to play in the first half, Army trailed 7–6.

Navy extended its advantage before halftime with a pair of field goals while Army's offense didn't come close to replicating the success that led to the Black Knights' first-half touchdown. The Midshipmen ran 40 plays during the half and outgained the Cadets in total yards, 162 to 55. Of Dahman's four completions, the longest was the 10-yarder to Alexander that kept the touchdown drive alive. The good news for Army was its absence of turnovers and holding Candeto, who had run for six touchdowns and thrown for one more against them a year earlier, to 15 yards rushing and 20 passing. Eckel, though, had rumbled for 76 and Navy averaged 4.2 yards per rush. How could Army succeed if Navy was constantly gobbling yards at such a pace? Esiason saw a scoreboard that read 13–6 in favor of the Middies but viewed a game that was almost out of reach for the Black Knights: "You really feel like Navy is going to take over any minute."

The Midshipmen took the second-half kickoff and needed just six plays to reach Cadets territory. They faced a 3rd and 2 at Army's 30, and Esiason identified the next play as critical if the Black Knights wished to stay in the game. Candeto handed off to Eckel, who plowed ahead for six yards—giving him 101 for the game, with more than a quarter and a half to play. Navy was back in the end zone three plays later, the lead growing to 20–6.

Turnovers then reared their familiar, ugly head for Army. Dahman threw interceptions on the Cadets' next two possessions, both inside Navy territory. The Black Knights gave up the ball on downs at Navy's 30 early in the fourth quarter, and the Middies converted that into another touchdown for a 27–6 lead. The designated visitors added another touchdown on their next possession to move ahead 34–6 midway through the final period. With the game decided, both teams finished out play with many of the game's starters sent to their respective benches. For Army's final drive of the season, Davis snapped the ball back to Dahman while Stewart took over at left guard and Waudby played right tackle. The three seniors, while obviously drained and distraught because of yet another loss to Navy—a loss that completed a winless season—felt a measure of pride in getting to take the field as Army football players one last time. When Tom Farrington tackled Navy's Lamar Owens on the game's final play, it occurred to him that the last play of his high school career was his recovery of a fumbled snap in that summer all-star game after he had severely injured his right hand. As a Shaler Area Titan and as an Army Black Knight, he had played to the final whistle.

The Army players gathered before their fellow cadets and sang their school song, then begrudgingly stood behind their Navy counterparts as the Midshipmen sang second for the second consecutive year and the third time in their four years at West Point. The Army players then jogged off to their locker room, Temple's dressing room at the Linc, but John Mumford wasn't done coaching. It wasn't difficult for him to identify players who would return to play for Army in 2004, and he urged each one whom he came into contact with to remember the day's defeat. If Mumford felt any sense of relief that a nightmare of an Army football season was over, that wasn't conveyed in his postgame comments to the media. He sternly said, "Losing to Navy is terrible. It's the worst thing at the United States Military Academy to do in anything." Army owned the ball for 12 possessions and failed to record a first down on seven. The Cadets' overall losing streak reached 15 games, the longest at the time in major-college football. The defeat shaved Army's lead in the all-time series down to a single victory. Hill was asked what was worse, losing to Navy or the winless season. Really, the two were cruelly intertwined. "The 0–13 is harder to swallow, definitely," Hill replied. "We came in with some high expectations. This really hurts." Over in the opposing locker room, Eckel was celebrated as the game's obvious selection by the media as most valuable player, rushing for 152 yards and two touchdowns. Candeto diplomatically cited that Navy suffered through a winless season only three years before building its current bowl team.

In the 2004 version of West Point's *Howitzer* yearbook, Woody later wrote the following synopsis of a disheartening campaign—more than four months' toil and draining investment of sweat, strain, and passion—that concluded without a single victory:

The Army Football 2003 season was a time that tried us mentally, physically, emotionally, and spiritually. The loss of our head coach and the worst record in Division 1-A football placed a heavy burden on all of our hearts and spirits. A feeling of disappointment was evident throughout the locker room. How this team reacted and dealt with these circumstances is what made it one of the greatest of all time though, not in the win column, but in character and personality. The moral fibers that these men were composed of are comparable to all of the great war heroes that have come from Army Football in the past. I say this because every time the odds were stacked against us or we were down by a lot, we would never give up; we were still out there sacrificing our bodies for the men next to us, and not for glory but for the love of the game and the brotherhood that this team was comprised of. As a team captain I could not ask for a better group of men who were as dedicated and selfless as they were. I would go into battle with any one of them.

—Clinton Woody '04, Captain

Chapter Ten

"LIFE IS NOT PREDICTABLE"

Army administrators, while trying to coax Frank Solich to board that plane in Nebraska, wisely kept in touch with at least one other coaching candidate. That was Bobby Ross. He coached Georgia Tech to a surprising share of the national championship in 1990, took the 1994 San Diego Chargers to the Super Bowl, and appeared to retire from the profession following the 2000 season, his fourth with the Detroit Lions. He apparently had some vocational itch left to be scratched a few weeks before his 68th birthday. A track record of success on major stages of football certainly worked in Ross's favor. So, too, did him being the graduate of a collegiate military academy—Virginia Military Institute. West Point moved quickly after the Solich courtship ended, and Ross was introduced as the Black Knights' new coach early the following week. The assistant coaches who worked under Todd Berry naturally assumed they would be let go as Ross assembled a staff, his people. John Mumford and his peers simply kept performing their duties until told otherwise, as they did a year earlier when suspecting the 2002 loss to Navy could result in Berry's dismissal.

Mumford was prepared to fly out on recruiting until Rick Greenspan suggested that he instead immediately accompany Ross to one of the highlight events on the college football calendar, the annual National Football

Foundation awards dinner in the grand ballroom of New York's Waldorf Astoria. That really wasn't on Mumford's to-do list. His first attempt at getting out of the engagement was to tell Greenspan that he didn't have a tuxedo. "Rent one," Greenspan said, and Mumford reluctantly acquiesced. Before the Army contingent that included Ross, Mumford, and Bill Lynch loaded up for the drive to Manhattan, Ross held his first meeting with the players at Washington Hall immediately following the cadets' lunch period. After the get-together, Ross told Mumford that he'd like him to remain on the coaching staff. It would be on defense, Ross said, though he wasn't yet sure in what capacity. The offer was bittersweet for Mumford, since he and Tucker Waugh, who coached receivers and coordinated recruiting, were the only Berry assistants asked to stay. But Mumford was primarily grateful to have a job and to continue at an institution that he greatly respected.

* * *

Days after Army turned over its football future to Ross, the future of Saddam Hussein drastically changed. Coalition forces had searched for him soon after the Iraqi dictator's hasty departure from his conglomerate of palaces in Baghdad in advance of the American military's march into the city back in April. Hundreds of troops were assigned to Operation Red Dawn to locate his hiding place, including Staff Sergeant Eric Maddox. The native Oklahoman conducted hundreds of interrogations to that end, the last one coming on the morning that he was scheduled to leave Iraq. That particular session was with one of Hussein's bodyguards. The gentleman was not only persuaded to identify Hussein's harborage but even led the team of Delta Force soldiers to the farmhouse in the town of Adwar, about 10 miles from Tikrit, under which the now-notorious "spider hole" was dug. What especially vexed the soldiers when they arrived was that they had already searched that house. And there was Hussein, who surrendered rather quietly. Among the US military personnel who took commemorative photos of the unlikely lair was one of the officers involved in establishing the perimeter operation for the capture—Captain Brody Howatt, who had served as a mentor during CTLT at Fort Hood during the summer of 2002. Howatt posed while holding a copy of the West Point hockey media guide.

* * *

In mid-December, there was a shake-up at the top of West Point's cadet hierarchy. The leader of the corps, the First Captain, was removed from the position because of "administrative actions" as stated in the academy newspaper *Pointer View*. Deputy Brigade Commander Grace Chung, the kid from Conyers who was ambivalent about attending West Point three years earlier, became First Captain. She became only the second female to do so.

For Christmas, Ryan Kent presented his parents and stepparents with presents that he hoped would express his overwhelming appreciation for the sacrifices that they'd made over the years in the name of his West Point football career. He had his game jersey from the 2002 Navy game framed and gave it to his father and stepmother. He presented his mother and stepfather with the practice helmet from his firstie season, along with a note containing the following message:

> No matter what happened, you two were always there to support me. You have missed 1 game my entire career. Thank you so much. You two are just as important to my football success as any coach or player. You have allowed me to become a leader through your support and guidance. Thank you. Love, Your Son #4

With the dispiriting West Point season over, Kent was the lone Black Knight with one more college football game to play, one to look forward to. He was chosen to play in one of the postseason all-star games, the East-West Shrine Game in San Francisco at the home of baseball's Giants in mid-January. Kent was stunned during the season to receive an invitation, which was sent to the Army football office. The players flew in the previous Sunday and began the week with lunch that afternoon at Fior d'Italia, a few blocks south of Fisherman's Wharf. An estimated 250 scouts from all 32 NFL teams carefully dissected each practice, perchance to discover something about a senior that they didn't know before the annual player draft three months later. Kent enjoyed the lunches, dinners, practices, outings (including Alcatraz), and rooming with University of Miami strong safety Maurice Sikes. But scouts didn't flock to him, didn't inundate him with questions like they did virtually every other player. A few team officials were polite and asked him about the season, but every scout knew Kent's immediate future had nothing to do with playing pro football. He was also one of the few participants still enrolled in school. The vast majority had already left their campuses to focus on training for the NFL combine that preceded the draft. (Sikes wasn't drafted, either, and never played in the NFL. Instead, he made his career in law enforcement.)

West Point's post-graduate active-duty military commitment prevented cadets from pursuing careers in big-league athletics, at least immediately following graduation. NFL franchises drafted football-playing cadets throughout the 1940s, '50s, and '60s, but no Army football players were drafted between 1969 and 1997, when Ronnie McAda, the kinetic quarterback from Texas, was the final player that year to have his name called, by the Green Bay Packers. McAda was dubbed "Mr. Irrelevant," as all the final draftees have been called since 1976. That meant an expense-paid trip to Newport Beach, California, for McAda and his girlfriend, a $2,000 Rolex, leading a Disneyland parade with Mickey Mouse, tee times in two golf tournaments, and more. All of this the brainchild of a former NFL player named Paul Salata, who decided during the mid-1970s that the draft's final pick each year should be suitably celebrated.

The most well-known military academy product to go on to pro sports fame is probably Navy grad Roger Staubach, the Pro Football Hall of Famer who played 11 seasons with the Dallas Cowboys. Staubach, though, didn't become a pro until fulfilling his active-duty commitment. But during the 1980s, Army personnel looked on as two Navy athletic stars ascended to the pro ranks through creative means. Running back Napoleon McCallum, a two-time All-American, was drafted in the fourth round in 1986 by the Los Angeles Raiders. McCallum was able to combine active military status, assigned to a nearby base, while playing that season and making five starts. He was then transferred to a base in northern California and didn't return to the NFL until 1990. Basketball star David Robinson was nicknamed "The Admiral," led the Midshipmen to their first appearances in the NCAA Tournament in a quarter century and was honored as the national player of the year as a senior in 1986–87. He'd been granted a waiver in 1983 to enroll at the Naval Academy at 6-foot-8, two inches beyond the maximum. The first two years of Robinson's college basketball career convinced him that he had a future in the NBA, and he considered leaving Annapolis before the Naval Academy's version of the third-year affirmation ceremony. Academy brain trust placed Robinson in a post-graduate program in which he would train civil engineers in the reserves and be bound for only two years instead of five. He was chosen first overall in the 1987 National Basketball Association draft by the San Antonio Spurs—taller than seven feet at that point. Robinson, an affable personality who provided an excellent advertisement for Navy athletics, played on two NBA championship teams, was named the league's MVP for the 1994–95 season, and was inducted into the Naismith Basketball Hall of Fame in 2009.

McAda attended summer training camp with the Packers—taking all his leave time at once and scheduling the latest possible date to begin officer basic school at Fort Sill—with full knowledge that he'd be leaving before the season began to start his military career. As the Pack's No. 3 quarterback behind Brett Favre and Doug Pederson (who coached the Eagles to a Super Bowl victory in February 2018), McAda was confident he would have been retained at least on the practice squad. He found the speed of the pro game unnerving, even in just calling plays; quarterback coach Andy Reid told him he'd assist with that. McAda played in one preseason game—he saw himself on the Lambeau Field Jumbotron running onto the field before the game because he was running next to Favre. He later fit in some NFL Europe time while under contract to Green Bay, returned to the Packers in 1999, and was cut during training camp. He made one last attempt to play in the NFL in 2001, with the Denver Broncos, but was again released before the season began.

Dawn and Bill Livingston made the trip to California for Kent's final collegiate football game—likely his final formal football game ever—and brought along his older brother. It was Eric who, while the family took in one of the midweek practices, was starstruck to see former San Francisco 49ers head coach Bill Walsh, then working in the team's front office, watching the East team's drills. Eric later chastised his parents for not taking a picture with football royalty. Kent finally wore No. 6 again—No. 4 was given to kicker Billy Bennett from Georgia—and lost again, the West winning 28–7.

A month after Clint Woody's final game as an Army football player, he finally took advantage of an opportunity to visit with Sue Petroff on a Thursday night at the Firstie Club, the on-post watering hole whose patronage was limited to, well, firsties. The two of them sat in a booth and talked for hours. It was difficult to determine who enjoyed that first extended meeting most—Woody, Petroff, or Skyler Munekata. It was Woody's loyal roommate who kept hustling other seniors over to the booth one at a time to embellish their buddy however possible. Not that Petroff needed such a nudge. She was already smitten during the rambling discourse, which included her noting the wood-frame couch back in her dorm room belonging to her roommate was broken. A week later, Petroff answered a knock at her door to see Woody and a bottle of wood glue. "Well, you told me you had a broken couch," he said matter-of-factly. The son of a North Carolina handyman proceeded to repair the couch and invited her to see a movie up in Newburgh the following night. She said yes, and their first date—if you don't count taking orders in a tank—was watching *Fifty First Dates*.

The bookend event to autumn's Branch Night for seniors was Post Night, in early February. That was when graduating cadets chose where they would begin with careers as officers. Most branches featured multiple locations to choose from, but that wasn't the case for Woody, Petroff, and the others who branched aviation—including Grace Chung. Fort Rucker, Alabama, was the army's sole training ground for helicopter pilots since 1942. For the majority of branches, Post Night resembled a fantasy draft, with many selections being greeted with a cacophony of yells, guffaws, and the occasional small object thrown at the selector—especially if the next cadet up just saw the final slot for the post of his or her choice coldly removed from the board.

A couple of the most popular armor locales—Alaska and Colorado—were gone when the count got close to Peter Stewart in a room within Washington Hall. He debated whether to begin his time in Germany or at Texas' Fort Hood. The Texan in him apparently took over, and he tabbed Fort Hood. The field artillery selection took place in a small, amphitheater-style auditorium in Bartlett Hall. It was conducted by Major Daniel Blackmon, with the aid of a projector that made the order of selection visible to even those seated in the rear of the auditorium. The 129 cadets were called one by one in order of their academic rank through the fall semester. Each one walked down to the auditorium floor, picked up a patch for the post of his or her choice, announced the selection, and signed the hard-copy log alongside the name of the post. Those who enjoyed making their peers squirm copied some of the "gotcha" antics that many high school football commits employed on signing day. They would pick up a patch that would raise a ruckus amid those who had yet to select, then put it down and proceed to the actual choice.

Hawaii, Germany, and Korea were the desirable locations in terms of geography, but most of the soon-to-be grads chose a post not for what would look good in a photo sent back home but for how it fit into military career plans. The first cadet to select was David Howald, who ranked 23rd overall in the class. On the clock for months in NFL draft jargon, the Missouri native calmly walked down the auditorium steps, turned and stood before his fellow cadets and announced for Fort Campbell, Kentucky in order to join the 101st Airborne Division. He received primarily good-natured applause since his choice didn't subtract one of the prime locations off the board. Ryan Kent was the first of the football players to select and chose Fort Hood, as did Brian Hill soon after. Tom Farrington and Anthony Zurisko hoped to join them there, but the Hood slots were gone by the time they selected. They'd previously decided that, if Hood was unavailable, they'd both take Fort Riley, Kansas. Brad Waudby also selected Riley. Josh Davis's reason for choosing Fort Sill was related in great measure to a lieutenant colonel who taught his psychology class. The instructor was headed there to command a training battalion and told newlywed-to-be Davis there would be an assignment there that would be unlikely to deploy anytime soon.

One of the last milestone events for the Class of 2004 took place on the final weekend of February. "100th Night" is a countdown toward graduation—100 days until the firsties will walk into Michie Stadium to receive their diplomas. The weekend included a night of skits at Eisenhower Hall entitled "Or Disciplinary Action Will Follow" and a formal banquet. Among the entertainers that weekend was Andrew Betson, who sang the national anthem before the 2003 Army-Navy game. A few weeks later, the cadets were on spring break when President George W. Bush appeared on national television to state his intent to expand the war on terrorism and, specifically, to free Iraq from the rule of Saddam Hussein.

With the end of the football season, the Army football seniors who'd been registered in the Selected Athletes Program since arriving at West Point were removed from those ranks. In taking the Army Physical Fitness Test for one last time in mid-May, about two weeks before graduation day, they would no longer substitute a 12-minute session on a stationary bike for the timed two-mile run. They would run and need to finish in 16 minutes and 36 seconds in order to graduate.

Peter Stewart weighed as much as 280 pounds when playing. He was told that, for his height (6-foot-2), his optimum weight would be around 205. By the time he lined up for the May 2004 APFT, he got down to 230—his weight as a senior at Nimitz High School—and he had no trouble completing the run in time. Brad Waudby passed the first two phases easily but needed 18:54 to cover the two miles. Waudby had completed all academic requirements for a bachelor's degree in systems engineering and pre-law with a grade-point average of 2.12. But his failure to run two miles in 16:36 prevented him from being recognized as a 2004 graduate. The best that West Point could offer him was a retest scheduled for late August, more than two months after the Class of 2004 would celebrate.

Josh Davis passed the APFT but ran into a different obstacle related to his size. A tape test was also administered, comparing the ratio of a cadet's waist size to his or her neck size. Any male under 28 years old in the army must have a ratio of 22 percent or below. Davis realized that could be an issue and began an extensive workout regime. But when Davis was taped, he was over by 0.3 percent. Suddenly, his carefully scheduled sequence of graduation on Saturday, May 29, followed by a wedding in Connecticut two weeks later was thrown into unimagined peril since West Point cadets aren't allowed to be married. If the academy followed procedure and scheduled Davis's next attempt to pass the tape test for the following fall, he would have to choose between postponing one very elaborate wedding and country club reception or kissing goodbye four years of West Point education excruciatingly short of graduation. His parents and other relatives were close to leaving Florida for West Point and the graduation ceremony and were jolted by the news. Cheryl Davis genuinely feared for her son's well-being, telling him, "If this doesn't happen, there's no need to kill yourself over this." Davis's desperate parents got on their cellphones, asking politicians at home to intervene. Craig Froehlich contacted the Department of the Army.

Davis was graciously given another chance—in fact, multiple chances. Academy officials allowed him to continue his efforts at losing weight with them standing at the ready to re-tape him at any time. Davis all but lived during the coming days either on a treadmill while wearing black trash bags to retain body heat or consuming a diet of skinless chicken, soup, or salad. And sleeping. That was it. He reached the point of exhaustion and didn't feel hungry despite the lack of intake.

The graduation week activities began, but Davis wasn't yet beneath the tape-test bar. He stubbornly attended the various events. The glee club held a concert. The gospel choir held a concert. Then, they performed a combined concert. The superintendent held receptions on Wednesday and Thursday afternoons for parents and other guests who were fortunate enough to get to West Point that early. On Thursday night, religious services were held for Catholics, Protestants, Jews, and Eastern Orthodox. Davis even attended practice for the ceremony itself, which threw off the organizers since his name was listed among those who would walk up and receive diplomas. He didn't want to suddenly be eligible to participate at the literal last minute and not be accounted for. That didn't happen. His last taping the day before the ceremony still left him over the limit. He left for Connecticut, where he'd already rented a house in anticipation of being married in a few weeks and continued his weight-loss crusade. The Davis family despondently headed home.

Of the 1,200 "new cadets" who had reported to R-Day in 2000, a total of 960 were listed on the graduation day roster. The guest speaker that day was Secretary of Defense Donald Rumsfeld. On a sunny Saturday morning, the gates to Michie Stadium were unlocked at 7 a.m. The firsties lined up for an entrance walk that would begin at 9:35. But before entering, they finished taking up a collection. Each was expected to contribute one dollar to the graduate who finished four years of West Point studies with the lowest grade-point average. The term of endearment for such an honoree is class "goat." George Pickett, he of Pickett's Charge as an officer in the Confederate army during the Battle of Gettysburg, was cited as being last in West Point's Class of 1846. George Armstrong Custer held down the position in 1861. West Point historian Steve Grove determined the label had nothing to do with the barnyard animal, though it proved to be convenient given that a goat is the mascot of the reviled Naval Academy. Instead, a West Point professor who'd taught classes that were considered at the low end of the academic pecking order sported a goatee, leading to the lowest graduating cadet being tabbed a "goat."

Given the monetary benefit for being a West Point goat, a measure of competition for the position can ensue moving into the firstie year. Or tanking, to borrow language from the pro sports practice of maximizing a franchise's chances of selecting first in the league's next draft. At the academy, such would require a nimble mind—to compile the worst academic average yet still be eligible to graduate.

The Class of 2004's goat was Jerry June, a member of the F4 Frogs from Portsmouth, Ohio, who majored in Foreign Area Studies of Western Europe. No tanking was involved; his was an atypical goat's tale. June dealt with significant medical issues while at West Point and was under the impression that he would need to return to the academy for the following semester, rescheduled to graduate in December. That all changed only six days before graduation day when he learned his inclusion in that weekend's ceremony was a go. As the goat, he was appropriately prepared that Saturday morning with a brown paper bag in which to collect "earnings" that totaled almost $1,000.

Rumsfeld noted that the graduates who sat before him didn't think they'd be going off to war when they walked into Michie Stadium for R-Day. "I suspect that when you first arrived in July 2000, you imagined that your most challenging times as an army officer might involve activities like enforcing peace in the Balkans," he said. "But, as we've seen, life is not predictable." Rumsfeld praised the example of 2001 West Point graduate Kristiaan "K.C." Hughes, who was severely wounded in May 2003 while evacuating soldiers from an enemy ambush. "The civilized world will win the war on terrorism because of people like Lieutenant Hughes and because of you here today. . . . The truth is we're closer to the beginning of this struggle, this global insurgency, than to its end." After the grads walked up and received their diplomas, they retook their seats on folding chairs on the football field. First Captain Grace Chung rose and stood before her peers. She ordered the class to stand and put on their hats. She then yelled, "Dismissed!" and the graduates threw their hats into the gleaming Hudson Valley sky and cheered themselves.

Cory Wallace never convinced anyone to throw him out of West Point. A member of the A2 Spartans, Wallace graduated with a major in arts, philosophy, and literature. Russell Burnett, a member of the H2 Happy Deuce, graduated with a major in Portuguese and a minor in systems engineering. Burnett played on the sprint football team as a junior and senior. The 2003 squad won the Collegiate Sprint Football League championship for a record 30th time, preventing Navy from claiming its 30th title. Thomas Roberts graduated after majoring in geography, inspired to do so by Colonel Gene Palka. Roommate Peter Stewart was his connection to the football team during their final two years at West Point. Roberts often marveled that "Stew-Dog" could wait until the relative last minute, complete an assignment on time and get better grades than him. With one-finger typing, no less. Roberts' mother, true to her word, returned to the academy for graduation day, her first visit since dropping him off on R-Day.

Brad Waudby sat in his barracks room, packing his belongings in order to move to different quarters for the coming summer, when he would continue training for his August run. His father and grandfather were at the stadium; Bradford Sr. insisted on attending so he could congratulate some of his son's friends, many of whom had become like sons to him thanks to their many visits to Oakland. He was present afterward inside the Kimsey Center, in a room with the back windows facing Michie Stadium's football field, when Tom Farrington, Brian Hill, Ryan Kent, Peter Stewart, Clint Woody, Anthony Zurisko, and senior manager Chris Klich were commissioned together by Colonel Patrick Finnegan. Each was pinned with their 2nd lieutenant bars—nicknamed "butter bars"—by various relatives and friends. It was a bittersweet experience for the elder Waudby, who could only wonder what his son was thinking and feeling. Afterward, Woody hustled down to Eisenhower Hall, where Sue Petroff and many of her graduating friends held their ceremony. She was pinned by her parents and commissioned by a cousin, Brian Anderson, an active-duty Marine captain. While Woody had met Petroff's family in Connecticut during the previous months, graduation day was the setting for Petroff to finally meet the Woodys.

Dennis Zilinski II and other seniors from the Army swim team conducted their commissioning and pinning in the academy cemetery, at the gravesite of David Bernstein. When Zilinski and the other '04 swim grads were plebes, Bernstein was a firstie and the team's captain. He was killed in Iraq the previous fall when trying to save his driver. When Zilinski graduated, he was dating classmate Marie Cicerelle. They'd met during plebe year, when they were placed in the same math study group. Because Cicerelle was a Rabble Rouser, Zilinski typically chose to stand toward the back of the Corps of Cadets during football games and focused his attention on the sideline instead of the playing field.

Back on Branch Night, Zilinski couldn't comply with his mother's desire to choose a relatively safe option, like finance or law. He and Cicerelle branched infantry. Zilinski was sent to Fort Benning, Georgia, for officer basic school while she was dispatched to Fort Jackson, South Carolina. During Christmas break, they rendezvoused in New York City. He took her to Central Park and proposed. They planned on a wedding in 2007 without setting a formal date. They were briefly reunited at Fort Campbell, Kentucky, before going abroad, the result of Zilinski doing some serious horse-trading to change his location. Cicerelle left in August 2005 for Mosul; Zilinski left a month later for Bayji, located about an hour south of Mosul. Just before Zilinski left for Iraq, his mother asked if he was afraid. "You know what I'm afraid of, Mom? Losing one of my soldiers and having to face his mother or father." Zilinski's parents traveled to Fort Campbell to tend to the house that he'd bought. "Big Dennis" tried to ease Marion's mind by stating the obvious, that many more fighting men and women return from combat than not.

The Stewart family had a pair of commencement ceremonies to attend that weekend. Nancy made the trip to West Point for Peter's graduation while Pete remained in Houston to take in the twins' big day from Nimitz High. Patrick was about to follow his older brother into preparation for a career in the military. He originally planned to join twin sister Anna and enroll at Texas A&M with a significant interest in joining the school's Corps of Cadets. Patrick, while intrigued by West Point, was leery of following in Peter's boot steps. Early in Patrick's senior year of high school, his father noted there were military academies other than West Point and suggested pursuing a slot at the Naval Academy. Patrick graduated in the top 10 percent of his class, which, by state law, earned him automatic acceptance to every state college, A&M being one of them. He pursued enrollment at the Naval Academy but wasn't accepted to either Annapolis or its prep school in Rhode Island. He was set to head up to College Station until Gene Green, the Stewarts' neighbor in Congress, called to say there was an opening at Navy's prep school, with about four weeks to go before the school's summer indoctrination program began. Patrick had four days to decide. He talked to the parents, his siblings, his friends, his teachers. Anna advised him to do what made him happy, that he could always come back to A&M if the Naval Academy wasn't for him. Patrick opted to attend Navy's prep school.

The week following West Point graduation, Josh Davis, still running and sweating and doing whatever possible to lose weight, drove back to West Point for another taping. He was at 24 percent. A few days later, after more intense exercise and dieting, he was measured at 21.4. Victory! He was finally, exhaustingly, eligible to graduate from the United States Military Academy. And, by virtue of that, his wedding to Misa Froehlich, the date by then only a week and a half away, could go on as scheduled. Part of the beleaguered groom-to-be's celebration was to treat himself to a chicken breast, skin and all.

Given the Davis family's financial commitment to traveling from Florida back north for the Connecticut wedding, his father was the only relative who was able to attend the personal graduation ceremony, held in the academy's distinguished Thayer Award Room—only three days before his son's wedding. It was part board room, part military museum. As stated in its name, it was the setting for the annual presentation of the prestigious Thayer Award, to a person who exemplified the academy motto of duty, honor, and country.

Mike Davis was dazzled by the décor, from its shields and crossed swords to a massive, stone fireplace. He thought it looked like King Arthur's court. While he was the only person able to return from Florida for the ceremony on such short notice, Froehlich naturally drove over, along with her father and other relatives. Lieutenant General William Lennox did the honors, accompanied by other West Point dignitaries. A professional photographer arranged by the academy shot photos. After Davis was handed his diploma, he even got to throw his hat. For all the angst that the previous weeks brought, Davis and those who accompanied him were pleased with the proceedings.

Misa Froehlich and Josh Davis were married the night of Saturday, June 12, 2004, at St. Joseph's Catholic Church in Brookfield, Connecticut, with the reception about 10 minutes away at Ridgewood Country Club in Danbury. Brian Hill was the best man. Tom Farrington, Ryan Kent, and Anthony Zurisko were among the groomsmen. The following morning, the alarm clock jolted them awake at 4:30 to catch a limousine for their morning flight from New York's LaGuardia Airport to Bermuda. Graduation from West Point and a picturesque wedding in Connecticut, imperiled only a few weeks earlier, were in the young couple's rearview mirror.

Chapter Eleven

LIFE AFTER WEST POINT BEGINS

That summer, Brad Waudby participated in a P.E. remediation program two hours a day, three days a week. He requested to report five days but was denied. His body fat had dropped from 33.54 percent in January, when he began efforts to lose weight and pass the APFT, to 21.55 percent in August. Though Waudby had failed only the run in May, his retest included all three portions of the test. He did 41 pushups to earn a passing grade for that. He followed with 51 sit-ups; two-for-two. For the run, he used a pace man. But Waudby finished in 18:35; while that was 19 seconds faster than his run in May, it was still well beyond the necessary clocking. Days later, Lieutenant General William Lennox recommended that Waudby re-enroll for the academy's fall semester for the sole purpose of taking the APFT one last time.

One of the perks for a handful of graduating West Point athletes each year is to begin their military careers assigned as graduate assistant coaches at either the academy or the prep school. There would no longer be any high-stress classes or mandatory marching, but the recent grads were again part of an athletic team, often in the sport they played at West Point. For the football program, that usually meant assigning a dozen or so graduating seniors. Not so for the Class of 2004. And neither Clint Woody nor Peter Stewart was interested in such an appointment. Each was ready to begin his chosen army career immediately. For Woody, electing to spend most of the 2004–05 academic year back at West Point as a grad assistant would have both separated him from Sue Petroff and staggered their respective aviation timelines. Josh Davis, Brian Hill, and Ryan Kent gladly accepted invitations to work with the Army football team during the 2004 season, beginning with summer drills and ending with signing day in February. Hill's parents were also elated with the opportunity; they held out hope that the conflict in Iraq could be resolved or at least made less volatile in a matter of months and their son wouldn't be deployed to a perilous war zone.

The four initial football graduate assistant assignments for Fort Monmouth went to Tom Farrington, Brad Waudby, Anthony Zurisko and, with no other Army football grads available, Hill's roommate, Mark Patzkowski. Among grad assistants for other sports was Josh Davis's old roommate, Bernard Gardner, for wrestling. The four football assignees arranged to rent a house in the nearby shore town of Manasquan, but Waudby's failure to graduate eliminated him from serving. In the short term, Davis was temporarily reassigned to the prep school as Army administrators tried to determine how to fill the position. Stewart had just arrived at Fort Knox, Kentucky, to begin armor's officer basic course when he received a call from Kent the night before the instruction began. "Would you be interested in coming back to coach?" Kent asked. Stewart was torn: "Yeah, I guess. If you need me to." That led to a follow-up communication the following day involving Major Bill Lynch, with Stewart noting that he'd started his OBC class that very day. Lynch indicated the football staff could get Stewart reassigned to Fort Monmouth. Stewart relayed the apparent change of plans to his chain of command at Knox, who was both surprised and somewhat perturbed: "You're already here. That's not going to happen." Stewart thought: "You don't have the pull that West Point does. I'm pretty sure this *is* going to happen." The following day, Stewart had orders to report to the prep school. Being the last to occupy the rental house, he was assigned the bedroom in the attic.

In many ways, being a football grad assistant at Fort Monmouth became the most "regular" college experience that those West Point graduates would experience. Once they completed their duties during the day, they were free to do as they pleased without the restrictions of academy life. The rental house was close to the cleverly named watering hole Leggett's Sand Bar. That's where Farrington met Kaitie Colligan, who likewise was sharing a rental home with a friend. Colligan grew up not far from the shore, in New Brunswick, was a 2003 graduate of Northeastern University in Boston, and was a standout swimmer for the Huskies. She swam one meet at West Point, an experience most memorable because her coach made the team members tour the academy grounds despite temperatures that hovered around zero.

Stewart and Gardner were enjoying dinner at the Boathouse Bar and Grill in nearby Belmar when they overheard a young woman talking about her recent trip to Australia. Stewart unabashedly chimed in, "Hey, I've wanted to go to Australia! Wow! What's that like?" Maura Sommers, from Manasquan, had just returned from six months' travel to the South Pacific before beginning a teaching career. The two chatted a bit and agreed to get in touch with each other upon leaving the restaurant. Neither realized that would be only minutes later, at a 7/11 on their respective drives home. "I live here," he said, pointing in the direction of the house that he shared with the other grad assistants. "I live down the block," she said.

Hill and Kent rented a house in Highland Falls along with a baseball grad assistant. Davis's new bride tried to rent one there, too, but instead settled for one in Connecticut because her father was a real estate agent and able to arrange an extremely reasonable rate. The downside was a daily commute of almost an hour each way for Davis. As the plebe prospects reported for Beast Barracks 2004, he typically left the house at 3:30 a.m. to be present when the cadet candidates' day began at 4:30. He often worked well into the evening and arrived back in Brookfield around 9 p.m., to repeat the routine only hours later. Halfway through a summer greatly spent on the backroads of western Connecticut, Davis reluctantly traded in the new Dodge Ram truck that he'd just bought for a more fuel-efficient Honda Civic.

Fort Rucker, home to the army's aviation school, occupies about 58,000 acres in the southeastern corner of Alabama. It's named for Edmund Rucker, an officer in the Confederate Army. The nearest town is Enterprise, a few miles west of the base, and is best known for its municipal adoration of the boll weevil. A monument graces the middle of Main Street, a statue of a woman holding aloft an oversized version of the insect. A nearby plaque details the boll weevil's unintended contribution to the local community in the early 1900s. A plague of the pests ingested about 60 percent of the area's cotton crop and forced the desperate locals to identify agricultural alternatives in order to diversify and keep the economy afloat; that began with peanuts. On December 11, 1919, the boll weevil monument was unveiled. (The replica bug was vandalized and pilfered enough through the years that it's now housed within a secure location while a reasonable facsimile resides at the intersection of Main and College streets.) Enterprise holds an annual Boll Weevil Festival on the last Saturday of October. It was on Sue Petroff's long trip to Alabama with her parents that she divulged to her mother the real explanation for why she had to march those 80 hours during her yuk year at West Point.

Clint Woody, at 6-foot-5, soon discovered that one size doesn't fit all when it comes to helicopter training. While he was accommodated just fine in the craft that began his high-flying driver's education, the second phase—moving from a civilian copter that resembles the ones used by most television stations for their news and traffic coverage into the military version of the same craft—was a far different story. The dashboard sat a little lower. When he fully pushed the left pedal to counteract the rotation of the blades, his shin made bloody contact with the dash. Nor was the headroom adequate; his helmet kept banging into the roof. His understanding instructor tried to ease Woody's plight by moving the pedals up, but that put his knees into his chest. The new student was deemed a safety risk in that environment and was shifted to a different copter to complete his training. Petroff, at 5-foot-6, faced no such issues. Also, she enjoyed something of a head start. During the summer before her firstie year, she spent a month at a flight school at the University of North Dakota as part of a first-year partnership program with West Point, learning many of the basics. While a solo flight at Fort Rucker was done with two other students aboard, the solo at UND was literally that.

The US Army's three general categories of helicopters are Apaches (attack aircrafts), Black Hawks (used primarily for transporting individuals), and Chinooks (also used primarily for transport, able to accommodate more individuals than Black Hawks plus substantial volumes of cargo). Aviation students are assigned their copters during flight school based upon their flying aptitude. Petroff certainly didn't want to be assigned to an Apache; she readily admitted not wanting to swoop down and shoot at the enemy.

* * *

During Army's 2004 football season, Davis primarily worked with football players in the weight room. On game days, he was involved with pregame warmups and stood on the sideline during play. Hill and Kent helped the offensive and defensive staffs, respectively. They broke down film on future opponents during the season, documented formations on game days up in the coaching booths, and pitched in on office work during the offseason when the assistant coaches were on the road recruiting. While Kent dearly missed being able to suit up and hit someone on the field, G.A. duty didn't really feel like work. He considered coaching as a possible vocation, and being a grad assistant was a terrific way to see the inside workings of what such a job would entail that he wasn't able to witness as a player. Part of that was first-hand knowledge of the time commitment, which gave him pause.

Bobby Ross's approach to volume on the football roster resembled that of Bob Sutton and not the path taken by Todd Berry. The 2004 plebe roster numbered 75, actually dwarfing the amount of freshmen in the 2000 signing class that was first recruited by Sutton and later by Berry. Among the '04 newcomers were a couple of players who began impressing Ross and his staff early on: fullback Mike Viti from Berwick, Pennsylvania, and cornerback Caleb Campbell from the Texas panhandle town of Perryton. Viti could have walked on at Penn State or Maryland or played at any number of Ivy League schools. But the 9/11 attacks during his sophomore year of high school instilled in him a desire to serve his country. The chance to play FBS football at the same time was simply an added bonus. Campbell's only FBS athletic scholarship offer coming out of Perryton High came from Tulsa, and that was before a coaching change took place there. He took a recruiting trip to West Point on his own and called home to say he had signed with the Black Knights. Campbell spent a year at Fort Monmouth and then earned a starting Army position midway through his plebe season.

Eleven months after Rick Greenspan fired Todd Berry, and less than two weeks before Ross debuted as the head football coach on the Hudson, the Army athletic director resigned to assume the same duties at Indiana. Greenspan would become the Big Ten school's fourth A.D. in slightly more than three years. Justin Rodriguez's report in the *Times Herald-Record* quoted former Army football players from the 1980s and '90s who essentially said good riddance. "He put the football program back five or six years by hiring his buddies with no real concept how the academy works," said Ron Rice, a center who played on the Cadets' first two bowl teams under Jim Young.

* * *

The opening game of the 2004 football season was a Conference USA matchup at Michie Stadium against one of the contenders for the league championship. Bobby Petrino's Louisville Cardinals scored the first 24 points and cruised to a 52–21 victory to extend the Black Knights' school-record losing streak to 16 games. Army then went on the road to face another conference opponent, albeit one projected near the bottom of the league standings: the Houston Cougars. Hill and Kent were part of West Point's traveling party for that game. As usual, there was a team dinner on the Friday before the game followed by meetings involving coaches and players late into the evening. (The grad assistants were invited to the dinner but excused from the meetings.) Hill took advantage of the opportunity to arrange a meeting with a young woman whom he'd met the previous summer, Morgan Hesse, at the University of Texas in Austin. Hill brought along Kent, and Hesse brought along Kristen Keefhaver, her friend since fifth grade and current roommate. Keefhaver was initially unenthused about making the trip, and Hesse didn't really want to go by herself. Keefhaver agreed at the relative last minute, and they were off for the 160-mile drive to Houston that Friday afternoon. The four of them hung out that night, not staying out terribly late since all members of Army's football party needed to be up and at 'em at an early hour for Saturday's game. The social group reconvened briefly the following morning before the team left for the UH campus. The game itself was another disappointment for the Black Knights and their followers, as Houston broke a 21–21 tie with about seven minutes to play and won by two touchdowns.

Army's losing streak reached 19, longest in the country at the time, with subsequent losses to Connecticut and TCU before West Point finally savored sweet victory for the first time since November 2002 with a 48–29 win over Cincinnati in front of a joyous and relieved gathering at Michie Stadium. Zac Dahman, who yet again succeeded Reggie Nevels as starting quarterback early in the season, threw two touchdown passes, including a 93-yarder. An Army program that had gone years without one win then strung together two, winning at South Florida with another solid offensive display (42–35). Was West Point football "back," as the media often declared?

Not really.

The victory in Tampa was the Black Knights' last of the season. A 2–9 finish represented progress when compared to the 2003 record but was far from what Army fans ultimately desired. The season ended with another overwhelming loss in south Philadelphia to Navy, 42–13, to run the Midshipmen's winning streak in the series to three and retain the Commander-in-Chief's Trophy. The day provided a different, almost painful experience for Kent. In what had been the most important day of his football life during the previous four years, he could only stand on the field before kickoff wearing a sweatshirt and think, "Man, I can't believe I can't play!" Freshman cornerback Caleb Campbell played in every varsity game that season, starting the final six, and fullback Mike Viti played in 10. They were among seven plebes to earn letters that fall. That same month, West Point hired Oregon State associate athletic director Kevin Anderson to become the academy's new athletic director.

Having completed all of West Point's core courses, Brad Waudby enrolled solely in electives in fall 2004 as he prepared to take the physical fitness test again in December. One of his classes was a special operations course taught by a former Green Beret. The major took Waudby aside a week into the semester and said he knew why Waudby was back at West Point that fall. "Hey, big boy," the major told him. "We're going to get you through this. Monday morning—5:30. MacArthur Statue. Meet me there. We're gonna go run." Waudby and the major (not identified here because of his current secure military status) ran on Mondays, Wednesdays, and Fridays, the major wearing a weighted vest. Waudby progressed to covering the first two miles of their jaunts—uphill stretches—20 seconds faster than the required 16:36.

With Waudby "on campus" but with afternoons free after doing his training and taking his electives, he was eligible for the first time to pursue a mission that he'd coveted throughout his time at West Point. That was to carry the American flag at a New York Yankees postseason game. Team owner George Steinbrenner was a huge Army booster and enjoyed having cadets involved in that capacity. Waudby was a member of the cadet color corps that rode to the Bronx for the second game of the American League Division Series against the Minnesota Twins. The cadets finished their early afternoon practice—marching in from left field to the infield—in time to relax and watch batting practice. Being a Yankees fan since childhood, Waudby relished hanging around the batting cage to watch the likes of Derek Jeter, Alex Rodriguez, Jason Giambi, Bernie Williams, and Jorge Posada take their hacks. Soon after manager Joe Torre and bench coach Willie Randolph walked out of the dugout and onto the field, Randolph peered toward the batting cage and seemed to recognize his son's former Indian Hills team-mate: "Brad, is that you?" Randolph walked over and chatted with Waudby, which left the other cadets speechless. Randolph then introduced all of the cadets to Jeter and Rodriguez.

Six weeks into the workout sessions with the special ops major, Waudby felt light-headed and experienced tingling in his left arm, which halted training for several weeks. When it resumed, Waudby was told by the academy's physical education department not to employ the major any longer, and he curtailed his workouts. His third attempt to pass, and be eligible to graduate, took place in early December. Waudby planned to have a pace man again but was told he couldn't. He breezed through the pushups (42) and sit-ups (53) before doing the run, the major cheering him on. Waudby finished in 17:27, 51 seconds over the allowed maximum. Days later, Waudby's TAC officer recommended that he be allowed to graduate but not be commissioned as a 2nd lieutenant. In mid-December, the major filed a written assessment of Waudby's efforts and "strongly recommended" retention. In five breakdowns, he awarded Waudby four "top" grades and one "middle." Responding to the question, "What leadership potential is shown?" the major's remarks included: "If we fix this run time, I expect to see this soldier five years from now as a competent professional that soldiers admire. He will excel in command positions. He loves soldiers and respects NCOs. He has a solid work ethic." In a space available for general comments, the major expounded on Waudby's situation. Parts of that entry: "Based on my interaction with him, I strongly recommend that we retain CDT Waudby in our army . . . We have asked CDT Waudby to be a big offensive lineman and develop explosive, fast twitch muscle fibers—until 12 months ago. Then, we asked him to develop endurance, increase performance, and simultaneously lose weight. It's a tall order, even for an athlete of his caliber." The major noted that Waudby ran the first two miles of an informal three-mile run 20 seconds faster than the required time for the fitness test before experiencing an "injury/health scare" that set him back. The major further stated Waudby told him that, if he didn't graduate and wasn't commissioned as an officer, he was willing to enter the army as a non-commissioned officer or even an enlisted soldier. "That attitude reflects a level of 'inspiration' that I want from soldiers in our army," the major wrote.

On December 28, 2004, Lieutenant General Lennox recommended that Waudby be separated from the academy, denied the bachelor's degree that he'd pursued, be discharged from the army, and be responsible for academy restitution of $190,005. The stunned Waudbys responded by filing suit in federal court. Their legal team included Frederick Klepp, a retired army colonel. Their suit was reported in the *Record*, with West Point officials declining to comment on their story, but, the story noted, "they acknowledged that the biannual physical fitness test has been modified for others in the past." A few months later, Waudby received a Certificate of Completion of Academic Programs from West Point.

During Ryan Kent's stint as a West Point football graduate assistant, he committed to pursue a slot in the elite Ranger School. The topic was suggested to him by two former West Point football players on staff whom he greatly respected. Rick Roper and Joe Ross, he of the Center for Enhanced Performance, were members of the Class of 1995 and majors in the army. They not only played football together but lined up in the same backfield, Roper the quarterback from Houston and Ross the running back from Maryland. Given the spellings of their last names, they lockered next to each other all four football seasons. They were even Ranger School buddies. When Roper contracted trench foot following the constant rains of the school's opening weeks, the bottom of his foot was all but torn away. Their Ranger instructor told Roper, "Either your Ranger buddy carries you, or you're out." Roper gave Ross a quick look, hobbled behind him, jumped on his back, and said, "Let's go, Joe." To which Ross replied, "You bastard." Fortunately for Ross, the day's duties were devoid of unreasonable physical stress. Also, fortunately for him, Roper was able to negotiate on his own after that. Later in Ranger School, Ross broke his back while jumping from a helicopter. He didn't tell anyone—for years. Ross deployed to Kosovo in April 2001 with the 101st Airborne, 502nd Infantry Battalion, Bravo Company—a companion to the "Easy Company" of "Band of Brothers" fame. Ross's group captured two of the CIA's ten most wanted insurgents, and he developed a program to institute "visualization" into battle strategy that was adopted by the Pentagon.

Roper explained to Kent that no one day of Ranger School was more difficult than any football practice, but the cumulative effect of going days with little to eat and little sleep would make it extremely taxing. Ross encouraged all graduate assistants to take a shot at Ranger School. In Kent, he saw a young man of relative average football talent who excelled on the field thanks to effort and intense preparation. The two majors emphasized that Ranger School provided the best leadership training in the army. Kent concluded that passing on the chance to go through Ranger School would be a decision that he'd later regret.

Clint Woody and Sue Petroff enjoyed Valentine's Day weekend in 2005 only hours from Fort Rucker, in the Florida Gulf Coast town of Destin. They spent a day at the beach and shopped before enjoying a quiet dinner. At the restaurant, Woody pulled out a heart-shaped box that resembled one that would contain chocolate candies—but was much deeper. There indeed were chocolates in the box but also a bottle of wood glue, a reminder of him repairing her roommate's barracks couch. There also were some dollar bills folded into a box, similar to the dollar-bill heart that he configured a year earlier when paying off a basketball bet. Petroff opened the box to find another bill shaped like a heart—and a diamond ring.

The young couple initially planned to be engaged for a year or more but soon realized that status might not assure them of being assigned to the same location after graduation from flight school. Their Black Hawk flight course would end around Memorial Day, followed by their officer basic course. They requested a 10-day leave and a delay of only a few weeks before starting OBC. The plan was to hold their wedding at a location relatively near the academy on a day close to when the third of the Woody brothers, Clay, began his own West Point career—including an invitation to join the football program, as a tight end—at R-Day on the final Monday of June. By having the wedding on the preceding Saturday only a few hours away from West Point near Petroff's home in Connecticut, the North Carolina Woodys would have to make only one extended trip to the northeast for two important family events. Permission granted.

The hastily scheduled festivities made it problematic for some intended guests. That included Skyler Munekata, deployed to Iraq then. Some serious wheeling and dealing of R&R cycles with a benevolent maintenance sergeant was required for Munekata to land a two-week slot that allowed him to travel to Connecticut. He only learned that he'd be able to attend the wedding two days before the ceremony and kept that fact under wraps to make a dramatic entrance. Clint Woody and Sue Petroff were married on June 25, 2005, at Emanuel Lutheran Church in Manchester with a reception at the nearby Nutmeg restaurant. They reported back for duty in Alabama the following Wednesday. Two days after the wedding, 6-foot-4 tight end Clay Woody experienced the joys of R-Day. He was one of 77 Army football newcomers in what Bobby Ross called his first full recruiting class. Forty-eight of them came straight from high school and 29 from Fort Monmouth, where the prep team's 2004 record of 6–3 included wins over Navy and Air Force.

In April 2005, West Point allowed for its athletes to perform only two years' active service like David Robinson had during the 1980s. The first Army athlete to take advantage of the policy change was baseball player Josh Holden, a 2003 graduate. The outfielder signed a minor-league contract with the Cincinnati Reds and spent four years in their farm system before being released. After Holden's pro baseball career ended, he reapplied for active military duty. Also that April, Navy enabled fullback Kyle Eckel to sign as an undrafted free agent with the New England Patriots and trained with them by locating his active-duty assignment at its prep school in Rhode Island.

Eckel was administratively separated from the navy that fall and played in the NFL for three seasons for three teams. In July of that year, Army published another policy change entitled "Early Separation to Participate in Activities with Recruiting or Public Affairs Benefit to the US Army."

The Woodys and all of the other students in the aviation officer basic course were given their helicopter assignments based, just like post assignments, on their standing in the West Point Order of Merit. An officer entered the classroom and informed both Woodys that they would be flying Black Hawks. The same procedure determined where the students would be stationed after graduating from Fort Rucker. The Woodys were a combined "entry" holding the second and third slots among the Black Hawk pilots since they were enrolled in the Army Married Couples Program. (If circumstances dictated that a husband and wife couldn't be stationed together, the US Army would have provided a monthly separation stipend.) The Woodys chose Germany.

The grad assistants left their respective posts in February 2005. Peter Stewart made his "return" trip to attend OBC for armor at Fort Knox along with Bernard Gardner, caravanning from the Jersey shore to Kentucky. Josh Davis, Tom Farrington, Brian Hill, Ryan Kent, and Anthony Zurisko were bound for Oklahoma and Fort Sill. They creatively scheduled a side trip for their reporting date to Austin, Texas. Hill and Morgan Hesse reconnected in person as their interaction developed into actual dating. Kent got better acquainted with Kristen Keefhaver. Farrington, Hill, Kent, and Zurisko then settled into their living quarters on the base. Davis, the only married man among the group, rented a house in Fort Sill's "hometown" of Lawton. He was also the only member of the group who would remain at the post following OBC.

Hill's destination following OBC was Fort Hood, where he was assigned to the 4th Infantry Division. Soon after, he learned he would be deployed to Iraq within a matter of months. But not before spending a month at the National Training Center in Fort Irwin, California, for instruction within a setting that was designed to simulate the conditions that the military personnel would find in Iraq. And not before attending Hesse's graduation from the University of Texas with a degree in English. And not before he watched the telecast of the 2005 Army-Navy Game in early December at a friend's house along with Hesse. He was amped up, ready to take the field, in part because the Black Knights went to Philadelphia riding a four-game winning streak, their longest since the Ronnie McAda team of 1996. She wore his Army football jersey, and he was compelled to bring along his helmet. The Midshipmen matched their scoring prowess of the previous year, winning 42–23 for their fourth consecutive victory over Army and held the Commander-in-Chief's Trophy for a Navy-record third straight year.

At Fort Knox, one of Stewart's charges was a congenial solider from Walpole, Massachusetts, named Andrew Bacevich Jr. Second-generation military, Bacevich joined the army in July 2004, about a year after his graduation from Boston University. Bacevich's energetic, capricious personality was endearing to his friends and sometimes disarming to those who didn't know him. His father was on the BU faculty, teaching history and international relations. The elder Bacevich was a 1969 West Point graduate and had taught at the academy; Andrew Jr. was born at West Point. Andrew Sr. served in Vietnam in 1970–71 and returned with an appetite for diplomacy and military strategy, earning a master's degree in American History and a PhD in American Diplomatic History, both from Princeton. He was sent to Iraq during Operation Desert Storm in the summer of 1991, retired as a colonel, and became a prolific author and contributor to professional journals and major US newspapers and magazines.

As a student at BU, Bacevich enrolled in the ROTC program but was removed when a routine physical during his attempt to go to jump school revealed childhood asthma. But as a young adult, Bacevich became an avid distance runner; his collection of medals from completed marathons included twice running Boston's storied version. After graduating, Bacevich was convinced the childhood asthma red flag that disqualified him from ROTC would likewise prevent him from serving in the military and turned his attention to politics. He worked for multiple Massachusetts politicians, including then-governor Mitt Romney. A friend of Bacevich's father informed the family that the army had changed its acceptance rule regarding childhood asthma; it was no longer a deal-breaker. Son followed father's lead into the military, enlisting as a private. Bacevich struck the following deal upon his entry—if he completed basic training, he'd be commissioned as a 2nd lieutenant. Which he did, at Fort Benning

Andrew Bacevich Sr. became one of the military experts who dissected and analyzed the United States' involvement in Iraq. He contributed a commentary to the *Los Angeles Times* in late March 2003 that questioned the government's decision to invade. The piece closed:

Seduced by images of war rendered antiseptically precise, we have lost our bearings. We have deluded ourselves into believing that the best hope of safety and security lies in dispatching the cadre of military professionals whom we proclaim to be "our best and brightest" on a mad undertaking to transform the world—or, if need be, to conquer it. In Iraq, President Bush has opened up yet another front in his war against evil. Committed, we must win. But the long march to Baghdad should give Americans pause: Exactly where is this road leading us.

Chapter Twelve

"THINGS ARE GOING GOOD OVER HERE"

Flight school at Fort Rucker included training that had nothing to do with maneuvering copters or airborne skills of any kind. "SERE" stands for survival, evasion, resistance, and escape. It's a worst-case scenario times four. Trainees are taught how to survive in the wilderness, evade capture, resist the enemy's efforts if captured and, in the event of that unfortunate turn of events, escape. The first portion might have resembled an episode of *Survivor*, with participants eating roots, building fishing nets, making spears, etc. Chicken could be on the menu as long as you did the killing, skinning, and quartering. Instructions for such an effort recommended digging a hole in which to kill the chicken since the bird, even after beheading, was liable to run around like—yes—a chicken with its head cut off.

The newlyweds were part of the same SERE assignment, which delighted many of their fellow trainees. "Lt. Mr. Woody" and "Lt. Mrs. Woody" became the couple's names on first reference. Sue was assigned to be a team leader, which she initially disliked—it was bad enough having to endure all of that without being in charge of others—but came to enjoy it as the course progressed. The Woodys' team was in the lead because she'd just killed a rabbit. That apparently called for special recognition. Husband and wife were called up in front of the group. They were asked how long they'd been married ("Three weeks, sir."), if they'd had a big wedding ("Yes, sir."), if the reception included a toast ("Yes, sir."), and if that toast included linking arms. ("Yes, sir."). All of that information worked against the newlyweds. Lt. Mr. and Mrs. Woody were then asked to lock arms, and Sue suddenly realized where that was all going. The delicacy in that backwoods celebration of matrimony would be the eyeballs of the rabbit; for practical value, it was noted the saline in the bunny's eyeballs would provide nutrients in a situation of dire need.

The two orbs were popped from the unfortunate hare by an eager officer. Sue had been forewarned about this aspect of SERE school and was prepared to decrease the foulness of the activity, if that was possible. For one thing, a healthy swish of Gatorade before consumption was said to mute the taste. Sue lucked out in that she was given only a portion of an eyeball and was able to gulp it down whole. Clint's *hors d'oeuvre* was more substantial and couldn't simply be swallowed whole. The rest of the class applauded and howled—some of them grimaced—as he chomped away at his ration. It kept slipping from between his teeth until he reluctantly resorted to holding it in order to get a satisfactory bite.

The Woodys graduated from flight school that August and were assigned to a base in Germany, Katterbach Kaserne (Kaserne means post), near the Bavarian city of Ansbach, as part of the 4th Brigade, 1st Infantry Division. Their West Point friend, Grace Chung, was also sent to Germany along with her husband—fellow '04 academy grad Andrew Chung. Grace and Andrew shared the same last name before their betrothal; since they even finished their academy careers in the same company, their portrait-style photos in the *Howitzer* yearbook were side by side. With a relative glut of lieutenants, the Woodys had to initially settle for jobs that had little or nothing to do with flying. Clint soon became a platoon leader for an aviation maintenance company, Sue an executive officer—a can-do position that entailed making sure a variety of tasks at the headquarters company were performed, such as refueling copters. They bought used BMWs for almost nothing from a generous local car dealer and moved into a townhouse off base. They were pleasantly amused that fall by advertisements in the local grocery stores showing families cheerfully gathered around a holiday turkey given that there is no

Thanksgiving holiday in Germany. The Katterbach assignment afforded them the ability to travel throughout Germany and across Europe, including acting as tour guides for visiting family and friends. They waved at Queen Elizabeth as she was driven in a carriage across London during a national birthday celebration. They saw the popemobile on a visit to Rome. At home in Katterbach, most of their neighbors were enthralled during the summer of 2006 with Germany hosting soccer's World Cup. In the Woodys' neighborhood, folks set up lawn chairs in a driveway and projected telecasts of the matches on a garage door. The festivities to celebrate the couple's wedding anniversary in June 2006 included buying a DVD of the film *Fifty First Dates*. Clint moved into an actual flight company, planning and managing flights for his platoon. He and Sue were assigned to different battalions within the same brigade and often worked schedules that didn't coincide. The lengthiest conversation between them during a week might be all of 20 minutes.

Clint resumed his football career that spring following a two and a half year hiatus, playing for a semi-pro team based in nearby Rothenberg called the Franken Knights. Their opponents included the likes of the Wiesbaden Phantoms, the Munich Cowboys, and the Königsbrunn Ants; the Ants' helmets shamelessly replicated an outdated New York Giants helmet's underlined block lettering of *GIANTS* and simply lopped off the first two letters. The games were played at facilities built for soccer with seating that was comparable to American college football at schools in the NCAA's lower divisions or the NAIA. The players were essentially compensated in beer and all-they-could-eat meals. Most of them smoked on the field just before kickoff. They promoted the games by dropping off fliers at grocery stores and were expected to clean the field's surroundings after a game.

The Knights were quarterbacked by another American. Dan Burns played at Peru State College in Nebraska, an NAIA school. Woody's status as a recent Division I-A player immediately elevated him to team leader. Before one game in which the opposition was considered particularly challenging because of a hot-shot running back, he was asked to give a talk in the locker room before kickoff. The players gathered in a nearby gym, standing in a big circle. An emotionally charged Woody assured that if they immediately "punch 'em in the mouth," the loyal opposition would back off . . . which is exactly what happened, and the Knights led by a touchdown at halftime. Maybe he should have given another talk then, as they would end up losing the game. Clint's parents visited during the season and got to see ol' No. 81 back in action. As Clint drove the family to the field for one game, Clint spied an ad for the team on a billboard and dryly noted: "I think that's a picture of me." Not only was that a photo of him, but the image was also reproduced on that game's ticket stub.

* * *

Dennis Zilinski and another Army swimmer who graduated in 2004, Charlie Lewis, were assigned to the 187th Infantry Regiment of the 101st Airborne Division known as the "Rakkasans"—the Japanese word for parachute, which was adopted after World War II. Zilinski was assigned command of the 1st Battalion, Bravo Company, third platoon, known as the Bulldogs. They were sent to Iraq in October 2005, stationed at Forward Operating Base Summerall within the Sunni triangle. The platoon interacted with sheiks in the northeastern corner of their patrol zone. The area was frequented by insurgents given its strategic location, convenient to Mosul to the north, Hadifa to the west, Kirkuk to the northeast, and Tikrit to the south. The resistance efforts elsewhere, in Anbar Province, dominated media coverage then back in the United States, but American forces in Bayji often dealt with four or five roadside bombings daily. Zilinski reported to Major Matt Bartlett, who almost immediately recognized a trait in his new lieutenant that was common among Army athletes. Team building came relatively easy to them thanks to their experiences at West Point. Bartlett saw in Zilinski a natural leader with charisma, one who didn't need to be told anything twice. Only one conversation was needed to convey the danger that Zilinski and his Bulldogs would face in Bayji.

On Saturday, November 19, 2005, Zilinski and his platoon had recently returned from an early detail, and his next priority was to recruit for a pickup basketball game. He was about to change out of his uniform when a colonel noted that a captain who was scheduled to head out that afternoon to visit with one of the sheikhs would likely meet with an uncooperative party.

"That sheikh won't even talk to me," the colonel said. Someone suggested, "Take Lieutenant 'Z' with you." And Zilinski was soon off on his second mission of the day. He rode in the third vehicle amid a convoy of five. The vehicles headed down a dirt path known as Smugglers' Road, bordering the Tigris River. The road was congested, and the convoy decided to take a different route. Two Humvees made it through a blocked-off road before an explosion rocked the third. Dennis Zilinski II was the Class of 2004's first wartime casualty.

"Big Dennis" often monitored the Department of Defense's website, particularly when he and his wife had gone a few days without receiving an email from their son. They tried to accept that there would be days when circumstances made it extremely difficult for Zilinski to make contact, leading to the assumption that he was safe. Marion sent emails every day. She always finished with "Ask Jesus to be your partner." But on that Friday, she altered her closing for no apparent reason: "Walk with God." That Saturday, her husband read about a roadside bomb blowing up a Humvee in Bayji, resulting in the deaths of five members of the 101st Airborne. He didn't mention that to Marion and tried to go about his business, trying to make it feel like a routine Saturday. Each passing hour without any contact from a military official helped convince him that everything was fine . . . until two officers wearing Class A uniforms came up the front walk to their door that night at 11. Their son had explained what that would dreadfully mean. Three weeks later, they received the letter that Zilinski wrote in accordance with military practice for delivery to next of kin in the event of death. It included: "I want to thank you for this wonderful life that I have lived." It also mentioned that the $100,000 death benefit would go to the family's church.

* * *

Fort Sill is the US Army's home base for field artillery, the "King of Battle." Its members have been known as "redlegs" since the early 1800s, when the various branches had color-coded uniforms. Josh Davis remained at Fort Sill after his fellow F.A. football alums had moved on to other assignments. By the fall of 2005, he was a platoon leader for 85 soldiers learning to fire howitzers as well as a maintenance officer, a supply officer, and the battery's fire direction officer—with wife Misa expecting their first child in January 2006. He was responsible for 29 howitzers, 21 wheeled vehicles, and related equipment plus supplies that totaled about $70 million. In what spare time Davis had, he began pursuit of a master's degree in economics through a remote program offered by the University of Oklahoma. At West Point, he earned a bachelor's in psychology. Davis chose psychology as his major thinking such courses would help him understand people and become more well-rounded. A master's in economics, he figured, would make him more marketable upon his exit from the military.

Lawton, Oklahoma, was quite a cultural shift from Connecticut. Suffice to say Misa Davis wasn't OK with Oklahoma. Davis was prepared to seek what in the civilian world would be called a transfer; the army lingo was permanent change of station. Such a move, though, would have likely increased the chance of him of being deployed relatively soon. Davis was hopeful that having a newborn would brighten his wife's opinion of their surroundings. Leighton June Davis arrived on January 3, 2006, nine days short of the due date.

Early in 2006, Davis became the executive officer of the battery and the range safety officer for all live fires. Privates typically spent 14 weeks at Fort Sill for instruction on the big guns. That included nine weeks basic training, four weeks of advanced individual training, and one last week before graduation. Overnight live-fire exercises—target practice—included shooting at a target area located about a football field away with forward observers being stationed at a watching point on Potato Hill, about a mile and a half from the target, to confirm if a shell landed in the desired area. The simplified lingo for firing amid the "King of Battle" was: "Pull rope. Gun go boom."

Each private was required to load, fire, and clear a howitzer four times. After Davis's first go-round supervising the exercise as a range safety officer, his immediate superior, Captain Woody Gebhart, reported that the lieutenant "is a phenomenal officer and leader. He executed with remarkable success. He is an excellent Lieutenant and will, without a doubt, be an outstanding Commander."

Anthony Zurisko learned in May 2005, at the end of his officer basic course at Fort Sill, that he would be sent to Fort Riley late that summer and have only weeks to settle in before deploying to join a unit in the 4th Battalion, 1st Field Artillery Regiment that was more than halfway through its tour in Iraq, scheduled to return early in 2006. Zurisko was eager to get into battle, to do what he had trained for and make a contribution. He phoned his parents that night to inform them of his impending deployment. His father shared Zurisko's enthusiasm, or at least sounded that way on the phone, while his mother was more apprehensive. The quick turnaround created a stressful time crunch for completing what needed to be done before heading to Iraq, including two weeks' training to catch up with his unit. Tom Farrington hosted him on his apartment couch during Zurisko's final week at Fort Riley while providing a complementary drive to the departure point.

Fort Riley was founded in 1853 and was named for Major General Bennett Riley, a hero of the Mexican War and the first to lead a military escort along the Santa Fe Trail. Much of the post's construction was done with native limestone that was readily available in the area; the same was true in the building of nearby Kansas State University. Fort Riley featured a Custer Avenue and a Custer House because Brevet Major General George Custer came there in 1866, fresh off an applauded performance during the Civil War, to take command of the 7th Cavalry Regiment. He and the regiment departed on a campaign that took them to the western side of Kansas and into Colorado. Custer was ordered to remain at Fort Wallace, almost 300 miles from Fort Riley. He instead returned to Fort Riley to visit his wife, Elizabeth, which resulted in a court martial and year-long suspension from the army. More serious events would, of course, take place for the rambunctious Custer years after his return to active duty.

On a Friday, Zurisko learned that, instead of leaving for Iraq the following Thursday, his unit would be shipping out the following day. Also, the itinerary varied greatly from the original plan of bussing about an hour to Topeka and flying to Baltimore. Instead, they would bus all the way from Fort Riley to Baltimore—24 straight hours on the road. From Baltimore, it would be a 10-hour flight to Germany, followed by stops in Italy and Kuwait before reaching Iraq. Zurisko took two duffle bags, a ruck sack plus one backpack with personal belongings—a CD player and a couple of books. He was in the middle of one book then—*American Soldier* by Tommy Franks; Zurisko became a fan of the general after he spoke to the West Point Class of 2004 during its firstie year.

Zurisko required about a week to get fully acclimated to his new surroundings at Camp Taji. He was pleasantly surprised to learn he wouldn't be pitching a tent in the desert. He and his fellow 1–4 Field Artillery officers, located about 17 miles north of Baghdad, had private quarters in air-conditioned trailers within relatively secure compound walls beneath multiple guard towers and a loop of barbed wire—secure except when the occasional rocket or mortar was aimlessly fired over the walls. There were multiple gyms where personnel could lift weights and play basketball. And the mess hall featured KFC, Pizza Hut, Subway, Taco Bell, plus Baskin Robbins.

Zurisko soon learned that the cherished brotherhood among former Army football players in combat could have its acerbic side. Since Zurisko was a kicker for the Black Knights, the other former players called him "The Foot." His battery commander was Captain Mike Coerper, an Army linebacker during the late 1990s. Coerper frequently reminded Zurisko that he played on West Point's most recent bowl team. But no matter how the former players treated each other, most of them perceived that they were collectively held in high esteem. The assumption was a former Army football player was dependable, with above-average dedication, work ethic, courage, and skills that would be of benefit on any mission.

Zurisko was a platoon leader, supervising about 30 soldiers on missions in and around Taji. That included raids, searches, and patrols during which they resembled a friendly police presence. That was a primo assignment for an incoming lieutenant; many of his peers were stuck behind desks. He soon learned that many Iraqis had limited access to running water and electricity, maybe for an hour each day. Some of their homes had no doors. Some houses that were the size of a small American apartment were home to eight people. His patrol area included the spirited Taji market. A vendor of live chickens and fruit might be next door to an auto-parts dealer. Goats and cows were slaughtered right there in the dirt, the blood running off into pools. Soldiers weren't often welcomed in the market; for one thing, vendors were forced to move their vehicles to accommodate the military Humvees.

If life in the camp, complete with extra crispy and chocolate ice cream, somehow made Zurisko feel like he wasn't in a war zone, he certainly was jolted back to reality late one night in early October 2005 when he was nearly shot. He was standing on the Grand Canal Bridge about a mile and a half from Camp Taji on a major north-south road running through Baghdad, MSR Tampa (main supply route). Zurisko was directing his soldiers beneath a street lamp to unload some barriers with a crane when a sniper shot into the crane's window about 20 feet from him. No one was hurt, not even the crane operator. The lesson learned was that setting up at night under a light source provided the enemy a much easier target.

A few days later, Zurisko's convoy came to an abrupt halt at the sight of a decapitated man on the side of a road. It was obvious the man had been extensively beaten before the beheading. The site was too much for Zurisko's Iraqi interpreter, a 28-year-old with a physics degree who hoped aiding the American forces would lead to a future in the United States. "Scorpion," as he was called to protect his identity, regurgitated, and Zurisko nearly did, too. The headless corpse served as a warning to any Iraqis who were inclined to cooperate with the Americans.

On Route Cobra about two miles from Taji, Zurisko and his men were inspecting the dirt road when an IED exploded seconds after they'd passed it, with no one hurt. He soon determined training needed to change every few months to keep up with the insurgents, like opposing coaches who adapted their game plan at halftime. The enemy was building different IEDs, bigger IEDs, and devising new ways to hide them. Such adjustments for the American forces didn't come cheap; it cost billions of dollars to update equipment, plus the time for such changes to be budgeted, researched, and finally distributed. Zurisko also learned early on that the collegial relationship between the Coalition forces and the Iraqi troops didn't always run smoothly or produce the desired outcome. His 30 troops teamed with a like number of Iraqis on a cordon-and-search mission in the market, with his men essentially providing peripheral security. The task was supposed to last three hours but ended after 90 minutes; the Iraqis apparently lost their interest in the mission and wandered off.

In October 2005, the Iraqis held a watershed election to ratify their proposed constitution. Camp Taji dropped or postponed much of its daily agenda to ensure the three polling sites in its area operated without incident. Security was increased weeks before the vote took place. It took 10 days to tabulate the votes, many voters proudly displaying the finger that was dipped in purple ink as proof of participation. The balloting was a landslide of approval, 78.6 percent to 21.4 percent. Zurisko was proud of his unit's role in making sure the election in his small portion of the country was conducted without incident.

* * *

As of August 2005, Tom Farrington planned to be stationed at Fort Riley into 2009 and anticipated his first deployment before the end of the year. Farrington was a fire support officer in the headquarters battery of the 1st Battalion, 5th Artillery Regiment. Lieutenant Colonel Chad LeMay took command of the 1–5 earlier that year. LeMay was a 1988 West Point graduate and captain of the baseball team. The battalion boasted the longest unbroken lineage of any active duty unit in the army, back to the Revolutionary War under the direction of Alexander Hamilton. Hence the nickname "Hamilton's Own." Among Farrington's first duties at Fort Riley was arranging for funeral detail for retired officers who had lived in the region assigned to the post—Kansas and parts of Oklahoma and Colorado. Ten soldiers were required to work each service, providing a 21-gun salute and presenting the colors.

The town closest to Fort Riley is Junction City, which featured businesses that might appeal to soldiers: the Wild West Gentlemen's Club, Club Alibi, and the G Spot. Twenty miles to the east is Manhattan, home of Kansas State University. "The Little Apple" is its popular nickname; in 2002, the city of 50,000 borrowed from its New York namesake the tradition of dropping a ball to mark each new year. In lieu of the high-rise One Times Square building, Manhattan's ball drop was staged outside Varney's Bookstore in the entertainment district called Aggieville (Kansas State Agricultural College's original athletic nickname was Aggies instead of today's K-State Wildcats). If soldiers cared to make the drive over, they could kick back and rub elbows (or bend elbows) with the college students in establishments like The Salty Rim, Rusty's Last Chance, and the So Long Saloon. Farrington lived in

Manhattan, in an apartment that he shared with Kaitie Colligan. She landed a job as a pharmaceutical sales representative, missed not having a Dunkin' Donuts in the area, bemoaning the presence of only one local Starbucks. Among the apartment furnishings was a West Point saber of Farrington's hung in an elaborate case that was given to him by his grandparents.

By early fall, speculation of impending deployment for Farrington's unit ran rampant, and he simply hoped to know something by the end of October. Those involved could only joke about it on occasion. "Tomorrow we're going to go," became something of a catch phrase. One of Farrington's fellow lieutenants created a video as part of the early December celebration of St. Barbara's Day, honoring the patron saint of field artillery, that lampooned the delay. Set to *Star Wars* music, the clip showed military personnel boarding a plane in anticipation of entering a war zone, only to be told they weren't going anywhere that day. The satirical production even made a couple of colonels chuckle. With vehicles and equipment—even maps, dry-erase boards, markers, pens and pencils—having been dispatched to Texas' gulf coast for shipping to Iraq, Farrington and those left waiting were limited in what they could accomplish at Fort Riley. He was able to keep in touch on occasion with Anthony Zurisko, who said he enjoyed going out in convoys on patrols.

New Year's came and went with no deployment. Farrington's unit was reorganized and rescheduled for deployment, hoping to learn in late January 2006 when they'd be sent. Preparing for what he assumed would be his first of multiple deployments, he was already pondering whether to stay in the military beyond the minimum commitment. That didn't mean staying for 20 years, which allows an officer to retire with full benefits, but he wanted to command a battery or a company. That would be an enjoyable experience and look good on his resume when seeking corporate employment. Another factor to consider was his relationship with Colligan. He was planning to propose, and the prospect of multiple military relocations with a wife and family wasn't attractive to him.

Then, there was the continuing issue related to Farrington's right hand. He couldn't ignore that he was losing feeling in it. When he held a hot pan that contained the couple's Thanksgiving turkey, he didn't realize his right hand was being burned. His worries grew to the point that he visited the base doctor. Army business often requires a prolonged series of events to put a routine event into motion; such wasn't the case regarding Farrington and his hand. The physician insisted that Farrington travel to Brooke Army Medical Center in San Antonio, Texas, within a few days. There, he saw specialists and underwent nerve tests. Farrington soon appeared before a medical board and was told by a doctor that he couldn't be trusted to defend someone else in any kind of battle situation. Back at Fort Riley, he was assessed on whether he could fire a weapon with his left hand. Farrington passed all phases and was hopeful that he could continue with his unit, though the prospect of taking some sort of desk job wasn't terribly appealing. That wasn't what he had planned for when pensively beginning the 1999–2000 school year at Fort Monmouth, when he struggled to hold onto the pulley during the "Slide for Life" at Camp Buckner, when he resorted to concocting different tackling angles on the football field because he couldn't grip an opposing player with his right hand, when he threw his hat into the air on graduation day. But in March 2006, he was told he would be given a medical discharge. Tom Farrington was told he would need to leave the army within 30 days.

It took weeks for Farrington to reconcile the fact that his military career was over. His commanding officer, Lieutenant Colonel LeMay, was similarly crushed. LeMay regretted losing him, recognizing he would have been an outstanding officer in combat given how he approached his daily duties at Fort Riley. It didn't escape LeMay that Farrington maintained his dedication to military service throughout the review process though the young man feared the episode would end with his departure from military service. Farrington's next mission was to find civilian work. After all, he was planning to pop the question to Kaitie Colligan soon. He sent an email to the Army football alumni group with the goal of locating contacts in the financial industry in New York. He didn't simply ask for a job; he also sought advice. Should he go to New York immediately? Should he instead attend a business school? One of the 60-or-so replies recommended attending one of the job conferences that were organized for veterans.

In March 2006, Farrington and Colligan enjoyed a weekend trip to Kansas City. They stayed at the Sheraton near the square with dinner reservations at Ruth's Chris Steak House, followed by a ride in a horse-drawn carriage. Farrington initially sought to buy an engagement ring through a local jeweler but was unhappy with the asking price and instead went through one in Pittsburgh. The proposal went off without a hitch, and they made plans to move back east that May. Farrington attended a job conference in Washington, DC for graduates of all three military academies and returned to Kansas on a Saturday morning only hours before a farewell party with them scheduled to hit the road the following morning. Everything that they owned was packed in two cars save for an air mattress. They got all of four hours' sleep before Anthony Zurisko joined them for breakfast in advance of the caravan that set out for New Jersey. The couple initially moved in with Colligan's parents with plans to rent a house at the shore if Farrington was hired in the financial district of lower Manhattan.

In June 2006, a cancerous polyp was discovered in his father's colon. Young Tom immediately headed to Pittsburgh for the surgery, which was essentially the repeat of a procedure performed four years earlier. His father had stood by him through so much, and he was determined to do the same. Everything from the previous surgery looked good until summer 2005, when blood work showed unusually high protein levels. Tom Sr. told his son after the surgery that he was in a lot of pain. While young Tom was there to support his father, he was also there to bust his chops. Farrington told his father than it was easy for him to complain, which brought a smile and a laugh to them both. Subsequent chemotherapy would last for six months. Tom Sr. said he was ready to fight. He sounded a great deal like his son did in December 1998, his right hand dangling from the complex apparatus that helped hold it together.

* * *

During Ryan Kent's early days at Fort Sill, he expressed an interest in Ranger School and was told what requirements he would need to achieve to land one of the coveted slots. He passed, realizing there was no turning back. The move to Oklahoma placed Kent within a few hours' drive of Kristen Keefhaver. She never really knew her father, who left home when she was a child. The primary male influence in her young life was a grandfather,

Clarence Linton, who graduated from West Point in 1945 and served in the US Army Air Corps, later the US Air Force, and retired as a lieutenant colonel. He finished his military career at Carswell Air Force Base in Fort Worth.

After Kent and Keefhaver met in Houston the previous autumn, the two had kept in touch, talking every few weeks. They were able to get together regularly following his arrival in Oklahoma. When Kent traveled to New Jersey to be the best man in his brother's wedding on the Saturday of Independence Day weekend—he choked up while toasting the groom and confessed: "I'm just like my dad."—he hustled back to meet Keefhaver in Fort Worth, essentially midway between Fort Sill and Austin, and squired her around in his new GMC Sierra. That included the very Texan experience of the Willie Nelson July 4 Picnic concert in the city's popular Stockyards behind Billy Bob's Texas.

As Kent prepared to leave for Ranger School in summer 2005, he verbalized the obvious to Keefhaver. They were staring at months in which he'd be unable to contact her. They could commit to a serious relationship in advance of the personal communications blackout or she could enjoy life back at school without any binding tie. Keefhaver chose the former, to the considerable relief of the Ranger hopeful. The three-month test to determine whether Kent had what it took to be called an Army Ranger began on Sunday, July 10, 2005, at the starting point for the 61-day test of physical and cerebral will at Fort Benning, Georgia. It would continue to two other locales, the mountains of northern Georgia and the gulf coast of Florida. The phases are succinctly described as "crawl" followed by "walk" followed by "run." The 258 other hopeful candidates included Zachary Kaye, his West Point buddy and former Army football teammate. Kent and Kaye were in different platoons, but they figured to see each other at some point during the proceedings.

The Rangers trace their roots to the seventeenth century, when English settlers in North America learned to defend themselves against attacks from the native inhabitants. Their motto—"Rangers lead the way"—grew from an exchange between officers on Omaha Beach during the D-Day invasion in 1944. In today's US military, the Rangers are revered in the same way as the Navy's SEALs as an elite, special-forces unit. (SEAL is an acronym for

SEa, Air, and Land.) Ranger School was started in 1950 at Fort Benning, which is located outside the city of Columbus on the Georgia-Alabama line. It previously contained a fourth phase, in the desert, during the 1980s and '90s. The opening chapter is called the Darby phase, located in and around Camp Darby and Camp Rogers within Fort Benning. That begins with RAP Week, for Ranger Assessment Phase. RAP Week is to Ranger School what Beast Barracks is to enrollment as an official plebe at West Point. In a typical Ranger School class, more than half the candidates who either elect to leave or are dismissed for not meeting the requirements during the entire three months won't advance beyond RAP Week. Kent, despite being part of a group from Fort Sill that physically prepped for Ranger School by doing additional physical training, stood in formation beneath the unforgiving Georgia summer sun upon a bed of large rocks and thought, *How in the heck am I ever going to get through this thing?*

The would-be Rangers' first assignment was to dump out their heavy packs for superiors to ensure they had included everything that was cited on the voluminous and detailed list that each candidate had previously been given. Each would soon learn one of the first connections between himself and his new Ranger buddy. If either didn't have everything on that list, they both dropped and did pushups on the uneven surface. As a helpful reminder not to commit such a mistake again, the pushups were followed by shoulder pressing their duffle bags. All of that was complemented by a substantial dose of ear-piercing screams from commanding officers. Kent recognized early on that such reactions to the candidates' shortcomings wasn't meant to simply hear themselves yell but emphasize that such mistakes out in the field could be life-threatening to the Ranger and his buddy. For anyone who had come through four years at West Point, that wasn't a new experience. It was then on to the standard Army Physical Fitness Test. Kent arrived at Benning with shoulders that often ached following all his years of hits on the football field. The initial day of RAP Week was a dispiriting experience. At least he was still part of the group; more than 60 departed that first day for falling short of some aspect of the day's travails.

Ranger School's grading system consisted of demerits of varying severity; there were major minuses and minor minuses. In Ranger School math, three minor minuses equaled one major minus. Compiling three major minuses during the course's three phases, for a total of nine, meant being recycled; the candidate was pulled from the class but was allowed to restart at a later date. Even an attendee who completed all three phases but ran afoul during the week between the end of the concluding Florida phase and the graduation gathering at Fort Benning—let's say he celebrated a little *too* vigorously—could result in a delinquency report and a recycling. It was difficult to determine if continuing through the demanding yardsticks of one's mental and physical fitness proved to be more difficult for a candidate whose military career track required attendance or for those who subjected themselves to this voluntarily and could conceivably surrender at any time. The latter would result in an officer being tagged with "LOM" on his permanent record (lack of motivation). As candidates dropped out, there were no formal announcements to inform the remaining class members of the subtraction among their ranks. For instance, the group might reassemble for the afternoon conducting of the APFT lacking one or two candidates from the morning session. Such individuals would report to an officer and state the desire to discontinue, and that would be that. The exception, in terms of class-wide awareness of someone's departure, would be when a candidate failed to pass a timed run.

Day Two dawned with a five-mile run that had to be completed in 40 minutes, with a recommended pace of 7:30 per mile to finish in 37:30. When Kent finished his pre-Ranger training at Fort Sill, he could cover the distance in 35 minutes. Alas, that wasn't accomplished following the arduousness of Ranger School's first day. The good news was Kent beat the cutoff time; the bad news was that doing so left him feeling nauseated for the rest of the day. He didn't drink any water for fear of throwing up. Next came the chin-up test, on which he easily reached the minimum of six. That was followed by Combat Water Survival Assessment (CWSA), which was done at three stations. There was the Log Walk Rope Drop (climbing a 35-foot tower, walking across a narrow, 70-foot log that featured three steps in the middle, a commando crawl along a rope and over water followed a 35-foot drop—all while wearing a combat uniform, boots, and a flotation device), swimming out of the pond to Ranger School's version of the "Slide for Life," and a 15-meter swim (in uniform and boots). During training that night, the lack of ingested water resulted in Kent cramping. He realized if someone was identified as a heat casualty, said candidate wouldn't be long for the group. He made it through the final session, was given intravenous fluid later that night, and didn't experience the same difficulty during the rest of Ranger School.

Each of the phases lasted a few weeks with a travel day sandwiched between them. The attendees had no access to phones or computers. They were allowed to write letters, but that would mean staying up another 20–30 minutes on a day that ended at midnight with the following day's schedule beginning in a mere four hours. Kent wrote to Kristen Keefhaver often and found himself in the minority of those who took advantage of that option. Most candidates in that Ranger School class wrote maybe once a week. But most of those candidates probably didn't address and stamp 60 envelopes to his girlfriend and 20 more to his parents before even arriving at Fort Benning.

"Road march" was something of a euphemism in describing the 12-mile jaunt just to reach the initial training site. The "road" wasn't pavement but sand and gravel, making the task that much more difficult. Zachary Kaye's feet were never previously prone to blistering before he experienced the seemingly incessant marching during the early weeks at Fort Benning, and foot powder was only so effective. He finally resorted to taping his feet. Another characteristic of the Darby phase was to minimize the amount of sleep. Kaye came perilously close to becoming a heat casualty during one of the road marches. He had difficulty breathing, seemed to stop sweating, and developed a debilitating headache. At a stopping point, he was dragged into a shaded area and allowed to hydrate.

Ranger School's middle phase was conducted at Camp Merrill, just north of Dahlonega, Georgia. Kent's class started that go-round with 88 candidates (down from the initial 259). One challenge related to the elements—at least during mid-summer when that group went through—was the temperature extremes present in the mountains of northern Georgia. It was difficult for many candidates to realize that a day spent amid wilting heat could be followed by frigid conditions that night at the patrol base. Kent encountered a foot problem similar to what Kaye agonized with during the Benning phase.

The constant moisture led to a case of trench foot. Kent brought the issue to the attention of his superiors and was allowed to sleep barefoot until the problem passed.

The terrain allowed instructors to teach skills such as mountaineering and knot-tying plus further develop platoon-level techniques. The continued limitation of food and water, after experiencing the same at Fort Benning, took a cumulative effect on the candidates. If a candidate drops out during the second or third phase and takes another shot at graduating, he returns to the program where he previously left off. Such returnees become valuable resources for the first-time attendees. Nine more hopefuls were subtracted by the time the class left for the gulf coast, leaving 79 still grasping the goal of graduation in a matter of weeks.

The Florida phase was held within the swampy environment of Eglin Air Force Base and was something of a hands-on, practical test of lessons administered during the Darby and mountain phases. The candidates were put in simulations and expected to react appropriately, including how to maneuver small watercrafts, as well as through water without the benefit of any craft, no matter the obstacle. That included opportunities to volunteer for leadership roles. The last days of the phase were a grueling test of the candidates' physical and mental stamina. That class came through Florida when Hurricane Katrina battered the Gulf of Mexico. In Zachary Kaye's group, a commander asked if any candidates had family in the New Orleans area. Only Kaye raised his hand; his godparents and their extended family lived there. He was then excused to take five minutes to make calls on a borrowed cell phone to determine that his relatives were safe. For the balance of the phase, Kaye was occasionally assigned duties that would allow him access to the outside world—typically newspaper articles—that enabled him to keep up with the storm's aftermath.

The graduation ceremony for Ranger School was held back at Fort Benning, at the end of Babbit Road on the south bank of Victory Pond, enjoyed by family and friends—Dawn and Bill Livingston among them—who packed into a covered grandstand. The visitors and the grads themselves first witnessed a demonstration of some of the tests that the students performed, like the Log Walk Rope Drop and the "Slide for Life." Mock battles were also staged, the explosions drawing enthusiastic applause from the crowd. The graduates stood in formation, trying to express interest and appreciation for the demonstrations while really just wanting the ceremony to end so they could return to the real world (and catch up on some much-needed eating and sleeping). Finally, the new Rangers received their Ranger tabs, similar to the West Point graduates being pinned. From the initial group of 259 zealous candidates, 64 individuals—roughly 24 percent—were recognized that day. (As of summer 2017, that beat the norm of 15–19 percent.) Also among the graduates was Kaye, who'd left 25 pounds along the school's three phases, his parents and Ann Cox in attendance. Kaye had spent the bulk of his Ranger School term in a four-man team that included a sergeant from the 10th Mountain Division, a captain who was previously a military intelligence lieutenant in the process of going through special-forces training, plus a private first class from the 3rd Battalion, 75th Ranger Regiment. Kaye willingly acknowledged that, without the support of his three teammates, he never would have made it to Victory Pond. Cox pinned the Ranger tab on her boyfriend. Despite his relative skin-and-bones appearance, she managed to draw blood. Kaye's father presented his son and Kent with special battalion coins. The Kent contingent, the Kaye group, and virtually every other graduate plus his family and friends then made a beeline to nearby restaurants to immediately put back on some of the weight lost during the previous 60-plus days. For the next month or so, each of Kaye's stops at a gas station would include a walk into the adjacent convenience store to pick up a Snickers ice cream bar.

* * *

Weight loss was an issue for Peter Stewart soon after he arrived at Fort Hood in July 2005, but that was a positive. He was down to 217 pounds, below what he weighed as a high school senior. He still experienced knee problems and had surgery that fall. At Fort Hood, he was reunited with one of his soldiers at Fort Knox, Andrew Bacevich Jr. The laid-back Texan enjoyed spending time with the kinetic personality from Massachusetts. On Bacevich's birthday, they celebrated at a bar in nearby Killeen to watch an Ultimate Fighting Championship title card. Just before the main event began, Bacevich suddenly decided they should continue the revelry in Austin. Off they went, and Bacevich overwhelmed another group of unsuspecting strangers with his *Bah-ston* charm, amusing Stewart by telling one young lady that the two of them were cousins, then telling another they were brothers.

In September 2005, the Waudbys filed a civil complaint related to their efforts to have Brad Jr. officially recognized as a graduate of West Point despite not having passed the APFT. Subsequent depositions taken by the government from cadets, including some of Waudby's football teammates, stated that he continued to eat heavily, drink heavily, and smoke while attempting to get into better physical shape that would allow him to pass the test. Some stated that Waudby professed confidence that he'd pass the test. A graduate assistant coach for the 2003 season stated that Waudby had been penciled in as a starter for the coming season until he returned from his CTLT training in Hawaii out of shape.

In May 2006, the Waudby suit was thrown out. US district judge Jose Linares agreed with the defense motion that the court didn't have jurisdiction. The Defense Finance and Accounting Service informed the family that it was expected to either pay the full $190,005 within 30 days or make monthly payments of $5,597.04. Waudby still had the option of transferring his four years of West Point credits to another university in New York State and, with a $1,500 payment, receive a diploma from that institution. He declined that opportunity. A columnist for the *Record* argued on behalf of Waudby in a piece entitled "Big guy deserved a break." "If you ever wondered why the West Point mascot is a mule," Mike Kelly wrote, "look at the story of Brad Waudby." Kelly's stance drew the ire of *Record* reader E. Paul O'Connell, a retired US Army lieutenant colonel: "I find it somewhat surprising that an individual with the physical ability to play college football at the varsity level could not pass the APFT given multiple chances, and the time, coaching and opportunity to train for it."

* * *

During fall 2005, Brian Hill was down to counting the number of weeks before his deployment. He talked virtually every night to his concerned mother. Hill attempted to steer her thoughts away from the prospect of her oldest child dropping into a war zone: "Maybe I'll do some cool things. Maybe I'll learn a lot about life and not taking things for granted. I'll have cool pictures and tell good stories when I get back." He politely told her that it would be better if she didn't travel to Texas to see him off. She understood that was a somewhat common request, that the young officer wanted to keep a different picture in his head of his mother happily tending to her business back home. Hill asked Morgan Hesse to check in regularly with his mother. Hesse did and tried her best to keep the conversations positive, yet it seemed like each one ended with Nancy in tears.

Hill's schedule had his birthday and Christmas falling while he'd be in Iraq. So, his family gave him early gifts for each in hopes of him taking them with him. Such a luxury was virtually impossible. In addition to his military gear, which included various notebooks and manuals, he elected to bring a laptop, iPod, a couple of digital cameras, and a PlayStation.

Hill's battalion was assigned to Camp Taji, replacing an armor battalion that worked with Anthony Zurisko's field artillery battalion. Hill was technically a member of a field artillery battalion but had been "tasked out" to an artillery battalion as a fire support officer. His routines included conducting raids on civilian homes that were suspected of housing active insurgents and boarding copters for air assaults. His emphases were working with detainees plus intel and information operations. The air assaults were exhilarating, like being on the kickoff team and racing downfield, looking for an opposing player to plow over. One night, they shocked the unsuspecting subjects by landing a copter in the home's front yard. The take that night was a dozen insurgents, AK-47s, grenades, Iranian rifles, materials for making IEDs, other ammunition and propaganda CDs. But not all the missions required kicking down doors and interrogating suspicious locals. Hill's battalion built a playground with equipment, accompanying gravel, concrete, plus the construction tools donated by a major US toy manufacturer. They also installed generators, paved roads, and helped upgrade the local schools.

With Brian Hill's unit replacing Anthony Zurisko's, there was some overlap during which the two '04 West Point grads caught up. They watched the New Year's college bowl games in Zurisko's quarters since his room had a television. Hill and roommate Emiko Terry, the former West Point cornerback, shared a trailer that resembled Zurisko's, with heat and air-conditioning. They joked about how similar their living conditions were to the academy. Between the PlayStation that Hill had brought over and the DVD player that Terry had shipped to him, the pair didn't lack for entertainment options. The mess hall included cafeteria-style options, fast food, stir fry, pasta, a salad bar and, of course, Baskin-Robbins. To keep the Candy Bar Mashup and other ice cream flavors from weighing down America's fighting forces, the complex also included two gyms.

In April 2006, Hill emailed home to family and friends with an update plus a collection of photos taken "on the job" that included shots of him working with the local sheikh in the town of Hor al Bash. "Things are going good over here," he wrote. "The insurgents have been quiet lately and seem to want to fight each other more than us which is good."

For Mothers' Day, Hill and his siblings bought Nancy a high-end camera. "I tried finding one that was easy to use. I know how your electronic skills are!!" Hill emailed. Nancy didn't know what to think when the doorbell rang and she was handed the package by a delivery driver. "No one ever comes over," she wrote in reply. She said it was the perfect gift since she was "picture crazy" and conceded that she would likely lean on daughter Caroline to learn how to use it.

It took Zurisko and his fellow returnees six days to traverse from Camp Taji to Fort Riley in mid-January, enjoying the luxury of flight arrangements into Topeka instead of bus transportation halfway across the country. At the post, they were welcomed home by family and friends with an official recognition ceremony. Tom Farrington was there to provide a ride back into Manhattan and more short-term shelter. The first two weeks back at Fort Riley for Zurisko *et al.* included instruction in stress management and suicide prevention. Before leaving Iraq, Zurisko and seven of his military comrades mapped out a week-long R&R trip to Rio de Janeiro during Brazil's upcoming Carnival. However, there actually wasn't much of R *or* R in their adjoining two rooms one block from Copacabana Beach. The revelers put to pragmatic use the military training that helped them maximize performance on little to no sleep. They hit the beach about 11 a.m., returned for dinner, began an expedition of various clubs around 10, and took advantage of closing times around 7 a.m. Rinse and repeat. Since Zurisko wasn't a surfer, he settled for body surfing but found the waters treacherous. Mike Coerper, who *was* a California surfer, wasn't even spared; he broke an ankle in the unrelenting waters. Amid the frenzy of Carnival, the visitors avoided confrontations with the locals with the exception of the night when one indignant bartender insisted one of them had not paid his $100 tab. Two *gendarmes* were summoned, and the tourists elected to pay the bill twice rather than escalate the disagreement.

Soon after Zurisko's leave time began, he traveled to Pittsburgh to visit his parents, relatives, and old Springdale friends. Eager to see his family after being away for so long, Zurisko was somewhat flummoxed when Damian chose to make multiple stops along at the way, at this grocery store and that gas station. Such delays had a purpose given the flight's early arrival; they allowed dozens of relatives to arrive at the Zuriskos' home in time to greet their favorite son for a surprise party. That included young kids, who were allowed to skip school to join in the fun.

* * *

More than six years after Zachary Kaye and Ann Cox began dating, Kaye surprised her with a proposal while she and some girlfriends were enjoying a weekend at the casinos on the Mississippi coast in February 2006. The date was set for July 1, which happened to be only weeks before his scheduled deployment to Iraq with the 82nd Airborne. They were married at the First Methodist Church in Tuscaloosa with their reception at the NorthRiver Yacht Club on the banks of Lake Tuscaloosa. Part of the military adornment to the ceremony was a custom for welcoming a new bride into the ranks, so to speak, with the newlyweds walking through an arch of swords or sabers. The men of the wedding party, in full dress uniform, faced each other and formed the arch with their swords. As man and wife passed the final pair, they were told the price of passage was a kiss and gladly complied. One member of that final pair of groomsmen is then required to playfully strike the bride on the backside with his sword and proclaim, "Welcome to the Army, Mrs. So-and-So!" As the newlywed Kayes left the church and walked toward their limousine, that duty fell to Ryan Kent. During rehearsals of the sequence, he gently tapped her with the sword. Following the actual ceremony, Kent's swing contained much more vigor. The sword met the new Mrs. Kaye with enough force to briefly separate her from Mother Earth. The look on Ann's face as she peered back over her shoulder at Kent, her mouth agape, indicated she was hardly expecting that brief, unscheduled episode of free flight.

Chapter Thirteen

"WE RESOLVE THAT THEIR SACRIFICE WILL ALWAYS BE REMEMBERED BY A GRATEFUL NATION"

Brad Waudby spent much of the summer of 2006 working at a mortgage company and doing security on Thursday nights at the Blu Restaurant and Lounge in Rochelle Park, New Jersey. It was a far cry from involvement in public service, which he sought in the absence of a military career. Waudby was accepted into the police academy for the Waterfront Commission of New York Harbor to pursue a detective position. The course included instruction in state law on both sides of the Hudson River, physical fitness requirements, defensive tactics, the use of weapons (pistol, shotgun, baton), and training for dealing with terrorism. In his family's ongoing disagreement with West Point related to his departure from the academy, they did as the court had asked. They contacted the Army Board for Correction of Military Records in Washington, DC and asked for a personal interview. On one of his first days at the harbor academy, he received a call from an unfamiliar number, let it go, and wasn't left a message. He soon after received an email from a member of the board, passing along that his file was being reviewed.

* * *

Brian Hill enjoyed 15 days' leave in July 2006, first visiting Morgan Hesse in Texas and then spending time with his family in Florida. There was Saturday dinner at Stonewood Grill & Tavern in Port Orange, followed by a Sunday cookout at home. Brother Scott came down from Gainesville, and the three Hill children just hung around the house like old times. Nancy cherished the sight, wanting so much to fuss over them as much as humanly possible but recognizing it was best for her children to simply enjoy their limited time together.

In August 2006, Tom Farrington began his civilian business career as a financial analyst for Bank of America in Manhattan, hired as a result of an academy job conference that he attended in Washington. He commuted from the home of his fiancée's parents in New Jersey, getting up at 4:45 a.m. to take a 5:30 bus, arriving back home around 7 p.m. Farrington and Colligan bought their own home in June 2007 and were married a month later in Morristown, New Jersey. The couple's preference was to be wed somewhere at the shore, but there wasn't a facility large enough to accommodate the planned guest list. The rehearsal dinner was held in the atrium of the fashionable Madison Hotel. Hill, Waudby, and Anthony Zurisko were among the groomsmen. Guests rode to the ceremony in rental party buses that were stocked with beer, with the bridal party having its own limo. The newlyweds honeymooned in St. Lucia for eight days. At the reception, Hesse first met Waudby and Zurisko's girlfriend, Brigit McGuire—sister of a fellow officer at Fort Riley and Iraq and a participant in the Carnival adventure.

Back in Iraq following leave, Hill went out one day with a small mission team that included Private 1st Class Ian Faggerstrom from Illinois as the driver. They were in the lead vehicle in a three-vehicle convoy on its way back into Camp Taji on Highway 1 around sunset. About 600 yards from the camp entrance, they stopped near a gas station to inspect an odd-looking bag and a pile of dirt in the median. Hill looked to his right into the setting sun and thought he saw a man at the station. But he couldn't see anyone there and flipped down his night-vision glasses. Hill then saw the man pop out from behind the building and alerted Faggerstrom. That was only seconds before an IED exploded about 40 feet from the convoy.

None of the vehicles were damaged, but dirt and rocks flew everywhere. Hill and Faggerstrom jumped from their Humvee and took off after the man, who apparently didn't immediately recognize that he was being pursued and was late breaking into his own run. For the former linebacker, sprinting after a running back while wearing football pads was a relative breeze compared to chasing down an insurgent while wearing combat boots and full gear plus carrying a weapon. Speaking of the weapon, Hill understood that the rules of engagement prohibited him from shooting at such a target in that situation. All he could do at that point was yell at him to stop. Hill tripped on a rut in the gravel in front of the station and lost ground on his party. But, fortunately for Hill and Faggerstrom, their quarry chose to hightail it into an area that was fenced in and offered no escape from the onrushing Americans. It appeared to Hill that the man pondered running at the fence and leaping to climb over. If so, the Iraqi thought better of that plan. He tossed something behind a nearby bush, thrust his hands above his head, and yelled something in Arabic.

Hill's interpreter joined the gathering. The captured party—probably in his early 30s, standing about 5-foot-7 and 150 pounds—said he simply ran because he was scared, not because he had anything to do with the detonated IED. The "something" that he threw behind the bush was two cell phones. Hill's platoon sergeant determined the cell phones were indeed connected to multiple IEDs planted nearby, at which point the Iraqi essentially told the interpreter, "You've got me." Hill's men patted him down, took photos, secured his hands with zip ties, blindfolded and "seated" him in one of the Humvees wherever he fit best. The more thorough interrogation was delayed until the subject was back at the camp and could be questioned by those who were experienced in what to ask and how to ask it. The Iraqi was held in a jail within Camp Taji. If it was decided to release him after questioning, Hill's men would take him back out into the public. If the subject was prosecuted, the severity of the case against him would determine if he'd remain at Taji or be transferred to a more substantial lockup in Baghdad. In this case, Hill and others who were involved would likely be called to testify. That didn't happen here, but that didn't frustrate Hill. He was simply relieved that no one was hurt when the IED was detonated. Hill and Faggerstrom were each awarded the Army Commendation Award.

Hill was also feted for an extended period of meritorious service, awarded the Bronze Star for the period from mid-December 2005 to December 2,

2006. The certificate, signed by the Secretary of the Army, Major General James Thurman, read:

> For: Exceptionally meritorious service while assigned as a fire support officer and platoon leader during Operation Iraqi Freedom. First Lieutenant Hill's outstanding performance, expertise, and contributions were instrumental to his unit's overall success during combat operations. His actions reflect distinct credit on him, the 4th Infantry Division, and the United States Army.

Hill was initially recommended by Captain Mark Paine, Hill's company commander. Paine's hand-written comments were: "1LT Hill did it all: Fire support, IO, Platoon leader. His efforts at building an informant network were second to none. Strongly recommend!" Those were forwarded up to Lieutenant Colonel David E. Thompson, Hill's squadron commander, who added: "Always where the action is—made a huge difference." Those were passed on to Colonel James Pasquarette, the brigade commander, who contributed: "A super lieutenant that performed with distinction."

On a Sunday night in October 2006, Paine died shortly after an IED exploded near his vehicle just outside Camp Taji. Deployed since 2005, Paine, thirty-two, a 1997 West Point graduate, was also a recipient of both the Bronze Star and the Army Commendation Medal. He'd followed the example of his father, who was a US Army officer in Vietnam, and discussed the possibility of dying in battle years earlier with his concerned mother: "Mom, there are worse ways to die than fighting for your country." That conversation took place when Paine was seven years old.

* * *

Veterans Day 2006 fell on Saturday, November 11, nearly a year after Dennis Zilinski II was killed in Iraq. The following day, the first "Run with Dennis" was held at the PNC Bank Arts Center in his hometown of Holmdel to benefit the Lt. Dennis Zilinski II Memorial Fund. More than 1,400 people participated, raising more than $75,000. Among the participants were Brad Waudby and his father. It was the first time that Waudby had spent any appreciable time with former West Point peers and associates since his family had taken the academy to court. That included football teammate Tom Farrington and many of Zilinski's former teammates on the Army swim team. Waudby wondered how he'd be greeted, if he'd be treated like a pariah. Such concerns proved to be unfounded, and the experience proved to be somewhat therapeutic for him. After the post-race ceremony, the Waudbys introduced themselves to Marion Zilinski and expressed their condolences. She asked Brad what he was doing. "Well, ma'am, I'm out of the service." She replied: "Good for you. At least you're safe."

That same day on the other side of the globe, 1st Lieutenant Michael Cerrone, the E1 Viking who had explained the cannon firings on the telecast of Army's first football game under John Mumford in 2003, was killed in action. Cerrone was one of three members of the 2nd Battalion, 505th Parachute Infantry Regiment, 3rd Brigade Combat Team, 82nd Airborne Division from Fort Bragg on patrol near the Iraqi city of Samarra when his Humvee was struck by a car bomb. His father was Brigadier General James Cerrone, special assistant to the 18th Airborne Corps commander at Fort Bragg. Cerrone never wanted others to think he was riding his father's military coattails, eager to forge his own career path. His individualism certainly shone forth during his last two years at West Point, when his mode of transportation was a head-turning 1966 Pontiac GTO. Cerrone was promoted posthumously to captain.

Skyler Munekata had discovered something of a kindred spirit in Cerrone. Munekata was one of the few cadets whom Cerrone had confided in to explain that he chose the branch infantry in part to avoid any potential nepotism conflicts by going field artillery; at that time, his father commanded the F.A. training school at Fort Sill.

At times at West Point, the motto of "cooperate and graduate" could fall by the wayside if a cadet encountered desperate circumstances. Munekata recognized Cerrone as someone who would drop everything and help when, as he phrased it, "the poop hit the fan." When Munekata learned of Cerrone's death, he immediately boarded a plane to attend the funeral in Massachusetts—so quickly that he forgot to pack some of his dress uniform. When he met Cerrone's mother in the receiving line, he cried like a baby.

That Veterans Day weekend, many of the government officials most heavily involved in the war effort in Iraq came together at 1600 Pennsylvania Avenue to discuss potential changes. The group included Vice President Dick Cheney, Secretary of State Condoleezza Rice, and National Security Advisor Stephen Hadley. One of their priorities was to consider a significant increase in so-called boots on the ground. Such was a distinct possibility in great measure because of a related announcement made only days earlier. President George W. Bush intended to fill the void created by the upcoming resignation of Secretary of Defense Donald Rumsfeld with Robert Gates, the director of national intelligence. While Rumsfeld was determined not to grow the American forces in Iraq, Gates was known to desire an increase in troop strength. Amid the confirmation hearing, Bush informed the country in early January 2010 of the increase in numbers, by approximately 21,500, which became commonly referred to as "the surge." The surge required months to complete and actually added almost 31,000 troops rather than the figure that was virtually imprinted upon the national consciousness through repeated news accounts.

* * *

Nancy Hill resigned her position at Spruce Creek High in November 2006. She wasn't feeling well and believed that getting away from her busy routine at the high school would help. The coaches often approached her for help with this or that since they were so familiar with her with Brian and Scott having come through the football program, and she just couldn't tell them no. Another reason for her decision was a change of personnel at Spruce Creek; she didn't feel comfortable in such situations. And Hill's deployment was difficult for her to deal with given that her sons had never displayed aggression beyond the controlled environment of a football field. They'd never even played much with guns or pretended to be in the army. She was concerned that this would affect him for the rest of his life. She couldn't get it out of her mind, yet she didn't want to talk about it with him.

Hill soon after returned from deployment, arriving at Fort Hood by way of Kuwait, Ireland, and Bangor, Maine. With so many returning troops making a first US stop in Bangor, local veterans and others in the community formed an informal group in 2003 that made sure the weary military travelers knew they were appreciated back home. Thus began the Maine Troop Greeters. No matter the time of day or night, no matter the weather, members of the Greeters stood cheerfully in the arrival area of Bangor International Airport to offer a hearty handshake or a hug to each returning individual. The Greeters also provided snacks and, for any military that lacked access at the time to a cell phone, the use of one to contact their family.

The night-time welcome-home festivities at Fort Hood featured a soundtrack that included *Jock Jams*. The excited, appreciative gathering included Morgan Hesse. Luckily for them, a nearby steakhouse was still open after 10 p.m. The fluid travel connections left them without a lodging reservation that night. They settled for the Palace Inn, with a black light in the room, for about $30.

In January 2007, Hill was assigned to Fort McPherson in Atlanta, which he considered his second home. Hesse, having graduated from Texas, moved there, and they worked hard to master the routes of Atlanta mass transit. In his new surroundings, Hill was able to attend the NCAA Final Four at the Georgia Dome and the Masters in nearby Augusta along with his brother.

* * *

Ryan Kent's departure from Fort Hood in the fall of 2006 typified the common confluence of organization and chaos that a deployment can bring. The initial date was October 15, and his father allowed for plenty of visiting time by scheduling his arrival in Texas from Cincinnati on September 28 with a weekend trip planned for Houston. But Kent received word on September 20 that his date was moved up to September 28. Kent immediately phoned his father, each getting emotional at the prospect that the opportunity for a proper father-son farewell had been lost to military machinations. But David's supervisors at Kroger gladly allowed him to change plans and leave earlier, taking a flight on September 26 to Austin. Kent subsequently was told his date was changed again, to Tuesday, October 2. Father and son spent an enjoyable day in Austin with David then going on to Houston, Ryan to meet him there for a weekend holiday together. But as David was driving to Houston on Tuesday the 26th, Ryan was informed that his bag drop preceding deployment would be the following day with departure on Friday the 29th. Pragmatic chores that Kent had planned to perform over the weekend—set up bill paying during his absence, changing his insurance—had to be accomplished as soon as possible. David, Ryan, and Kristen Keefhaver enjoyed the time together, but each did so with a tightness inside knowing what lay ahead for Ryan.

Kent was initially told that he was being sent to Camp Anaconda but, at the relative last minute, was shifted to the forward operating base called Paliwoda. It was named for 1997 West Point graduate Eric Paliwoda, killed in Iraq in January 2004. In informing family and friends by email of the switch in locales, he wrote: "I know I know, I never told you, and thats b/c I just found out . . . surprised??" He added that while the living conditions would equal those of Anaconda, "the mission is better. Plus I probably won't be there the whole time and still spend some time at Anaconda. . . . And for the coaches . . . Go Army Football!!!"

Kent was part of the 2nd Battalion, 82nd Field Artillery Regiment in 3rd Brigade, 1st Cavalry Division as a platoon leader. He was one of only two Ranger-qualified lieutenants in the entire battalion. There was an opening for a scout platoon leader, which went to the other Ranger school grad, and Kent landed the other primo assignment. Senior officers could be sure a Ranger-qualified lieutenant could grasp a mission, work on his own, and eventually take on more responsibility. The daily mission for Kent's men: shoot when necessary. He enjoyed the duty, something he was trained to do. He likewise enjoyed the opportunity to regularly work out in the base gym and maintain steady communications with his parents and visiting with Keefhaver via webcam almost daily. Their conversations were routine, which somewhat delighted her. From Keefhaver's perspective, a boring day in Iraq was a great day. Since Kent was unable to provide much detail about where he was or what he was doing, Dawn Livingston concocted ways to enliven what could become a "Not much. How are you?" email exchange that often fell back on recapping how Philadelphia's sports teams were faring. One method was to say hello in as many languages as possible, converting simple conversation into almost a competitive endeavor for a son who couldn't resist competition. Keefhaver graduated from Texas that winter and moved on to nursing school in Galveston, Texas, the following spring. Kent's duties at Paliwoda evolved. His work days became 12-hour shifts that decreased the ability to keep in touch with family and friends back home.

Peter Stewart left Fort Hood for Iraq in September—weeks before originally scheduled—to become an executive officer (XO) for the headquarters and headquarters troop (HHT) of the 6th Squadron, 9th Cavalry Regiment at Forward Operating Base Normandy. The FOB was located in Muqdadiyah, about two and a half hours northeast of Baghdad. Stewart was able to perform most of his duties from his living quarters and typically got to the gym so late at night that he'd work out by himself.

Stewart adored his siblings even if, as a youngster, he regarded older sisters Amy and Abby as extensions of his parents' authority. Such devotion was displayed from the other side of the globe in mid-November 2006 for Amy Hogatt, living near Dallas. He managed to email a morning host of one of the market's more popular country music radio stations with a request. He asked host Amy Bishop to bid his sister a happy birthday over the air. Bishop was more than happy to comply. Talk about your long-distance dedication.

Stewart's assignment as an XO rarely required him to leave the FOB gates. There were occasions when he ventured over to the brigade office to drop off paperwork, but that convoy trip took less than an hour's drive along a relatively safe route. A scheduled influx of new lieutenants, like a draft of rookie players, would probably mean new assignments for many of the officers, some rising to the squadron level. Stewart, if given a choice for his next duty, would have preferred something in civil affairs, interacting with the locals with the intent of improving their community.

Christmas 2006 was a relatively relaxed day at FOB Normandy, as each troop sent out only one patrol. Stewart's regular morning meeting was cancelled, and he slept in until 11. The officers and upper enlisted men served Christmas dinner to the soldiers with main-course choices of turkey, ham, fried shrimp, and T-bone steak. Stewart dished out mashed potatoes and stuffing. That night, some field artillery men shot rounds of flares in an attempt to form a cross. It looked more like a trapezoid, but the effort was roundly applauded.

Stewart and Maura Sommers communicated frequently, practically daily, though technical difficulties were often an obstacle. Stewart's internet access was often unreliable. He was patient during such episodes; she wasn't. "What did you do today?" she'd ask. "I woke up, went to a meeting, took care of some work, ate, worked out," he'd reply. "Oh, So, pretty much the same thing you did back at Fort Hood," she'd say. "I guess," he'd answer.

In January 2007, Stewart learned of the death of one of his Fort Hood platoon soldiers, which was a first for him. Specialist Nathan "Chris" Fairlie, twenty-one, died from injuries suffered when a pressure-wire IED detonated near his Bradley Fighting Vehicle in Baqubah, the capital of Iraq's Diyala province northeast of Baghdad. Fairlie was the driver, had two passengers, and was the only soldier killed in the explosion. He'd joined the US Army in 2004, less than a year after graduating from high school in the small upstate New York town of Candor, located a few miles north of the Pennsylvania state line. Fairlie had been a lineman on the Candor High football team. As a sophomore, he was in physical education class when everyone stopped to watch the 9/11 attacks on television. His head football coach, Mike Swartz, recalled Fairlie being particularly unnerved by what he saw on TV and "wanted to take care of things," according to the *Press & Sun-Bulletin* of Binghamton, New York. On the snow-crusted route that led from Fairlie's funeral service in Allen Memorial Baptist Church to Maple Grove Cemetery, people lined the sidewalks and held American flags.

Stewart was told about Fairlie on his way to the mess hall. He recalled that the last time the two crossed paths, Fairlie was leaving the mess hall and was obviously exhausted. Stewart asked how he was, if he'd been going to the gym. Fairlie replied he'd been run ragged with obligations. But he'd said that matter-of-factly, not complaining. Stewart struggled to absorb the news of his friend's death, took his food back to his room instead of eating in the mess hall and couldn't finish. Stewart and others who'd served with Fairlie at home and abroad knew him as a funny guy who could turn a simple fast-food run into an adventure. That humor was sometimes used to break the tension of the moment. Stewart saluted his former soldier in an online tribute: "Even when he was mad, he still had a great attitude. He was one of the hardest working guys in the platoon. I never heard him complain and he always did his best at every mission he performed. I am honored and privileged; he was and always will be a part of my life."

Stewart had already planned how to spend much of his leave time upon returning from Iraq in October 2007. Bernard Gardner, one of his friends from both G.A. duty at the prep school and armor OBC at Fort Knox, owned a cabin in Wyoming. The two would go deer hunting. But on April 11, 2007, Robert Gates, who became Secretary of Defense in December 2006, announced that military deployments would be extended from 12 months to 15. The decision didn't surprise those whom it affected in the wake of the surge. In order to add at least 30,000 or so servicemen and servicewomen on the ground, keeping many of those currently on duty in theater was somewhat inevitable. "This recognizes . . . that our forces are stretched," Gates told the media, as quoted by the *Washington Post*. He termed the extension "difficult but necessary."

Stewart made sure his parents became aware as soon as possible that, instead of returning in October 2007, it would be more like January 2008. Given that deployment movements are often difficult to precisely schedule, he might make it back for Christmas. His email began:

> *hi momma,*
> *well, I don't know if you heard the news about us getting to spend 15 months over here instead of only 12. i am excited. i love it over here so much. everyday is something new and exciting. yeah. but it's ok. i understand why they are doing this. at least this way the guys who just got home will get to spend time with their friends and loved ones for at least a full year.*

Stewart wondered if he would still have a girlfriend by the time he returned and didn't know what to do with three months' additional pay while in Iraq:

> *man, there are just so many positives to this. well I love you and will try to give ya'll a call this weekend to talk to everyone. tell cuervo i miss him and i can't wait to see ya'll.*

* * *

March 2007 brought a change of command for Fort Sill's Bravo Battery of the 1st Battalion, 40th Field Artillery—the "all-for-one battalion." Josh

Davis was replacing Captain Gilberto Reyes. The ceremony featured the passing of the guidon, or the battalion's battle flag. Among those whom Davis thanked during his acceptance speech was Captain Woody Gebhart, calling him both a mentor and a friend. He recalled that their first encounter ended with Gebhart telling Davis, "By the time you leave this battery, you will be ready to command." Davis said: "Well, sir, mission accomplished. . . . It gives me great pleasure to know I will be leading a battery who carries out one of the most important missions in the army—training and preparing the future soldiers who will fill our ranks. Once again, I thank you all for attending today's ceremony. This we'll defend—all for one!" Misa Davis, holding baby Leighton, was presented with red roses.

Stewart and Ryan Kent were among those in the American military whose plans for communicating back home on Mothers' Day were scuttled by a communications blackout. Such events were typically employed in connection with a death, for the purpose of directly informing the family of the tragic event instead of word somehow informally leaking out. Three days after the "commo" blackout, Stewart learned the reason for it. It was another death that shook him to his core. Andrew Bacevich Jr., who'd attended OBC at Fort Knox with Stewart and was one of his running buddies at Fort Hood, was killed by an IED in Balad, northwest of Baghdad. He died of wounds suffered from a device detonated near his unit as it patrolled across Salah Ad Din province. Bacevich, twenty-seven, was assigned to the 3rd Battalion, 8th Cavalry Regiment, 3rd Brigade Combat Team, 1st Cavalry Division out of Fort Hood. He was deployed to Iraq in October 2006, scheduled to return in January 2008.

Stewart learned of his friend's death and the details that led to it in an email from another fellow armor OBC graduate, John Forehand. According to Forehand, Bacevich stopped a suspicious car. Two of the three occupants immediately jumped out and ran while the third remained at the vehicle to set off the explosive, which went off seconds later. Bacevich was able to kill the two who ran but was gravely wounded and died in route to a hospital. Stewart couldn't hold back the tears and began randomly punching whatever he could lay his fists on. He then went outside and smoked a Black & Mild cigar and recalled that night back in Killeen, when Bacevich abruptly urged them to continue their night out in Austin. Stewart also recalled an email exchange that the two had after they'd learned that one of their fellow OBC grads had been killed. "I'm not gonna lie," Bacevich wrote. "That took the wind out of my sails." Bacevich's death certainly sucked the wind from Stewart's sails.

Andrew Bacevich Sr., by that time, had long questioned the nation's involvement in Iraq. In April 2007, he revisited his question from March 2003—where exactly is the road to Baghdad leading us?—in the *Los Angeles Times*: "'What's your plan for Iraq?' was the right question back in 2002 and 2003—although it went largely unasked and almost completely unanswered then. But as we approach the 2008 presidential election, though the tragedy of Iraq continues to unfold, that question is moot. The one that matters is this: As President Bush departs and leaves the United States bereft of a coherent strategy, what should fill that void?" Bacevich noted in the May 2007 issue of the *Atlantic Monthly*: "The thousands of Americans killed in Iraq include no members of Congress and not a single general."

A standard condition of media interviews with Bacevich Sr. during the course of his public commentaries was there be no mention of his only son serving then in the military. Andrew Bacevich Jr.'s parents laid him to rest in Massachusetts instead of Arlington National Cemetery to allow relatives better access. Three days after Bacevich's death, his father released a statement: "Andy was a born leader, who felt called to serve his country. His determination is exemplified by his struggle to become a soldier." The family received hundreds of messages of condolence in the following weeks, but there also were two that offered quite the opposite. Bacevich Sr. addressed those in a contribution to the *Washington Post* soon after:

"Both held me personally culpable, insisting that my public opposition to the war had provided aid and comfort to the enemy. Each said my son's death came as a direct result of my antiwar writing . . .

"What exactly is a father's duty when his son is sent into harm's way? Among the many ways to answer that question, mine was this one: As my son was doing his utmost to be a good soldier, I strove to be a good citizen . . .

"I know my son did his best to serve his country. Through my own opposition to a profoundly misguided war, I thought I was doing the same.

In fact, while he was giving his all, I was doing nothing. In this way, I failed him."

* * *

Back at Fort Riley, Anthony Zurisko wrestled with an awkward feeling. His schedule wasn't overloaded, as it often was at Camp Taji. There were no missions or patrols, no potential danger, as was the case almost every time that he left the compound gates. With no midnight excursions, his work days ended at a reasonable hour. Good riddance, right? But, in some way, Zurisko missed that existence. It wasn't that his work at Fort Riley wasn't meaningful, but it didn't feel as important as what he had done in Iraq. Zurisko soon transitioned to work that was at least meant to resemble Iraq. He trained national guardsmen who came through Fort Riley for 60-day stretches before deployment as advisors. Such training had been touted by President Bush as essential to success in Iraq but scathingly criticized in 2005 by Lieutenant Colonel Nick Demas as a "phenomenal waste of time," according to a *Wall Street Journal* story written by Greg Jaffe. The mechanism was overhauled with inclusion of Fort Riley officers who, like Zurisko, had been there, done that. The guardsmen were schooled in operating field artillery, adapting to Iraqi culture, conducting raids, and doing patrols. Fake villages were set up and roads contained simulated IEDs that, when detonated, sprayed baby powder. Zurisko was thrilled to see the guardsmen make progress after only a few weeks.

Zurisko was invited by the head of Springdale's chapter of the Veterans of Foreign Wars to participate in the town's Memorial Day 2007 parade and speak afterward at the small memorial park, located next to a mini-golf course and Glen's Custard Stand. He wore his green Class A dress uniform amid the late-spring heat and sweated even more when he had no place on which to set down his printed text as there was no podium. Using a handheld microphone, Zurisko simply delivered the five-minute speech that he wrote in two hours one night from memory to a gathering of about a thousand people. That included a couple dozen Zuriskos—plus Brigit McGuire. He quoted Douglas MacArthur and cited the first major ground battle of the Vietnam War in November 1965, when 200 Americans were outnumbered

8-to-1 in the Ia Drang Valley. Zurisko closed: "Today we pray that those men who have made the ultimate sacrifice have found peace with God, and we resolve that their sacrifice will always be remembered by a grateful nation. May God bless America." Some people told Damian Zurisko that his son's speech moved them to tears.

Chapter Fourteen

"THERE'S NEVER A GOOD TIME IN THE ARMY TO HAVE A BABY"

The summer of 2007 marked the occasion in which the graduates of West Point's Class of 2004 who were still active military were promoted from the rank of 1st lieutenant to captain. For any of the six who planned to leave the army after the minimum active-duty obligation of five years (longer for aviation), being a captain would most likely be their highest military rank. The ascension was based on service time that began with their graduation date of May 29, 2004, though any of them theoretically could have been denied the upgrade on the basis of some sort of unlikely unappealing military behavior. In some cases, the promotion ceremony was delayed because of logistical particulars related to the recipient, the availability of pertinent officers or something connected to the post itself. Ryan Kent was promoted on July 1, but the pinning ceremony took place two nights earlier—in conjunction with an infantry awards presentation—because his battalion commander was scheduled to go on leave. The result was Kent being pinned in front of scads of soldiers who didn't know him, without the opportunity to say anything. He and the other new captains that day simply marched off.

Josh Davis was technically promoted a few days after the others since he graduated a few days after them following the agonizing tape-test episode. His duties changed greatly following the change of command at Fort Sill that spring. Previously, as an executive officer, his work was primarily done behind the scenes. As a commander, he had subordinates who handled details such as confirming resources. Davis eagerly anticipated being the highest ranking officer who would have daily interaction with the soldiers under his command. A major or a colonel would deal with a captain and not have the same connection with those who actually pulled the ropes and made the guns go boom.

Davis's pinning ceremony was performed by his mother and his grandfather, Allen Delamater. Afterward, Davis took them on a personal tour of the post. His grandfather, a huge Civil War buff, was enthralled with the Sherman House (so named because General William Tecumseh Sherman stayed there during a visit in 1871) and the grave site of Geronimo (he died from pneumonia at the fort in 1909 at age 90). With the promotion came a commitment with the artillery training center, which nearly assured that Davis would spend the rest of his commitment at Fort Sill. Given the minimal chance of being deployed, he backed off earlier efforts to seek a change of station that would be closer to his wife's family in Connecticut. He'd sought a position in Virginia as a general's aide de camp. When someone else landed the slot, Davis was disappointed but also relieved given the responsibilities of that position. While the Davis family would have been closer to the Froehlichs, he would have been at his new boss's beck and call at virtually any moment. Family life might have suffered significantly.

And that family was growing larger. The Davis's second child was born on December 28, 2007, also at Fort Sill's base hospital. He was named Crew, after the character Cru Jones in a 1980s movie about BMX racing; they eschewed adopting the movie's unconventional spelling for fear that the teachers in Misa's family might revolt. Little Leighton turned 2 only a few days after Crew's arrival and was enamored with her brother, trying to pick him up only weeks later.

In August 2007, Brian Hill and Morgan Hesse traveled to Cabo San Lucas, Mexico, for a vacation that she suspected might include a wedding proposal given that the couple had recently window-shopped for engagement rings multiple times around Atlanta. She joked that he should buy one close to where he planned to propose in the event that she declined; he played along, asking her to provide a ballpark percentage for her saying yes. Proposal or not, they were already discussing where to live. Hill, with family roots in Atlanta, liked the idea of staying there after his time at Fort McPherson ended, while Hesse's first choice was her native Texas. The night before the couple left for Mexico from Dallas/Fort Worth International Airport, Hill met with Charlie Hesse and showed him the ring. Hill had already alerted some of his friends to his plan, and many of them didn't have the timing quite down. The night before the flight, his phone practically buzzed off the nightstand with call after call asking if he'd popped the question.

The question was popped a few nights later, on a beach in Cabo around midnight, with just enough light coming from both the resort behind them and the moon above. Hill pragmatically wore cargo pants that allowed him to stash the ring in one pocket and a camera for capturing the momentous occasion in another. He got on one knee, grasped her hand, held it close to his chest, and said, "I can't imagine my life without you. Will you marry me?" Hesse, while obviously anticipating the moment, was still somewhat frozen and didn't immediately respond. "Well," he offered, "say something." Finally, she said yes. They hugged, and it was then it was his turn to forget something. "Oh, the ring!"

* * *

On August 30, 2007, the Army Board for Correction of Military Records awarded Brad Waudby a West Point diploma, officially recognized him as a member of the Class of 2004 with a bachelor's degree in system engineering and pre-law, which also dropped the demand for restitution totaling $190,005; official notice of the latter would arrive in the mail on New Year's Eve. "The Army knew or should have reasonably known that, after encouraging the applicant to gain weight and easing fitness requirements, that it would be difficult, if not impossible, to meet commissioning standards," a member of the board wrote. A representative of the board attempted to contact Waudby directly with the news, but he was unavailable, even by cell phone, while in training for the waterfront patrol. He learned of the decision that night at home, told by his overjoyed father. Waudby broke into tears—but tried not to get too excited until he actually saw the diploma with his own eyes. Bradford Sr. emailed word the following day to relatives and friends: "The lesson that Brad and I learned through this whole ordeal is if you believe you are right don't let anything get in your way and leave no stone unturned." The following day, Waudby's patrol class started its law studies with each student asked to introduce himself or herself. For the first time, he identified himself as a 2004 graduate of the United States Military Academy. When his fellow class hopefuls days later complained about being constantly yelled at by their superiors as part of the training, Waudby smiled and recalled Beast Barracks. But the Department of the Army soon let it be known that, while it agreed to waive the recoupment, it still refused to recognize Waudby as a West Point graduate worthy of a diploma. That sent the Waudbys back to court.

* * *

Clint and Sue Woody left Germany for the Middle East in the summer of 2007. They spent two weeks in Kuwait before moving on to an air force base in Balad. The giant logistics center base was often referred to by helicopter pilots as "the duck pond" because they were routinely fired upon during takeoffs and landings. Each person is allowed to account for 400 pounds, including body weight. Aviators are allowed an extra 100 pounds, the dispensation in deference to their additional flight gear. Clint's personal belongings included a laptop, a small CD player, and some aviation books.

While the Woodys were deployed together, they were assigned to different battalions in the same combat aviation brigade numbering about 2,500. The US Army's only obligation was to locate the husband and wife within 50 miles of each other. She was executive officer for her company, second in command overseeing aircraft refueling, wheeled vehicle mechanics, cooks, medics, and other staff soldiers. He initially was an officer in charge—she got to fly much more, which made him somewhat jealous—before he became a flight platoon leader. Sue updated many of the couple's friends in an email a few weeks after their arrival in Iraq:

> Hi again everyone,
> We're doing just fine here in Camp Anaconda (Balad). . . . Obviously, the weather is warm. It has cooled down from the 130 in Kuwait, to

117, and now we're seeing right around 101 every day. Honestly, it really does feel cooler . . .

Clint is staying very busy, and working long hours as a Platoon Leader. He's studying and working hard to earn Pilot-in-Command status before he moves to his next job as the Supply Officer for the Battalion this December 1. I know he'll make it!

As for me, I'm still working as the Operations Section for the Battalion and doing well. My hours are not as taxing as Clint's, since my boss gives us 4 days off a week to be at the flight companies we fly with. . . . . I'll also move to be a Platoon Leader in December, so I look forward to that.

We miss everyone very much and wish you all the best.

Hugs to all!

Love, Clint and Sue

Leslie Woody was constantly concerned while her son and daughter-in-law were deployed in Iraq, further distressed by the complications of communicating with them on the other side of the globe. She often just avoided following news from the war. Clint and Sue tried to assure her that no news was great news. That was of little solace when a US Army Black Hawk crashed in northern Iraq in August 2007, and the 14 Americans on board were killed. That happened on a rare day when Leslie was listening to the news; she immediately turned off the radio. She fought to retain her composure—no news is *great* news—but that became more difficult after receiving phone calls from anxious relatives and friends. Leslie suddenly questioned whether she was taking the situation as seriously as she should. She began to research where the crash happened and determined it occurred about 40 miles from where she figured Clint and Sue were. It was another excruciating day and a half before Leslie and the other Hayesville Woodys received an email from the Iraq Woodys and learned they were safe.

While parents of all deployed personnel lived in fear of what the day's events in Iraq might bring, families like the Woodys and Petroffs dealt with the uncertainty of both their offspring plus his or her spouse being imperiled.

Max and Kimberly Voelz deployed together to Iraq in 2003 in the same unit—explosive ordinance disposal out of Fort Knox. Only one of them returned home alive. Kimberly, the only woman in the 17-person unit, was killed that December while attempting to disarm a bomb; she was 27. The army officially recorded the incident as a fluke, noting that she had done nothing wrong.

The couple met at bomb school in 1997, on Valentine's Day. They were married in June 1999 and made informal plans to retire from the army. While members of the same unit, they were assigned to different disposal teams. Kimberly was in a medically induced coma when Max arrived at the hospital at the Baghdad airport. "The nurses were telling me to talk to her because they assured me that they had seen people come out of comas before, and that they remembered hearing things that people said," Max told NPR's "Story Corps" in 2011. "I mean, what are you going to tell your wife, who's dying? That you love her, and you don't want her to die." Max decided he should be the military person to inform Kimberly's parents of her death rather than the protocol officer in uniform with a cold-call knock at their front door in Pennsylvania. At the funeral, Kimberly was posthumously awarded the Bronze Star and the Purple Heart. Max was sent home soon after the tragedy. The condolence letter that he received gave no indication that he, too, was active military, certainly not that he was present when his wife died. "I am an army widower; I don't think there's very many of us," Max said. What was and wasn't contained in the letter, he added, "just makes it seem like nobody knows we exist." He left the army a few years later.

* * *

For Clint's twenty-sixth birthday in September 2007, he received a pragmatic present from the second of the Woody brothers, Reid. Two years younger, Reid had planned to follow Clint into military aviation and set his sights on attending the Air Force Academy. But as his senior year at Hayesville High wound down, his love for a sophomore name Shandalee Buchanan grew even greater. Reid eschewed a future in the US Air Force to pursue his second great interest, engineering, at Clemson, and the couple was married soon after Shandalee graduated from high school. For Clint's present, Reid installed LED lights in the tips of the index and middle fingers of his pilot gloves. That allowed him to see maps and other things in the cockpit without interfering with infrared night vision. Reid placed a round switch smaller than a Cheerio in the thumb.

As a pilot-in-command, Clint began transporting troops from base camps to hot-spot positions. Sue became a platoon leader in the 5th Battalion, 158th Aviation Regiment and part of Alpha Company, whose duties included transporting VIPs across Baghdad. No passenger was more important than their most frequent flier, General David Petraeus. A typical "work day" found members of the command aviation company taking Petraeus from his living quarters and primary working space in a lakeside palace built by Saddam Hussein to his secondary office at the US embassy. The flights took five minutes, Petraeus accompanied by his aide and sometimes a handful of other staffers in a Black Hawk helicopter. He was typically all business, even doing business during the brief flight, and didn't have time for chit-chat with the flight crew beyond a polite "Hello" when boarding. Petraeus liked to fly fast, even during such short excursions, given what he needed to accomplish during a work day that routinely lasted at least 15 hours. He would express this desire over the intercom system by saying, "Bend 'er over, chief." That was when Sue signaled to the male lead pilot that she would handle the response rather than him. In her best "girly" voice, she'd say, "Roger that, sir!" A *Stars and Stripes* article published in March 2008 noted that Petraeus liked to detour over particular neighborhoods to assess the military's reconstruction efforts. The story also quoted Sue on the general's need for speed: "We go as fast as the birds can go for General Petraeus. He's real quick to speak up . . . Literally every second of their day counts."

The pilots in the daily shuttle service had to be at the ready for whenever Petraeus's workday ended. A trailer was provided in which pilots could rest, and a coffee shop inside the compound was a popular spot in which to relax, play board games, read, or work on personal projects while remaining prepared. The crew sometimes remained with the aircraft unless it was loaned out for another purpose. The general never took any spur-of-the-moment trips; his days were meticulously scheduled. The biggest variable came when a meeting at the end of the general's day ended earlier than expected.

While Petraeus didn't interact much with the flight crews, he did occasionally invite the members to his living quarters for dinners and cookouts. The VIP "travel service" often included visitors who would be escorted around Baghdad by Petraeus, from high-level government officials to entertainers visiting the troops. It ran the gamut from Vice President Dick Cheney and Senator John McCain to boxing promoter Don King. The couple's long work days were rewarded with three weeks' leave that allowed them to travel to New Zealand. This allowed them to perform such husband-wife bonuses as holding hands in public. But just before going on leave, new orders resulted in Clint being moved to Taji, with Sue remaining in Baghdad.

* * *

Peter Stewart was one of four 1st lieutenants promoted at FOB Normandy. The ceremony was held outside, the thermometer reading 115 degrees. That was followed by a reception (inside) that featured chicken wings and cake. The next stop in Stewart's military career was to become a brigade executive officer at FOB Warhorse, located about 35 miles northeast of Baghdad. The job would resemble his previous one, reporting to majors rather than to captains. Stewart wasn't particularly keen on change—change of scenery, change of schedule, change of officers, change of problems. But, at the very least, Warhorse figured to provide a better mess hall with healthier choices. Stewart's new duties left him little time to watch television despite having a TV in his office. He did manage one day to catch General Petraeus testifying before Congress about the US troop surge and afterward heard one of the network pundits noting that a great man who'd served his country was now getting ridiculed. All Stewart could think was the American public was often making conclusions about the war without knowing many of the facts.

Shortly before Stewart left Iraq in December, he passed through Balad and attended a Carlos Mencia benefit comedy show for about 600 military personnel. The crowd was such that he couldn't locate a vacant seat and settled for sitting in one of the aisles. Stewart thought he heard someone from the seating area call his name. It was actually more than one someone; it was Clint and Sue Woody. When Balad was the Woodys' duty station, they often ran into fellow West Point grads and other military acquaintances who were either beginning or ending a deployment. Days later, Stewart hopscotched his way from Iraq to the United States in typical army fashion, encountering a band of welcoming patriots in the Bangor airport. About 300 members of the 3rd Brigade Combat Team returned to Fort Hood's 1st Cavalry Division's parade field on December 9, 2007. Following a succession of predictable postponements getting out of Iraq, home—at least the Fort Hood version—was only a few minutes away as the plane approached Robert Gray Army Airfield. There was a substantial layer of fog that obstructed more than the passengers' view of the homecoming crowd below, which included Nancy and Pete Stewart. The pilot announced: "We're going to have to circle around for a little bit. We'll see if it clears up. If not, we might have to land in Austin." That news naturally drew the ire of the eager—and exhausted, in most cases—passengers. The ranking officer aboard, a colonel, left his seat and prepared to approach the cockpit, probably with some words of abrading encouragement for landing right then and there. Before he reached his destination, the pilot came back on the intercom: "Uh, they just realized who we are. They're going to go ahead and let us attempt to land. So, they're going to guide me in."

And land they did. As the soldiers exited the plane from their multi-continent odyssey, some shook hands with eyes barely open. There was still much to do before meeting with family and friends waiting at the parade ground about 20 miles away. Inside the terminal building, the soldiers swiped their ID cards to officially register that they'd returned. Then, it was on to a nearby warehouse to drop off weapons. Next, they loaded buses, 40 at a time, for the drive to the ceremony. They were officially greeted by Brigadier General Fred Rudesheim, first at the air field and then with a ceremony at the 1st Cavalry parade field. At the parade ground, both the returning military and those welcoming them were anxious for the general's remarks to end and the long-awaited reunion to begin. Rudesheim wasn't a rookie at that, having learned from a previous episode to keep his speech as short as possible while still properly expressing appreciation for the returnees' service to the country. He understood that his words might be tuned out like the cartoon character Charlie Brown often did to his schoolteacher: *"Wah, wah, wah."* Finally, Rudesheim reached words that everyone present understood: "Join your troopers!"

Soon after Stewart got his military affairs settled at Fort Hood, preceded by his long-awaited reunion with the Chinese super buffet located on the main drag into the base, he was off to see Maura Sommers in New Jersey. Their holiday itinerary included a Saturday night performance of the Blue Man Group at the Astor Place Theater in New York. As the two waited in line to enter the theater, someone connected with the performance approached Stewart and asked him if he'd like to be a participant. He said yes, probably with hesitancy that resembled his response when he was asked to leave armor OBC school the night before it began to become a football grad assistant at the prep school. Stewart was next seen on an on-stage video screen that provided a view of what was happening backstage. He was clad in a white painter's suit. A helmet was placed on Stewart's head just before he was painted blue. He was guided across the room, laid down and tied by the ankles, then suspended upside down. For the next few minutes, Stewart became a human paint brush, swung repeatedly into a white canvas with the blue paint splattering in the general shape of a silhouette. Then, the screen went blank. A cart was then rolled out onto the main stage with a small box atop it. The box was removed to reveal a blob of giggling orange gelatin. Multiple Blue Men began hacking away at the blob until they revealed Stewart's blue-painted head. What the audience didn't know was that the helmet was actually a mold filled with the gel—dangerously close to Stewart's face, as far as he was concerned. (He was considerately asked beforehand if he was claustrophobic.) Fortunately, the gel wasn't hot. Stewart finished the routine unscathed and received hearty applause from the crowd and a comforting hug from Sommers.

* * *

Summer 2007 became fall at FOB Paliwoda, but not before Ryan Kent experienced a little long-distance joy thanks to a combination of the limited availability of the one all-sports channel at the installation and similarly brief internet access. Kent learned that his beloved Philadelphia Phillies pulled off one of the more astonishing comebacks in major league history. Trailing the first-place New York Mets in the National League East by seven games with only 17 remaining in the season, the Fightin' Phils amazingly caught the Mets with three games to play and finished one game ahead to win the division—for the first time in 14 seasons. Kent's delight was made all the more enjoyable because he worked daily at the FOB with three die-hard Met fans, whose rooting souls were damaged a little bit day after day after day down the stretch.

Kent's deployment ended late that year, capped by a month in Kuwait before returning stateside. Dawn Livingston planned to surprise him by attending his welcoming ceremony in Texas. His group was scheduled to arrive at 7 p.m., but instead touched down three hours early, just before her flight landed. Kristen Keefhaver was able to salvage some element of surprise by taking Kent from Fort Hood over to Killeen's commercial airport and quickly concocting a story that they were headed there to, uh, pick up a friend—only for Kent to see his mother walking out of the terminal. Over the holidays, Kent spent Christmas with his father and stepmother in Ohio, then New Year's with his mother and stepfather—and Keefhaver—in New Jersey.

Kent didn't remain at Fort Hood for long. He left in early February 2008 to seek membership in a Ranger battalion. That required another strenuous test of body and mind similar to Ranger School, akin to pursuing a military master's degree, called the Ranger Orientation Program (typically called "rope"). The session took two weeks compared to the longer Ranger School. There also was a different mindset, a different attitude toward the candidates. Ranger School hopefuls were treated like West Point plebes, but ROP attendees were accorded some dignity, an acknowledgment that their military accomplishments had earned them a higher level of respect. There were no 4 a.m. wakeup calls or 20-minute, shovel-down-your-throat meal periods. There was less emphasis on identifying the candidate's level of discipline; it was assumed that wouldn't be an issue. ROP was more business-like, though clearly military training once again. After completing the program, Kent stood before a board of officers who declared him fit to serve in the 3rd Ranger Battalion, numbering about 450, at Fort Benning. Officer assignments to Ranger battalions are usually for a duration of three years; the thinking is that such members of the army's elite should be able to exhibit their skill sets across a wide range of the fighting force. Keefhaver, who graduated from nursing school in Texas in April 2008, joined him in relocating to Columbus, Georgia.

* * *

In mid-December 2007, Nancy Hill was hospitalized to have fluid removed from her lungs. Her condition deteriorated within a few days, which prompted Brian to hurriedly drive home from Atlanta. He arrived late on a Wednesday night, and the doctors were already recommending hospice. Mother and son visited for a few hours; by the next morning, she was unresponsive. Nancy died that Friday morning. The service was held on Sunday, December 23, one day before what would have been her fifty-third birthday.

The following April, Hill spent time at Fort Sill to attend a course on joint operational fires and effects that included members from the other military branches. The trip afforded Hill a rare opportunity to see Josh and Misa Davis and their two young children. Davis was about to leave for Fort Riley to train for what Misa had long feared in the back of her head for years—her husband's deployment to Iraq, later that year.

Weeks earlier, Misa was leaving a follow-up visit to the base hospital following Crew's birth and coming off the elevator when she locked eyes with Josh, who was there to drive her home. She was immediately unnerved by the expression on his face—and his unusually pale complexion. Josh tried to deliver the news calmly; he was to be assigned to a MITT—a military transition team—that would go to Iraq and train an Iraqi unit. The deployment would be for a year, preceded by three months' training at Fort Riley. The team would be under the command of Major Dennis O'Neil, who'd taught psychology at West Point and was a mentor to the football team's offensive linemen when Davis attended. It would be a small, elite group consisting of the major, five captains, and five senior non-commissioned officers. The training would be a combination of counterinsurgency and just enough basic training—how to take the Iraqis through standard military tasks. One aspect was made clear: the goal would be to improve the Iraqis' methods of fighting and providing security; not trying to mold them into adopting American approaches. On the trip home from the hospital, Josh shed a few tears; Misa cried for the entire ride.

* * *

Brad Waudby graduated from the waterfront police academy in February 2008. He was one of two detective grads among the class of 63 that gathered in a ballroom of a Hilton Garden Inn on Staten Island. The ceremony began with bagpipes, a favorite touch of the Waudbys. The family held a reception back in New Jersey at the exclusive Brownstone restaurant. Waudby drove over, taking sister Ashley and his long-time friend Matt Graf. (Back when the Waudbys lived at the funeral home, it was young Graf who had to help Waudby pick up the broken pieces after the fishing-rod episode.) Waudby was decked out in his new police uniform. Graf had never pictured his buddy in a police uniform but thought it suited him well and had not seen him this happy in years.

Waudby attended Brian Hill's bachelor party in Atlanta along with Tom Farrington and Anthony Zurisko. It included a stop at Turner Field for a Braves game. While Hill and Morgan Hesse were unsure where they would make their home, they'd picked the site of the wedding for that July—the Barr Mansion, an 1898 Victorian home located about 30 miles outside of Austin, Texas. On the morning of the ceremony, Charlie Hesse brought the bride-to-be her favorite breakfast—taquitos from Whataburger. The official high temperature recorded in Austin that day was 99 degrees, 11 above normal, but many of the guests were certain that it hit triple digits. The reception was held in downtown Austin, on a paddleboat on the Colorado River before the newlyweds headed to the Florida Keys.

* * *

Early in 2008, Peter Stewart embarked on the next phase of his military career. Becoming a captain meant enrolling in the army's three-month captains' career course. His was scheduled for Fort Benning. Stewart would then continue his career at Fort McPherson in Atlanta as an operations officer, or S-3. He was afforded other options, but most of them involved deployment to a war zone. If Stewart had been given the opportunity to become a recon mentor and teach Afghans to be scouts, that might have swayed him. But one downside to that would have been the lack of facilities in which to exercise, as he'd done regularly in Iraq. That was more important than usual since he had recently been advised to have shoulder surgery. Plus, he was looking forward to Sommers joining him and the two being a real couple for the first time. She graduated from respiratory therapy school that spring.

* * *

Brad Waudby's first appearance back at West Point was for the 2007 Army football team's second home game of the season, against Temple. The traveling party from north Jersey consisted of Waudby, his parents, Tom Farrington and his wife, Farrington's parents, and another former Army football player from New Jersey, Peter Salfeety. Waudby was again pleased and relieved to feel no ill will from old West Point buddies or academy personnel whom he encountered. The '07 season was the first with Stan Brock coaching the Black Knights. Bobby Ross's run ended with his retirement following three seasons during which Army never won more than four games in a season. His three-year record on the Hudson was 9–25, with a combined record against Air Force and Navy of 1–6. Ross's replacement was a promotion from his own staff. Brock had no previous major-college head coaching experience, was Ross's offensive line coach for those three seasons and played on the coach's Super Bowl team. Among Brock's former fellow assistants whom he retained was John Mumford. Alas, the early October 2007 win over Tulane that Waudby witnessed was likewise in the sixth game of the year and was Army's last victory of that season. Six consecutive losses followed for another 3–9 finish, capped by a 38–3 loss to the Middies that extended West Point's losing streak in the series to an Army-record six straight.

Clay Woody was a junior on Army's 2007 football team. He broke his arm for the second time in his Army career late in the season and finished his third year on the team without seeing varsity action. The combination of no varsity playing time, the time commitment that was drained away from studies, and the physical toll that practicing was taking on his body convinced him it was time to leave the football program. The difficult decision was made slightly easier after talking to Clint and their father. Denny Woody had a way of cutting through chaff; he asked, "Just why did you decide to attend West Point?" Major Bill Lynch was aware of Clay's plight and tried to talk him out of quitting. Lynch spoke from experience. He'd gone from the high of playing on the varsity as a plebe to never lettering, his football career hampered by a shoulder injury sustained in his cadet boxing class. West Point academics were constantly challenging for Lynch, and he eventually realized leaving the team was necessary for him to graduate. It was the toughest decision of his life. Despite Lynch's imploration, Clay made an appointment with Brock, marched into his office, and told his head coach that he was finished with West Point football.

* * *

March 20, 2008, marked the fifth anniversary of the Americans' invasion of Iraq. It should have been a routine workday for Clint Woody as he participated in copter flights that shuttled military personnel among the FOBs scattered across Baghdad into the night. But he and the other pilots were startled late in their shift by what appeared to be bright-green tracer fire seemingly everywhere across the night sky. It turned out the night-vision goggles that they wore altered the appearance of harmless fireworks, roman candles, which were shot off to mark the birthday of the prophet Muhammad.

In April 2008, an Army football player became an NFL draftee for the first time since Ronnie McAda was "Mr. Irrelevant" in 1997. Caleb Campbell, one of the seven 2004 freshmen to letter, became a standout defensive back, and was chosen in the seventh and final round (218 overall) by the Detroit Lions. The most recent former Army player to seek an NFL roster position at that point was offensive lineman Peter Bier, who last played for Army in 2006. He signed a free-agent contract with the Packers in May 2007, was released during training camp, and then reported for active duty. The most recent former Black Knight to actually play in the NFL was tight end Ron Leshinski. He completed his Army career in 1996, did his two years, and played one game for the Philadelphia Eagles in 1999.

Campbell's selection was a media event, earning more air time during ESPN's live coverage than the typical seventh-rounder and greeted by the football fans who packed Radio City Music Hall with chants of "USA! USA! USA!" But such enthusiastic affirmation apparently wasn't universally shared across the country. A *USA TODAY* poll conducted days after the draft showed 52 percent thought Campbell should honor a five-year commitment.

Two other seniors off that 2007 Army team unsuccessfully tried to enter the NFL through free agency, punter Owen Tolson with the New York Giants and fullback Mike Viti with the Buffalo Bills.

Campbell agreed to a contract with the Lions, participated in the team's rookie camp immediately following the draft, and was prepared to start training camp in July in Michigan. That abruptly changed when Army athletic director Kevin Anderson called Campbell to say the alternative service option had been voided, trumped by the Department of Defense's overall rules for the three service academies that upheld the two-year service obligation. Campbell was ineligible to play for the Lions and was to report to West Point within 24 hours to become a football assistant. He concluded that Navy and Air Force assumed Army would never actually take advantage of the West Point rule and, after seeing the attention afforded to Campbell's drafting, cried foul. He was finally granted that release in July 2010 upon his graduation from officer basic school at Fort Sill. Campbell made his NFL debut in Dallas on November 21, 2011, and played in three games that season. He was released following the season and unsuccessfully tried to hook on with the Indianapolis Colts and Kansas City Chiefs over the next two years.

* * *

In early May 2008, Leslie Woody was startled by news from Clint and Sue—but it was news of a joyous nature. Sue was pregnant with a due date near Christmas. As per US Army practice, she would be leaving the war zone within a week or two and returning to Germany while Clint would remain in Iraq for another five months. The female doctor at the base clinic confirmed the pregnancy, congratulated Sue and added, "There's never a good time in the army to have a baby." She gave Sue some vitamins and told her to return to their living quarters and—providing instruction that seems ubiquitous for every military medical situation—drink plenty of water. Soon after Sue found out, she phoned Clint and asked, "So, what you do think about bein' a dad?"

Sue was worried about how her superiors would greet the news. Some commanders have guessed that pregnancy has been used to get a female out of a dangerous deployment. It's the phenomenon of *that* girl that begins at the academy level. Female cadets never want to be that girl who can't finish a run with all the males. Or that girl who can't finish a road march. Or that girl who gets pregnant. Sue called her battalion commander back in Balad, Lieutenant Colonel Jack Bone. She braced for some yelling and received just that: "This is the most amazing thing! I am *so* happy for you and Clint!" Clint, elated at starting a family, was also overjoyed that Sue's time in Iraq would end within days. When he first heard her voice on the phone coming from Germany soon after, he was overwhelmed with relief. Within weeks, Sue returned to Fort Rucker to participate in a training exercise for the unit that was scheduled to replace theirs in Iraq in autumn 2008. She was able to make a side trip to Hayesville, where Leslie Woody invited 25 people to join them for dinner at the big dining room table in Shooting Creek. Once back in Germany, Sue and Clint were able to talk nearly every night via Skype until his deployment ended that fall.

Chapter Fifteen

FIVE AND FLY

Graduation at Fort Riley for Josh Davis and his fellow members of the DN6 MITT team, also called the deployment ceremony, took place in early October 2008. His team was one of dozens to graduate that day. Lieutenant Colonel Christopher Wilbeck spoke: "You, as transition team members, are being sent by your country to embed and train Iraqi military personnel and security forces. As such, you will exercise a lot of power and influence over the indigenous forces. This influence will be the ultimate key to success—that is—their success. And in the global war on terrorism, their success equals our success." The ceremony was over in 14 minutes and included singing of the 1st Infantry Division's Big Red One song ("Men of the great division, courage is our tradition, forward, the *Big Red One!*").

The MITT team was sent to Mosul, the second largest city in Iraq. It was home to the core of Saddam Hussein's Baathist army and was the largest city in the country in which Sunnis made up the majority. Mosul, known centuries earlier as Nineveh, was ethnically diverse. The team settled into a compound on the east side of the Tigris River called Combat Outpost India, or COP India, that contained about 70 American military personnel with about 45 permanent residences. The compound was located within the larger al-Kindi base, home of the Second Iraqi Army Division, within a ring of 20-foot barriers topped by razor wire. Davis had his own room, about 7 feet by 20.

The need to train the Iraqi military to operate on its own grew greater soon after the election of Barack Obama in November 2008. One of the 44th President's campaign pledges was to scale back the American military presence in Iraq. One of the first manifestations of that was the commitment made on New Year's Day 2009 to remove US soldiers from the country's cities within six months. In late February, Operation New Hope began. Coalition and Iraqi military worked together to clear insurgents from neighborhoods across Mosul. Once an area was deemed cleared, a military unit moved into place and essentially began efforts to keep the locals busy and not as susceptible to enticements offered by operatives of Al Qaeda. It often amounted to a construction project that, once completed, would also benefit the surrounding neighborhood.

With the passing of the June 30 deadline, Davis's MITT team moved its operations to the west side of the Tigris River, to Forward Operating Base Marez. In terms of the physical plant, this was like leaving baseball's minor leaguers for the bigs, the latter accommodating multiple battalions of American soldiers plus air crews. The area that the team patrolled also changed greatly. East of the river was mainly residential, most of its inhabitants older. West of the river was home to younger residents with businesses dispersed among their homes. From then on, an Iraqi escort had to accompany the team on its missions, and the team's vehicles were painted to look like Iraqi vehicles. When someone who didn't appear to be Iraqi popped out of a turret atop a Humvee—basically, anyone who was white or black—he or she received double takes from the residents. The number of vehicles permitted out at once was reduced from ten to two.

One winter morning, Davis and the team were outside with soldiers from the battalion headquarters beneath Bridge 5, which spanned the Tigris. The Americans weren't wearing any helmets or protective vests as part of their good-will efforts within the compound. That also made them more attractive targets to the enemy. Davis was standing in a gravel parking lot and heard the first of three 80-milimeter shells sailing toward him and the others before he saw it. Fortunately for all involved, the shell landed in a small mud patch in the parking lot no more than five feet from Davis—making a *thud*—and didn't detonate. The next two incoming shells—one landing to the left of the first one, the other to the right—did explode, causing some injuries but no deaths. Davis, who was unharmed, suspected the shells were fired from the back of a moving truck on the bridge above the headquarters. Within minutes, copters sped off to locate the responsible party but had no luck locating it.

On another occasion, Davis and the team were patrolling through Mosul, driving along Route Buffalo. He served as the gunner in the last vehicle in the convoy, sticking out of the turret and almost always facing behind the vehicle. After reaching a point in which the road split, Davis noticed a red Volkswagen Rabbit about 100 yards behind the convoy that was being driven erratically through heavy traffic, even up on the sidewalk at times. A few minutes later, the Rabbit returned to the lane behind the Humvee, separated by only a few vehicles. Davis radioed to the team chief, Major O'Neil, about what he saw and was told to follow the suspicious car as closely as possible without staring at its driver. The Rabbit continued to move as if negotiating an obstacle course, darting from lane to lane for no apparent reason. When the convoy abruptly turned onto a side street to see what the Rabbit driver would do, the driver wasn't able to make the same turn, floored it, and made the next turn and got back behind the Humvees.

Ahead of the convoy lay multiple checkpoints, where traffic came to virtual standstills. O'Neil advised each checkpoint to pay close attention to the Rabbit if it followed the convoy's route and to conduct a full search. That didn't happen at any of the stops; the driver merely showed his ID and was waved on. By that point, Davis could see the Rabbit's back end appeared weighted down; he guessed explosives. The Rabbit was probably a dozen vehicles behind Davis's Humvee but gaining ground, still swerving this way and that like a Manhattan cabbie despite a slowdown in the traffic. Davis then made his intentions obvious, pointing his M240 Bravo Machine Gun at the Rabbit driver. That apparently gave the gentleman pause, and he backed off some. The convoy cleared the next checkpoint, continued on, and turned onto another road. And Davis saw the Rabbit catching up to his Humvee.

O'Neil convinced the Iraqi commander who was traveling within the convoy that the Rabbit was a plausible threat and needed to be stopped. When the car was diverted to a point where the driver could be questioned, Davis could see frustration and contempt on the driver's face. With the Rabbit no longer in pursuit, Davis heard a *boom* a few minutes later off in the distance and felt his turret rock. When the driver couldn't take out the convoy, he apparently identified a secondary target.

Davis returned home for a 15-day leave in April 2009. Leighton insisted on wearing her Cinderella dress to the airport and unwittingly alerted most of the people in the terminal when she spotted her father with screams of excitement. Crew, conversely, didn't recognize the unfamiliar man. Josh told Misa such a scenario with a very young child was common, which made him feel better. The thrill of having Daddy home caused Leighton to temporarily forget the potty training at which she'd been progressing. Crew finally said "Da Da" with only a few days left in Davis's stay. As the couple's days together dwindled and they prepared to return to their new normal, there was a degree of angst that wasn't previously there. Before the beginning of Josh's deployment, Misa had never experienced rearing two young children alone for an extended period of time. While she might have dreaded what it would be like when he initially prepared to leave for Iraq, the trepidation no longer was fear of the unknown—replaced by fear of the known; likewise for Josh regarding deployment. He previously could only envision what life in Mosul would be like. He enjoyed his last few days in Connecticut with full realization of what awaited him upon his return to the banks of the Tigris.

* * *

Brian Hill was sent to Kuwait in late August 2008 for about three months as part of his organization duties at Fort McPherson. "It's nothing dangerous," he assured family and friends in an email. "I won't even carry a weapon." While Hill was stationed by Camp Arifjan, south of Kuwait City, he caught up with Anthony Zurisko, who dropped in on Camp Buehring, north of the city.

For members of the Class of 2004, their five-year active-duty commitments were scheduled to end sometime during the spring or summer of

2009—except for those who branched aviation. *The New York Times* reported in April 2006 that more than one-third of West Point's Class of 2000 ended their careers as officers with that minimum obligation. The popular term for that practice among the military is "five and fly."

As Hill's time wound down toward spring 2009, he spent considerable time on his job search—though he still wasn't sure what he wanted to do or where he wanted to live. Staying in Atlanta still had great appeal thanks to his comfort level there and its proximity to Florida. Morgan's preference remained Texas. He worked with the Army Career Assistance Program and, shortly after completing his final deployment, attended a service academy job fair in San Antonio where more than 300 employers were represented. His interviews included Target, to be an Atlanta-based regional manager for asset protection. That essentially meant preventing theft and popping into stores at 3 a.m. Hill wasn't keen on such marching orders—or that everyone in the company, even officers, were required to wear red shirts. There was a Humana opportunity in Louisville, Kentucky, one for Proctor & Gamble in either Cincinnati, Ohio, or St. Louis, Missouri. Morgan was actually warming to the idea of staying in Atlanta, where she liked her job with Career Builder and had made plenty of friends. While Brian looked into such management positions, he still had a tug toward going into athletics. Coaching interested him some, but becoming the general manager of a big-league pro franchise would be even better. That, though, remained more of a dream instead of something that he pursued overtly. One thing that Hill made sure to attend to after returning to the States and before leaving the government's payroll was to have long-overdue knee surgery. In early December 2008, he had a microfracture procedure that his father proudly noted was similar to what Tiger Woods had.

Friday, March 26, 2009, was technically Hill's last day "on the job" for the US Army. He reported to Fort McPherson for his "final out," which meant completing his DD Form 214—Certification of Release or Discharge from active duty. Actually, he would still have to sign out the following Monday to go on terminal leave. He soon after began work in Houston for FMC, a chemical manufacturing company, beginning as a project manager and quickly rising to project coordinator. In early April, the Hills left Atlanta for Texas. Morgan put her English degree from the University of Texas to use, becoming an eighth-grade teacher in the Cypress-Fairbanks school district that ranked third in the state in size behind Houston and Dallas. In her Title I middle school, where almost half of the students qualified for free or reduced-cost lunches, one of her students had an after-school job. Another was pregnant. On the final day of the 2009–10 academic year, Morgan cried when they boarded their buses because she feared that some of them would someday end up in jail.

* * *

Ryan Kent left for Ranger deployment in early July 2008 for about three months instead of a 15-month term that "regular" army personnel received. An analogy for the difference could be found in comparing baseball's starting pitchers to "closers," whose job is to pitch almost exclusively in only the final inning. The intensity of the closer's mission—protect a lead of three runs or fewer—deems it a reasonable assumption that he shouldn't be required to pitch more than one inning. The same held true for members of a Ranger battalion. Kent wasn't able to tell Kristen Keefhaver that he was in Iraq; she only knew that he was nine hours ahead of Eastern Time. She got a job in the intensive care unit of Columbus Regional Hospital, where she found the gravity of the work fulfilling. Kent deployed to Afghanistan in autumn 2009 for a period of months that overlapped with the conclusion of his five-year active-duty military obligation, closing his army career as a special-operations fire support officer.

Kent and Keefhaver scheduled their wedding ceremony for the Saturday of Labor Day weekend in downtown Fort Worth, Texas. Kent was also in the process of trying to land a job. In the "regular" army, an officer is provided leave time during which he or she is provided time to pursue a civilian position before the military paychecks stop coming. That wasn't the case with Kent; the Rangers weren't interested in paying him to look for a job. He thought he had identified an efficient way to combine his employment hunt with planning for his wedding. He wanted to attend a headhunter's career conference for military officers hosted by the officer-recruiting service Cameron-Brooks in Charlotte, North Carolina, in August 2009—one week after his return from Afghanistan and one week before the wedding. If he missed that session, he would have to wait until year's end to attend the next one. Kent and Keefhaver drove from Fort Benning to Charlotte, where one of his interviews was with Los Angeles–based Technicolor. The interview led to the scheduling of a follow-up in LA on the Tuesday after Labor Day. The couple drove from North Carolina to Texas, celebrated their marriage, and Kent caught a flight for California the next morning. The honeymoon was put on hold.

Kent accepted an offer from Technicolor as a project manager, and the newlyweds were off for California. After leaving the military, he initially struggled to adjust to certain aspects of civilian life. He was frustrated when what appeared to be a simple task—having the cable company come and hook up your service—proved to be annoyingly complex or time consuming.

Four-and-a-half years amid the Los Angeles sprawl were more than enough for Ryan and Kristen Kent. He jumped at the opportunity during spring 2011 to move to Dallas to work for Ernst & Young as a manager in the performance improvement division within the financial services office. The job involved regular travel, which was initially invigorating but eventually burdensome, particularly when his family began to grow with the birth of son Casen in January 2014.

Kent wasn't overtly seeking a job change when he chatted at the gym one day in 2015 with Kevin Lavelle, founder and chief executive officer of the men's clothing retailer Mizzen + Main. But he took the plunge, leaving an established company with solid benefits to become a bigger fish (chief operating officer) in a much smaller pond. Kent made a priority of hiring veterans and consulted frequently with some of his former professors and mentors at West Point. He contracted with a company called Higher Echelon—run by former West Point football player and staffer Joe Ross—to help with much of the company's employee training. The Kents' second child, daughter Ryleigh, was born in October 2015.

* * *

Tom Farrington built a career in the financial district of lower Manhattan, working in sales of equities and equity derivatives for multiple companies beginning in 2010. His marriage to Kaitie ended in divorce. His father continued to battle cancer and died in October 2014 at age 63. Farrington moved back to Pittsburgh in July 2017 in part to be there for his widowed mother. He continued his career as a sales trader with Bay Crest Partners. He and his fiancée, Nikki, whom he met in New Jersey in 2011, scheduled a June 2018 wedding date in Aruba.

* * *

In mid-January 2009, Brad Waudby was driving back to his office in Newark, New Jersey, from Brooklyn along Manhattan's West Side Highway when a frantic call came over the police radio of a plane going down in the Hudson River. Waudby wasn't far from Ground Zero and shuddered at the thought of another terrorist attack staged in New York City. He was soon able to see the aircraft afloat in the water and realized it was a commercial airliner. US Airways Flight 1549 had incredibly been landed safely in the Hudson by pilot Chesley Sullenberger; America came to know him as "Sully." Waudby followed instructions to stand down in favor of law enforcement that was better equipped to handle such an anomalous situation.

* * *

Clint Woody's departure from Iraq in autumn 2008 typified how military movements, even leaving a war zone, are complicated and time-consuming. It took four hours for his battalion to get through customs at Ali Al Salem Air Base in Kuwait City. He made it through in only an hour, but that left a long wait for the others to join him as the morning sun quickly beat down. The procedure was done in a secluded area that prevented those who had already been processed from leaving the area. Tents were set up with air-conditioning, but the AC units were exposed to the sun. In late morning, the temperature already reached 100 degrees outside while it "only" hit the upper 90s inside, made warmer by the volume of people coming through. Woody bused to Kuwait International Airport, waited two hours, flew to Nuremberg, Germany, and bused again to Katterbach. There, it took relatively little time to turn in his weapons, work computer, and medical records. Finally, he and others who returned to Germany from Iraq were recognized with a welcoming ceremony in a hangar complete with a DJ blasting music off the walls. Woody quickly spotted banners personally welcoming him that were made by relatives back home at Sue's request.

In making plans for the delivery of the couple's first child, Sue decided, "When in Germany, do as the Germans" and chose a water birth with midwife Frau Wagner at a hospital in the nearby town of Neuendettelsau to minimize the pain. Blake Woody was born on December 16, 2008. His parents used the following criteria for determining his name: Clint insisted that it would sound good if announced at a rodeo; Sue's preference was also tied to a public introduction of a grown man. They identified five finalists before naming their newborn son—on the way to the hospital. As per the German practice for post-birth care, Sue remained at the hospital for almost a week. She returned to work in early February with the wife of an army chaplain who lived nearby coming over to watch little Blake.

* * *

In March 2009, most of the West Point graduates of the Class of 2004 were coming down the homestretch of their five-year active-duty commitment—not those who went aviation, like the Woodys. Their first opportunity to leave the military would come during the spring of 2011. But Clint was far from envisioning the finish line early in 2009. He had his sights set on a position that would extend his commitment well beyond 2011 in the prestigious 160th Special Operations Aviation Regiment. The 160th SOAR provided helicopter support to special-forces units, such as the Navy's SEALs, on missions relatively short in duration. Deployments with the 160th—the "Night Stalkers"—would last a month, maybe two, instead of the marathon of 15. Between deployments, the members did a great deal of training with other special forces across the country. Woody specifically assessed to fly Chinooks (with about 30 seats behind the pilot with a cargo limit of about 10,000 pounds), having to date flown Black Hawks (10 seats, transporting up to 4,000 pounds). The Woodys had discussed the possibility of Clint returning to school to earn a graduate degree in order to teach at West Point. Sue preferred that route, but Clint was eager to elevate his military experience to what he considered a greater purpose to more directly support war-zone troops than his previous roles in Iraq. Acceptance into the elite unit would keep him in the US Army for at least four years after he completed his training, likely into summer 2014.

The five-day assessment, or testing session, at Fort Campbell for the 20 candidates included marching with a ruck sack—they want to make sure the officer can still do it—shooting, combatants, flying skills, and navigation plus a final written test that contained 400 questions. Free time was technically built into the week's schedule, but it was usually syphoned off by the candidate's urge to put in more preparation for upcoming aspects of the assessment. The test was administered after the candidates had gotten little sleep. Some of the questions were repeated in a slightly different fashion to see how the weary students would react. Finally, the candidates appeared individually before a panel for a 30-minute grilling that ranged from interrogation of military knowledge to questions related to the candidate's personal life.

Woody spent most of the week doubting that he'd make the grade, which was the intended state of mind for a beleaguered candidate. The closing interview session was held on a Thursday morning at Feistner Hall, named for a fallen member of the Night Stalkers. Major Curtis Feistner was one of eight members of the 160th who were killed in February 2002 during a helicopter crash during Operation Enduring Freedom. Woody and his fellow contestants were called one at a time for the intense interview. He didn't know what to think when one of the candidates who preceded him came out crying. He was called in next and did his best to endure the mind game. When one of his replies ran longer than the board anticipated, he was rudely informed by one of the members: "You just wasted five minutes of my life!" Upon conclusion of the session, Woody was told to step out into a nearby office to wait with the other anxious hopefuls. The wait of 10–20 minutes felt like hours—again, the intent. When called back in, the candidate would hear one of three conclusions:

1. "You made it."
2. "You didn't make it and are advised to work on certain skills before assessing again."
3. "You didn't make it and aren't seen as fitting into special operations at all."

Woody was called back and first asked how he felt he had done. He blurted, "Pretty crappy from my standpoint." He was then told, "Welcome aboard."

Woody was both relieved and euphoric; only about half of the class passed. The 160th contained four battalions, two based out of Fort Campbell plus one each at Hunter Army Airfield in Savannah, Georgia; and Fort Lewis, Washington. Woody would begin at Fort Campbell and move on to Hunter. He was relieved, euphoric—and exhausted. When Clint called Sue to deliver the good news, he managed to say little more than: "We're in. We're going to Kentucky." before trying to catch up on lost shuteye.

The Woodys bade *auf wiedersehen* to Germany in April 2009 and returned to Fort Rucker, both enrolling in the aviation captain's career course that would run from May into the fall. Before they left Europe, Clint noticed that their belongings were marked for shipping to Fort Bragg, North Carolina, instead of Fort Rucker. He assumed someone saw him listed somewhere as being from North Carolina and made an incorrect connection. Clint noted the error to a soldier in shipping and figured all would be well. All wasn't well. The Woodys' worldly belongings—except for the baby bed that they mailed separately—were still sent to Fort Bragg. Furniture. Television. Silverware. Plates. They were forced to lean on Fort Rucker's Office of Army Community Services to borrow a card table, some folding chairs, utensils, an air mattress, a couple of pots and pans, plus similar items while waiting for their personal property to make its way from North Carolina to Alabama. That took almost two months.

While making the best of their new, sparsely appointed homestead, the Woodys began the captain's career course. It ran for 21 weeks, until mid-September, and included the third and final section of the survival instruction that years earlier saw them chomp down on rabbit eyeballs. That final instructional phase focused on "R" and "E"—resistance and escape. A description of the course written years later by a resistance training officer at Fort Rucker, stated "the SERE-C training approach exploits his or her weakness in order to induce the most amount of stress safely and effectively." That was taught both in a classroom setting and—literally—in the field. Aspects included food and sleep deprivation and worst-case isolation while an "enemy army" searched the woods for the student. By the time the Woodys began the

C stage, army brass had determined it would be best that a husband and wife not experience the session together.

Another Woody was soon headed to Fort Rucker. Clay graduated from West Point in 2009—commencement speaker Robert Gates admitted early in his remarks that "I am just about the only thing standing between you and a great party"—and followed his oldest brother into aviation. Most of the Woody family caravanned to the West Point commencement ceremony from North Carolina in two vehicles and stayed in nearby cabins. Military attire for the Woodys wasn't required, but Clint wore his uniform since he would pin Clay afterward. Sue enjoyed going "civilian casual." As the day's events unfolded, she felt like time had not passed since Clint and she enjoyed the same festivities five years earlier. Denny enjoyed the familiarity of experiencing West Point graduation the second time around and being able to tell first-timers what to expect. Gates also noted in his address that the 970 graduates in the Class of '09 had probably filled out their academy applications around the time of the second battle of Fallujah, during autumn 2004, and were undeterred by the nation already having spent about a year and a half involved in an agonizing war. "In doing so, you showed courage, commitment, and patriotism of the highest order." Clay and fiancée Lauren Rogers—they met at a Hayesville Middle School dance—were married a few weeks later.

* * *

Anthony Zurisko was scheduled to become a battle captain on a second tour of Iraq beginning late summer 2008. He did updated training at Fort Irwin, California, for a month the previous spring. The four-week stint was really two weeks of actual training sandwiched between one week each for unpacking and packing. The grounds simulated the conditions in Iraq, right down to herds of sheep and attacks in the middle of the night, the trainees being tracked 24/7 by dozens of supervisors. Their weapons weren't live; the instruction resembled an intense session of laser tag.

Soon after returning to Fort Riley from California, Zurisko proposed to Brigit McGuire. He bought the engagement ring before going to Fort Irwin, then took her to Tuttle Creek State Park near Manhattan. If McGuire was anticipating his proposal, she reacted with suitable surprise. They agreed not to set a date until he returned from his deployment but decided the wedding would be in St. Louis, her hometown. She had almost a year left in nursing school. Only days after the proposal, Zurisko learned from Kent that he was headed back to Iraq that week, six months after his most recent stint there.

Zurisko reported to Camp Justice, located in an area of northwest Baghdad called Kadhimiya. He began the deployment as a fire support officer, overseeing his brigade's projects and civil affairs in the area. When he and his fellow officers moved into their quarters, they pitched in to buy an office television and satellite connection. That purchase turned the office into a quasi-sports bar when his beloved Pittsburgh Steelers faced the Arizona Cardinals in Super Bowl XLIII. With his "Terrible Towel" hanging behind his desk, Zurisko cheered the Steelers on to victory.

* * *

Peter Stewart's younger brother, Patrick, graduated from the Naval Academy in May 2009 with a degree in engineering. Peter attended, enjoyed the display by the Blue Angels, and was impressed that the commencement speaker, President Barack Obama, shook hands with every graduate. West Point grads begin their military careers as 2nd lieutenants; Navy grads start out as ensigns. His first deployment was for seven months aboard the destroyer *USS Milius*, a ballistic defense ship, beginning in August 2010. Ensign Stewart shared living quarters with one other officer and enjoyed amenities like internet and TV access. To stay in shape, he and the others at sea could exercise in any of the ship's three gyms.

Chapter Sixteen

A WEBER GRILL, A SWIFFER MOP, AND A PURPLE HEART

Josh Davis and the DN6 MITT team left Iraq in October 2009, taking a C-130 from Mosul to Kuwait before going through customs—for 12 hours. Davis had five duffle bags plus a 100-pound ruck sack, pushing them along the floor a few feet at a time. With temperatures nearly reaching 100, the cattle call of going through customs left most drenched in sweat. He also carried in hand a change of shirt, socks, and underwear for the 17-hour flight from Kuwait to Ireland to Maine to Topeka, which would be followed by the bus ride to the team's technical home at Fort Riley. With his team's arrival time changing frequently over a period of days, it was convenient for Davis that neither family nor friends were waiting for him at the base when the buses pulled in around 10 p.m. After the standard welcome home festivities, the first stop for many of the returnees was the post's Class 6 store, where alcoholic beverages were available. Some resorted to taking cabs to the nearest post gas station for the same purpose. He made it back to his family's latest home, in Connecticut, in time to go trick or treating with his children.

Josh Davis's final day in the US Army was Monday, February 1, 2010. Ideally, the Davis' would have recognized the occasion with a night out. But Davis was preoccupied with looking forward instead of looking back—with finding a job—and was in no mood for celebration or nostalgia. His pursuit of a master's degree in economics concluded about a week before leaving Iraq, when he handed in his thesis to the University of Oklahoma. The topic was where post-2003 Iraq was positioned in relation to Rostow's five stages of economic development. Davis didn't spend as much time in Iraq online pursuing future employment as he had planned, instead essentially consumed by the events of each day. He did post his resume and scanned the job search site for the military academies. Davis dug into Monster, Career Builder, and Ladders. And there was the usual networking with West Point and military connections plus relatives, probably as useful as any site if not more so.

While Davis was deployed, he received letters from the elementary school class taught by his brother-in-law's wife back in the Connecticut town of Wilton. That fall, the teacher invited Davis to be one of the school's Veterans Day speakers. The guest who spoke immediately before Davis was Nick Davatzes, creator and developer of the cable networks A&E and The History Channel (his grandchildren attended the school). The two of them visited, and Davatzes soon after wrote a recommendation letter for Davis.

But Davatzes's letter, the West Point connections, and all of the networking ultimately had no nothing to do with Davis landing a job. He received a call from JPMorgan Chase five days after sending in his resume, made it through three phone interviews plus a dozen face-to-face follow-ups, and began work in Manhattan dealing in foreign exchange derivatives in early March 2010. Within months, the gainfully employed US Army veteran, husband, and father of two closed on a house in his wife's hometown of Brookfield, Connecticut. The commuter trains to and from New York usually traveled for about an hour and 15 minutes each way, his day beginning around 8 a.m. and sometimes ending around 1 a.m. It didn't take long for Davis to become involved in his company's recruiting efforts aimed toward transitioning military personnel. He participated in a job fair back at the academy's West Point Club that featured booths staffed by more than 50 prospective employers.

Davis became heavily involved in his employer's commitment to Carry the Load, a non-profit that was started in 2011 by two Navy SEALs who wanted to turn attention on Memorial Day back toward its original purpose instead of a holiday with barbecues and baseball games. The effort began as a march in Dallas, Texas, that lasted for 20 hours and 11 minutes in 2011, and it quickly expanded into a national remembrance with month-long relays of participants bound for Dallas from starting points in Seattle and West Point. Davis, wearing his combat boots, set out from the academy as part of the group that planned to cover the first 57 miles, to the site of the World Trade Center. The boots, it turned out, were his undoing. Davis had to retire to the accompanying support bus after 37 miles because of blisters. He then traveled to Dallas to help organize subsequent Carry the Load events, with Ryan Kent becoming involved in the Dallas portion. The Davises welcomed a third child, daughter Maggie, in February 2012; she came within hours of being a leap-year child. He left Morgan Chase as a vice president in May 2017 to accept an offer to hold the same position at Bank of America Merrill Lynch, again based in Manhattan.

* * *

Brian Hill returned to Fort Hood in November 2009, much earlier than he had ever anticipated and for a purpose that he had never imagined. Hill was part of an FMC team that made the nearly four-hour drive up from Houston soon after the tragic shooting by Major Nidal Malik Hasan left 13 dead and more than 30 wounded. The FMC contingent hauled the company's huge barbeque pit trailers and participated in the USO's "day for the soldiers" that included a concert and fair.

July 2010 saw another first for Brad Waudby in his gradual return to the social fold as a former West Point cadet and former Army football player. For the first time, he played in the annual summer golf tournament for ex-Black Knights football players near West Point. Brian Hill flew in and spent the previous night at Tom Farrington's place in New Jersey. Anthony Zurisko drove in, and they played in a foursome that day. On the Par-5 No. 18 hole, Waudby's drive of 370 yards left Hill speechless. It was the farthest drive that he had ever seen by an amateur golfer. Hill wondered how Waudby would be received, but everything appeared to go smoothly.

Zurisko finished out his time in the army at Fort Riley, where autumn 2009 was often warm enough to get in 18 holes at the public Colbert Hills course, designed by former Kansas State golf star and PGA Tour player Jim

Colbert. His time in the active military officially ended January 5, 2010, and his goal was to be employed 10 days later. During his final days in the army, Zurisko worked in a 9-to-5 staff position with a supervisor hovering over him. In seeking a new civilian career, he sought a position that featured variety. His efforts to find a job covered three areas: the online "iSABRD" (Service Academy Business Resource Directory), the executive recruiting company The Sterling Group (founded by former 1990s Army football player James Duncan) and another entity that assisted former officers start civilian careers called Alliance (run by 1985 West Point graduate John Todd). Zurisko aimed at landing something with the medical sales company Boston Scientific, selling defibrillators and other devices related to heart surgery. His target was Savannah, Georgia, because Brigit's sister was in the process of moving to Jacksonville, Florida, located about 90 minutes away. If that didn't work out, there was an opportunity in his native Pittsburgh, selling surgical robots.

Zurisko and McGuire were married in May 2010 at Holy Infant Catholic Church just outside St. Louis. The groom's brother, Jeff, was the best man while Farrington and Hill were in the wedding party. The newlyweds postponed their honeymoon since both were starting new jobs, she as a registered nurse; they traveled the following year to Ireland, where they kissed the Blarney Stone. One table at the wedding reception featured the Hills, the Farringtons plus Waudby and his girlfriend, Michelle. As the evening progressed, it dawned on Morgan Hill how different "the boys" were in their conversation. No one suggested heading out on a late-night excursion following the reception. The former football players and former military men were getting older and somewhat tamer.

Zurisko was hired by Synthes to work in medical sales at multiple hospitals in Jacksonville. He spent his days observing spinal surgeries and explaining to doctors how to use the company's equipment. To prepare for the position, he took a crash course in anatomy. Networking proved to be more important than the placement service. Mike McGuire, his brother-in-law and former fellow army officer, steered him to Synthes' vice-president of sales, who happened to be a West Point graduate. Brian Hill moved to Synthes in December 2010, taking a position in San Antonio with duties that were similar to Zurisko's. He worked medical sales, primarily for plates and screws used during surgeries that involved the head, face, sternum, or ribs. Zurisko left the medical sales field in 2015, his most recent employer being the water-analysis company Hach, still in Jacksonville. The Zurisko family grew to include daughters Molly, born in 2012, and Maggie, born in 2016.

The Hills welcomed their first child in February 2011. Ten days before Morgan's due date, a nurse noted her high blood pressure and urged admittance as soon as possible for delivery. The couple dropped off their dog, Magic, with a friend and made the 10-minute drive to the hospital. Morgan was surprised—stunned? disappointed?—that Brian confined his driving to the slow lane. Melynn was born, and Morgan was extremely impressed when her day-old daughter was able to hold up her head and turn it from side to side. The new family of three soon after spent Mothers' Day weekend attending a previous engagement, Kent Magueri's Saturday wedding in Lake City, Florida. Melynn grew noticeably tired during the reception but had difficulty falling asleep since the Hills were seated at the table closest to the DJ. When they returned home to Texas on Mothers' Day, Brian ordered takeout from one of Morgan's default restaurant choices, Chili's, and they dined on the "cuddle couch." A month later for the family's first Fathers' Day, Morgan prepared his favorite breakfast of biscuits and special sausage gravy and later presented him with a Weber grill. The holiday, though, didn't exempt Brian from lawn-mowing duty that afternoon.

Peter Stewart was technically eligible to leave the US Army in May 2009, but stayed on until the spring of 2010 to use up his accrued leave time—for yet another shoulder surgery plus post-op recovery time. His discharge would take place in April 2010. Stewart identified autumn 2009 as the perfect time for proposing to Maura Sommers because Halloween was her favorite holiday. Their first date five years earlier during his time as a Fort Monmouth graduate assistant, after they had talked for weeks over the phone, was at the pumpkin patch display at a garden center near the Jersey shore.

Stewart enlisted the covert services of one of Sommers' best friends back home, Nicole Zimmerman, and his future father-in-law to help construct an elaborate scenario for popping the question. Sunlight was fading while the two of them toured the pumpkin patch, Sommers still searching for the perfect potential jack-o-lantern. Zimmerman suggested she turn around: "Hey, 'Mo.' How 'bout this one?" Sommers turned to see two lighted pumpkins that were carved to spell out "MAURA WILL YOU" and "MARRY ME." Stewart was already down on one knee but didn't have time to repeat the question verbally before she said yes through tears. He then presented the engagement ring, which he had shipped to her father weeks earlier, so it wouldn't somehow be discovered by Sommers in their luggage. They set the wedding for October, naturally, the following year.

Peter Stewart and Maura Sommers were married in West Point's Catholic church, Chapel of the Most Holy Trinity, which is one of three houses of worship on the academy grounds. What's called the Old Cadet Chapel was built in 1836 and moved, brick by brick, to a location adjacent to the academy cemetery upon the construction of the current Cadet Chapel in 1910. The latter seats 1,500, serves the Protestant community, and features an immense organ (19,000 pipes and 312 "ranks"—a set of pipes that are set at the same timbre for each note). The Catholic chapel was built in 1900, and a Jewish chapel was added in 1984. Stewart and Sommers chose to wed at West Point in part because they had not established a real home parish given the moves that they'd made related to Stewart's career. Holding the ceremony in southern New York was at least geographically convenient for the bride's family. While there would be considerable distance involved for the Stewarts, there also would be a return to an overall familiar and comfortable setting.

Distance was more than considerable for Patrick Stewart, who determined early in the year that he would be deployed at sea when his brother walked down the aisle. How in the world could he be represented at the nuptial while on a destroyer halfway around the world? Sommers emailed Patrick about a month before the wedding with an idea. And on a sun-splashed Saturday in mid-October 2010, the seated guests watched the wedding party stroll in—one of them carrying a life-size cardboard photo poster of Ensign Patrick Stewart in his dress-blues uniform. The likeness was propped into place by a Swiffer mop. Patrick was at least able to phone the groom that morning and wish him luck. The reception was held at the West Point Club in a banquet room overlooking the Hudson. The Zuriskos were there. So was Thomas Roberts, living in Philadelphia with his wife. He made it a point to attend Stewart's wedding because his former roommate was the only one of Roberts' academy connections who attended his wedding.

The disagreement between the Waudby family and the Department of the Army over Brad's official academy status wasn't over. The military took them to court in January 2010. In March 2010, a New Jersey federal judge ruled in favor of the family, and he was finally sent a diploma from the United States Military Academy. Soon after, Waudby's career in law enforcement changed addresses. He was accepted to become a detective in the prosecutor's office in the New Jersey county of Bergen, which was where he'd grown up. From the initial duties that began upon his hiring, he added participation in the office's narcotics task force and regional SWAT team. Married in 2014, he and wife Erica have two sons—Joseph "J. J." and Tommy—and live not far from his childhood home in New Jersey.

The Army Physical Fitness Test will be replaced in 2020 by the Army Combat Fitness Test. It will be conducted in six phases instead of three but still ending with a two-mile run. The passing run time of 16:36 figures to be expanded since it will follow five previous events instead of two.

In February 2012, Major Rick Roper—the former Army quarterback and zealous salesman of Ranger School to Ryan Kent—earned his promotion to lieutenant colonel following a career that included two tours of duty in Iraq plus one each in Afghanistan and Bosnia. Roper's virtual next of kin since prep school, Joe Ross, beseeched him to hold the ceremony at West Point in front of the football team—which is what he did. With players gathered all around one morning following an early practice, the oath was administered to Roper by Lieutenant General Robert Caslen, chief of the Office of Security Cooperation in Iraq. "I'm one of you," Roper told the team. "This is the place where I learned so much, made so many friends and developed skills back then that I use today. People say that a lot, and it's not a joke."

With Clint Woody serving in the 160th's Alpha Company (Crazyhorse) in the 2nd Battalion (Darkhorse) at Fort Campbell, the Woody family moved in just over the Kentucky-Tennessee line in what was essentially the base's home-town of Clarksville, Tennessee. Sue became an officer in the 101st Airborne's division staff headquarters. His initial deployment was from November 2010 until early January 2011 in Kandahar, southern Afghanistan. The degree of classification of the mission was such that he got up that day at home, got in his car, left for work . . . and returned about two months later. The best that Clint could do for a farewell was send a text stating, "I miss you already. I love you." She saved the text and read it over and over during the weeks that followed. Clint was one of five pilots accompanying 10 crew chiefs and 20 maintenance people. They worked 14-hour days that began roughly around sunset and never left the camp—at least not on the ground, into the civilian world. He would finish his day's mission, eat an early morning dinner, and go to bed. He and others on the same mission lived in something of a trailer park with about 30 double-stacked metal containers that were converted into living quarters. Clint found the learning curve on this first deployment to be steep despite his six years in the military. The enemy would occasionally drop mortar rounds near the camp but rarely where the aircraft were kept. And there was the added bonus of a nearby water treatment plant, which graced the compound with an unmistakable stench when the wind blew in a certain direction.

Communication was a luxury. Sue knew email was probably the most efficient avenue, but Clint's online account, which was available via two computers in the morale welfare reaction area, required an inordinate amount of time to access. An email that contained an attachment with one or more photos could take five precious minutes to download. That vexed Sue because they enjoyed much more efficient email service during their time in Iraq. All she wanted to do was keep him apprised of what was going on at home, how the family celebrated events like Blake's second birthday. But replies were few and far between. They talked sporadically and for only a few minutes each time. Given the time difference, it was most convenient for him to call when it was around 10 p.m. back home. Sue saw her role as keeping things together at home. Even when she was feeling down or frustrated about something, she never carried that into the conversation. He couldn't provide any details about the classified work of his team, but just hearing each other's voice proved reward enough. The same degree of covert travel arrangements occurred when he first returned from Afghanistan in early January 2011. Sue was jarred awake at 3 a.m. on a Wednesday night by the sound of the front door opening. Only the subsequent clinking of a set of car keys on the key rack just inside the front door revealed to her that the noise was made by her husband and not by a burglar.

Dylan Woody was born in June 2010 at the base hospital at Fort Campbell, and let's just say the Woodys cut it somewhat close. Sue went into labor at home around midnight while her parents were visiting. Clint began the trip to the hospital up Interstate-24 in his Audi. Sue implored him to drive as fast as possible; he turned to her calmly and replied, "Is 105 good enough for you?" After subsequently hustling across in-town roads as much as reasonably possible, Captain Woody wasn't about to park in violation of military regulations. He backed in and out of spaces—at midnight, mind you—that he noticed were reserved for a command sergeant major and then for a chaplain. Clint settled for a 30-minute space; Dylan was born 20 minutes later, and Clint rushed out to move the car.

The second Woody birth again altered Sue's eligibility for deployment. She couldn't be sent until her newborn was six months old—December 2010. And because she would be joining a unit that was nearing the end of its time in Iraq, it wasn't likely that she'd be sent at all. The boys' day care was at a private home on post, with a woman approved by the US Army under the stipulation that she could keep only two children under the age of two. When they lived at Fort Rucker, Blake was originally sent to an on-post center until Clay and Lauren Woody arrived for his flight school and Lauren began looking after Blake. Sue was eager to watch her growing family full time. Her minimum aviation commitment of seven years made her eligible to end active duty around Memorial Day 2011. She returned to work for the 1st Airborne division headquarters in August and soon after began the lengthy process of filing paperwork that would culminate in her departure.

In the meantime, a third Woody joined the ranks of the nation's military aviation. Reid, who had ended pursuit of a slot at the Air Force Academy to marry his high school sweetheart, joined the Air National Guard. He graduated from officer training school in autumn 2010 and became a 2nd lieutenant based out of Maxwell Air Force Base in Montgomery, Alabama. Clint performed his commissioning while wife Shandalee and Clay pinned his bars. The fourth of the Woody brothers, Chad, sought to follow Clint and Clay at West Point. He didn't get an appointment and enrolled at North Georgia College, a former military school, and enlisted in the National Guard.

* * *

On Sunday, May 1, 2011, four copter pilots from the 160th provided transportation for the Navy SEALs quick-strike fighting unit to travel under the cover of darkness from Jalalabad Air Field in eastern Afghanistan into Pakistan based on the intelligence that Osama bin Laden was operating out of a walled compound near the town of Abbottabad. The mission was named Operation Neptune's Spear. Two of the copters were Black Hawks—dubbed Razor 1 and Razor 2, according to a book detailing the mission that was written by Chuck Pfarrer, a former member of SEAL Team Six—and would carry the SEALs into the compound. The two Chinooks would remain behind back near the Afghan border and be ready for any refueling needs encountered by the Black Hawks and to serve as backups if one or both Black Hawks encountered trouble.

Trouble occurred soon after the Black Hawks reached their destination and prepared to land. A one-in-a-million component failure aboard Razor 1 resulted in the copter veering out of control, crashing, and having to be left behind—destroyed, to minimize enemy forces learning anything about American aircraft by studying its remains. One of the Chinooks joined the fray to help carry raid members out of the compound. Operation Neptune's Spear accomplished its goal—Bin Laden was shot once in the chest and once in the head—and no American lives were lost.

The following Friday, President Barack Obama, accompanied by Vice President Joe Biden, traveled to Fort Campbell to privately congratulate the SEALs and the helicopter personnel from the 160th who provided support. The SEALs traveled from Virginia rather than have the president visit their headquarters. While at Fort Campbell, Obama would also publicly greet members of the 101st who had recently returned from deployment. Clint Woody missed the commander in chief's visit, his most recent deployment having begun three days earlier. Sue Woody, in her capacity with the 101st division headquarters, dealt with some of the arrangements of the public portion of the visit, of which they were given only a few days' notice. It was held in a hangar that was typically set up for welcome-home festivities. Given her role in the planning, she was granted a front-row seat for the president's speech.

President Obama informally spoke with members of the 101st before taking the stage and giving his prepared remarks to about 3,000 soldiers. It was obvious to Sue that he had done his homework or been skillfully briefed; the president knew all the units at Fort Campbell and their tactical call signs, which meant a lot to the soldiers. After the speech, Sue was in position to shake hands with Obama. Instead, she stepped out of the way to allow two PFCs who were sitting behind her to enjoy the privilege. The next day, she checked the local newspaper to see if, thanks to her primo spot in the crowd, she made it into the published photos of the event. No such luck.

After the public ceremony, Obama was taken to another portion of the base, viewed Razor 2, and met with the pilots and the SEALs in a windowless room. He was given a comprehensive review of Operation Neptune's Spear complete with a three-dimensional model of Bin Laden's compound, satellite imagery of the area, and complementary maps. Obama was presented with a framed American flag that was aboard the rescue Chinook, signed by the SEALs and the pilots. The president shook hands with each person involved. According to Pfarrar, he asked the SEALs, "So, which one of you guys took out Osama?" The unit's commander replied: "We all did, sir. It was all of us."

As a "working mother" who was an army officer, Sue discussed her potential exit from the military with other female pilots from her West Point class—Xenia Barnes and Holly Burke—who had juggled the same career and family life. The conversations went something like: "I did West Point. I'm in the army. I can fly helicopters. Have been deployed. I can handle a baby. How hard can that be?" They concluded that none of them were prepared for the magnitude of combining motherhood and being an officer. Sue decided she would leave the US Army at her first opportunity, in May 2011.

On the day that the last of Sue's paperwork for departure was finally ready, she waited 40 minutes to get her commanding officer's signature as he gave a safety briefing on dangerous plants to a battalion that had just returned from Afghanistan. If Sue was concerned about a long goodbye, such worry was needless; the major signed the forms and said, "Best of luck." The final step was out-processing, which proved nearly comical given a staffer's insistence on protocol. She waited in a hallway, was told to move farther down the hallway though almost no chairs were occupied. She returned to her original seat only to be told to go back down the hall. For better or worse, another exiting officer was forced to play the same game. (This could have been the inspiration for the scene at the end of *Meet the Parents* when Ben Stiller tried to board his flight.) After the last of Sue's paperwork was completed, she left the post and passed a couple of soldiers who saluted her. Sue felt like clicking her heels, but didn't.

Clint, deployed at the time, could only send a congratulatory email. Sue's co-workers honored her with a lunch at The German Corner, a small establishment at the end of a strip shopping center along the main drag outside Fort Campbell. After receiving a framed piece of art that everybody signed, she told them that she enjoyed every minute in the army and it was time to spend time at home with her sons. Sue looked emotional but held back tears.

Grace Chung also bore children while serving in the army and also left when her commitment ended to become a full-time mother—at least in the short term, as she had left aviation before leaving the service. While deployed to Iraq, she was intrigued by medical personnel who were dentists by trade but dealt with other needs at the front, such as head and neck trauma. Chung was told it was a worthwhile, satisfying vocation—particularly for people who liked to work with their hands. And that was right up Chung's alley. She transitioned from flying helicopters to dentistry, no easy feat at that point in her career.

* * *

In August 2011, a copter was shot down in Afghanistan killing 30. Initial reports indicated the craft was part of the 160th, but that wasn't the case. Confusion likely stemmed from a 160th crash that occurred the same day at Fort Benning as part of a training mission. Sue, months into her return to civilian life, was involved in her husband's Family Readiness Group along with other officers' wives. She was tasked with being a "key caller," making sure the other spouses knew there had been no crash in Afghanistan involving the 160th. There was still personal tragedy for the Woodys related to the training crash in Georgia. It killed one of their West Point classmates, a proud South Carolinian named John "David" Hortman. He was in Sue's final company at the academy, the H1 Root Hawgs, and they became good friends. The 160th held a memorial service for Hortman at Fort Campbell. It was the first military ceremony that Sue attended after leaving the service, and she badly wanted to wear her old uniform that day. As a Fallen Night Stalker, Hortman's name was added to the Night Stalker Memorial wall at regimental headquarters at Fort Campbell.

A year after the killing of Osama bin Laden, President Obama made a surprise visit to Kabul. Obama and Afghan President Hamid Karzai signed an agreement that provided details of future US troop totals moving toward the goal of withdrawing the last of the American forces in 2014. Clint Woody was among the officers and soldiers who afterward shared the stage at Bagram Air Base with the commander in chief, clad in a bomber jacket that featured his personal seal on a chest patch. "I recognize that many Americans are tired of war," he told the gathering. "As President, nothing is more wrenching than signing a letter to a family of the fallen or looking in the eyes of a child who will grow up without a mother or father. I will not keep Americans in harm's way a single day longer than is absolutely required for our national security. But we must finish the job we started in Afghanistan and end this war responsibly."

Woody was promoted to major in April 2014. He actually began his duties three months earlier because he was needed then to fill the role of deputy joint operations officer, which needed to be occupied by a major. Sue considered the ceremony "very Clint," with the guest of honor providing talking points about each of the family members in attendance for the presiding lieutenant colonel to address and saying very little about himself. In June 2015, following a year at the Command and General Staff College at Fort Leavenworth, Kansas, he moved to Hunter Army Air Field near Fort Stewart in Savannah, Georgia, and weeks later became the commander of Alpha Company, 3rd Battalion of the 160th SOAR for two years.

On a deployment to Iraq late in 2015, Woody was one of four passengers in a copter making a late-night administrative trip from Baghdad to northern Iraq. He was close to dozing off at about 500 feet when he heard a loud sound that he initially thought was a bird colliding with the aircraft. Seated on the floor on the copter's left side with his left arm up against the door, Woody felt a sting in the arm that he first thought was the door slapping at him. Actually, someone had fired shots from the ground. One came through the copter, struck his armored vest, and ricocheted into the magazine of ammunition that he wore. It hit the round but cracked the casing, hence no explosion. Had he been sitting in a seat instead of on the floor, the shot probably would have caught him in the left leg. The bullet didn't strike Woody, but it ripped off part of the vest with the shrapnel cutting into his elbow. There was so little blood that Woody didn't realize what had happened until after the copter made multiple stops and he saw that the bullet was lodged into his ammo magazine. The shrapnel was soon removed from his elbow, a small bandage applied, and Clint Woody earned a Purple Heart drawing less blood than when he tried to fit into the Alpha Charlie model of the Kiowa Warrior copter during flight training at Fort Rucker.

Woody and other Purple Heart recipients were invited by the Boot Campaign, a Texas-based non-profit that has given back to military veterans since 2011, to travel to the Lone Star State for a hunting weekend in February 2016. He was allowed to bring along one guest, and there was no question whom he would invite. A few months earlier, his father, Denny, went to see a doctor because of unusual difficulty controlling his left hand, which was particularly confounding since he was a machinist. He originally thought it was merely a pinched nerve. It took months to diagnose ALS in autumn 2015, and Denny's health was beginning to decline as father and son made the drive to Texas for the big hunting weekend.

The youngest of the five Woody brothers became the third to attend a military academy when Joseph entered the Air Force Academy. He landed a position as the one of the managers for the Falcons' football team. And, for a time, while Clint was deployed in southern Afghanistan, brother Clay was stationed in the northeast corner of the country.

The West Point Class of 2004's next generation of football talent took the field for the first time at the Effingham County recreation center just north of Savannah on a typically hot-and-sticky mid-September day in 2017. Blake Woody suited up for the under-8 Raiders (wearing black and . . . red?).

The son of an Army "lonely end" was a two-way lineman while seeing some time at linebacker. Dad schooled Blake on the fine art of an offensive lineman getting his hands underneath his opponent's shoulder pads. It was a skill that the youngster mastered early, but he had a tendency to maintain a firmer grip than recommended as he and his opponent made their way down the line, resulting in the occasional holding penalty.

With Woody scheduled for another deployment beginning in mid-October, those early weeks of the season appeared to be his only opportunity to watch his oldest son's first football season. That was time enough to walk Blake through his first injury, a twisted knee that left him limping to the sideline. Mom was suitably concerned, and Woody blandly noted: "This is a football injury, Sue." Blake's knee was iced for a few days, and he wore a sleeve on it before seeing the family doctor. The diagnosis was a deep bruise, and Blake immediately felt exceedingly better. The most painful experience of the season likely occurred when an opponent said "mean" things to him, and another stepped on his helmet.

Blake didn't let a bruised knee or cleat to the head slow him, and Woody was able to take in the entire season thanks to a relative last-minute swap of Afghanistan deployments at the request of a fellow major. On the deployment that Woody was initially to be part of, a Chinook crash in late October resulted in the death of Jacob Sims, a 36-year-old chief warrant officer 2 from Oklahoma with a wife and five children. It happened the night of the battalion's formal dinner back in Georgia, which offered the chance for the Woodys to leave the kids with the babysitter and enjoy a big evening out. Woody learned of the tragedy the following day, was obviously shaken by the loss of a skilled pilot and devoted family man, but also relieved that the other six crew members aboard weren't lost. The major who took Woody's place was responsible for coordinating the subsequent recovery efforts.

Blake Woody's football season concluded in early November with him being named to the all-star team. He successfully lobbied his third-grade teacher to let him stand before the class, announced the honor bestowed upon him, and also invited his classmates to attend the upcoming all-star game, the 52nd annual Rebel Bowl, to be played at a local high school field.

Blake played the entire game on both sides of the line, and his Effingham Blue Jackets took a 12–6 lead over the Barracudas into the final minutes. But the 'Cudas scored on the final play of regulation to tie the score and added the extra point on a run—Blake was one of multiple Jackets to make contact with the ball carrier but couldn't bring him down—for a harrowing finish to the game and the season.

Deployments became more emotionally taxing on Woody with his wife and children back home. The strain of being separated from family was only accentuated with the deaths of Joe Petroff and Denny Woody in 2016, only months after the couple welcomed Paige as their fourth child and second daughter. Sue's two brothers had relocated to Charlotte in 2013 on work-related moves, and her parents followed suit. Clint and Sue spent a year at Fort Leavenworth, Kansas, where he attended the Command and General Staff College. They relocated to Savannah, about a four-hour drive from Charlotte, in June 2015 with Clint's reassignment to Hunter Army Air Field. Joe Petroff was hospitalized that December, a few weeks after Clint went on a deployment, with agonizing stomach pain that turned out to be a perforated ulcer. Complications developed, leading to eight surgeries and more than a month in the ICU before he died. As Denny Woody's condition worsened, his children responded to increase their support. Stacy, the older of the two Woody daughters, moved back home to help her mother with growing care needs. Chad and his wife, Erin, left their home in Louisiana and returned to Hayesville. The youngest of the seven Woody siblings, Meaghan (who graduated from Hayesville High in 2018), was a source of strength, comfort, and joy to everyone in the family, particularly to her mother, Leslie.

Reid Woody likewise returned home related to his duties with the Air Force Reserves. He was transferred in late 2014 from Alabama to Dobbins Air Force Base in the Atlanta suburb of Marietta, Georgia, to fly C-130s. He was deployed to Iraq and Afghanistan in support of two operations, Inherent Resolve and Freedom's Sentinel. He took an engineering position near Hayesville that left him with a "commute" of about two hours to Dobbins. He also went into business with his father, starting a firearms company called Appalachian Arms. Reid and wife Shanda told Denny news that they had not yet shared with the rest of the family; they were expecting their sixth child. If it was a boy, they would name him after Denny. That was the last time that Reid saw his father smile. Denny Woody died in October 2016; Dennis Mark Woody was born in May 2017.

Having a spouse as part of an elite military unit, with its actions shrouded in secrecy, produced understandable angst for Sue Woody even while she was still active military. She understood their cross-globe communications would contain little more than pleasantries. When Clint was deployed out of Fort Campbell, they were able to visit every three or four days. While stationed in Savannah, the online opportunities were more frequent. Most of all, she tried not to fixate on the possibility there would be a knock on her door at any time of the night or day, typically able to shove such thoughts from her mind.

Clint Woody's stay in Georgia ended during summer 2018. With multiple options available for his next stop, he finally sought to land a position back at the athletic department of West Point. He was told at one point that he would be allowed to make the move, only to be informed later that day it couldn't be done. Instead, Woody was assigned to Homestead, Florida. The plan is to assume a staff position—a 9-to-5 desk job—and no longer be eligible for deployment. That was welcome for a family with a fifth child on the way, a third daughter due in August 2018. If the Homestead duty is for the anticipated three years, that would put Woody at 17 years served—three short of full army retirement and all the benefits that go with that. Not that he couldn't continue on. There could be the possibility of further intriguing possibilities. But there could also be the prospect of finding fulfillment outside the army—ministry within the family's church, growing fruit trees, tinkering with his truck, and watching as many little league games as possible.

Chapter Seventeen

"WE'RE HERE TO REMEMBER"

Stan Brock's tenure as head football coach of the Black Knights lasted only two seasons, each ending with a 3–9 record. Army replaced him in late December 2008 with Rich Ellerson, who compiled an impressive record over the previous eight seasons at Cal Poly in the NCAA's Division II. His father and two of his brothers were West Point graduates, one brother serving as a captain of the Cadets football team during the early 1960s. While such family history likely worked in Ellerson's favor, it was probably more important that he was a proponent of restoring the option offense on the Hudson. Soon after the hiring, John Mumford continued his unlikely streak by landing on the staff of a fourth West Point head coach. Ellerson also hired Joe Ross off the staff of the academy's Center for Performance Enhancement to oversee the fullbacks and special teams.

Ellerson's first Black Knights team took a 5–6 record into the Navy game. A victory would end the fatiguing losing streak to the Midshipmen at seven games and also, given what would be a 6–6 record, result in Army's first bowl trip since 1996—to the EagleBank Bowl in Washington. Army led 3–0 at halftime but couldn't muster any more scoring and lost to Navy yet again, 17–3. The following year, the 2010 Cadets won four of their first six games before playing Rutgers in the New Jersey Meadowlands. Army lost,

23–20, and the game attracted national attention for a tragic incident that happened during an Army kickoff return in the fourth quarter. Rutgers' Eric LeGrand broke through two double teams to tackle junior reserve running back Malcolm Brown, but the hit caused LeGrand to be paralyzed from the neck down.

The Black Knights won their next two games to improve to 6–2 and clinched a berth in the Armed Forces Bowl, ending Army's 13-year postseason drought. The game was based in Fort Worth, Texas, but would be played that year in Dallas, on the home field of SMU, because the bowl's host stadium was unavailable while being renovated. Army's opponent would be none other than SMU, making the Cadets the game's *de facto* visiting team; the host Mustangs went in as seven-point favorites. The gathering on a balmy, breezy day included Ryan Kent, Brian Hill, and Peter Stewart. The Black Knights took an early 7–0 lead on a 55-yard fumble recovery and increased the margin to 13 points later in the opening period on a 13-yard run by Malcolm Brown. Army led 16–0 at halftime before the Mustangs began to rally. One touchdown each in the third and fourth quarters pulled SMU within 16–14.

With about four minutes to play, SMU's attempt at a 47-yard field goal to take the lead drifted to the left of the goalposts. The Cadets' option offense under sophomore quarterback Trent Steelman consumed the rest of the clock, and the Black Knights, at 7–6, secured Army's first winning season since 1996 and the program's first bowl win since 1985. Among the black-and-gold fans who jumped over the brick wall that circled the field at Ford Stadium and onto the field to celebrate the win was Ronnie McAda, living back in the Dallas area, along with his 7-year-old son, Trip. Among the hugs that John Mumford gave and received outside the winning locker room came from Brian Hill and Ryan Kent.

Ending the weighty losing streak to Navy was another matter. It reached 12 straight in Ellerson's fifth season in 2013; consider that Army's longest winning streak against Navy, even with its storied history and multiple national championship, was five games. The loss in 2012 was especially agonizing for the Black Knights and their fans. Army, with the opportunity to win the Commander-in-Chief's Trophy for the first time in 16 years, was in excellent position to pull out a late victory at Lincoln Financial Field. Navy's lead with less than a minute to play was 17–13, but the Cadets had first down on the Midshipmen's 14-yard line. But on that first down at the 14, senior quarterback Steelman's seemingly routine handoff to sophomore fullback Larry Dixon somehow never connected. The ball instead fell to the turf and was recovered by a Navy defender. Yet again, Army sang first.

Ellerson didn't produce another winning season at West Point following the 2010 bowl team, and was dismissed following the '13 campaign. The subsequent hiring of Jeff Monken featured a degree of "if you can't beat 'em, join 'em." Monken was a Navy assistant coach from 2002–2007 under Paul Johnson while also coaching for him before that at Georgia Southern and afterward at Georgia Tech. So, Monken was both a practitioner of the option and was aware of any aspects of Navy's football program that could be adopted at Army. One significant change was to put some space between the younger players' summer military commitments to Beast Barracks and Camp Buckner and the team's offseason workouts. Also, players scheduled summer classes when possible that lightened their academic loads for the fall semester.

As Monken put together his first Army coaching staff, John Mumford was summoned for a one-on-one sit down that Mumford hoped would lead to yet another renewal of his position at West Point. Mumford had many observations regarding Army football from his 13 years there under four head coaches. For one, he was eager to point out that former Black Knights players often returned to the academy from their first few years in the military appearing to be in better physical shape than when they played. Mumford brought to the meeting a collection of his notes compiled over the years, but the session didn't last long after Monken indicated he had already identified another coach to fill his spot.

* * *

During the spring of 2014, former Army fullback Mike Viti enjoyed a corporate job in Las Vegas after retiring from the army as a captain. He couldn't get out of his mind that more than 6,800 of his fellow officers, soldiers, sailors, and other military personnel had lost their lives in the ongoing war against terrorism. His distinctive way to make sure that those lives weren't forgotten, that Gold Star families felt the appreciation of the nation, was to embark on a walk that would cover at least that many miles with his destination being the Army-Navy game that December. Viti loosely plotted a route that would begin in Washington state, dip down to Texas, then turn back up to the game's site in Baltimore. That would cover about 7,100 miles.

To make the game, he would need to begin in late April. Viti's employer said there was no possible way for him to be given that much time off. So, Viti quit his job. He set off from DuPont, Washington, and determined some of the details of his trek along the way. Viti was in west Texas when he realized he could be in Dallas on the 13th anniversary of 9/11. He then planned for that and, per his practice along the way, alerted some acquaintances there to join him for part of the odyssey. Among those who walked with Viti in Dallas was Ryan Kent and his young son, Casen.

Monken's philosophy on roster size echoed that of most of the recent Army head coaches; the initial head count was 170. His first two seasons on the Hudson only lengthened the latest streak of losing seasons to five, with finishes of 4–8 and 2–10; Mike Viti was added to the coaching staff months after the latter season. Monken's third campaign, in 2016, began with a 28–13 win at Temple that sent a message to players and supporters alike that something might be different that year. The Cadets took a 6–5 record into their game against Navy (8–4) in Baltimore. An Army touchdown that was scored with about six minutes to play provided a 21–17 lead that stood up. Black Knights sang second for the first time since Todd Berry's second season, 2001. Mind you, they sang without the accompaniment of the academy band. Its members had hopped out of the stands and onto the field to join in the long, gray celebration. Army's season ended a few weeks later with an overtime win over North Texas in the Heart of Dallas Bowl.

The issue of sports standouts at the military academies being eligible to go pro immediately following graduation regained national attention with the play of Navy quarterback Keenan Reynolds through his final collegiate season of 2015. Reynolds finished fifth in the Heisman Trophy voting and was drafted in the sixth round by the Midshipmen's "home" team in the

NFL, the Baltimore Ravens. Teammate Chris Swain, a fullback, signed a free-agent contract with the San Diego Chargers after going undrafted. Reynolds and Swain were extended the full blessing of Secretary of Defense Ash Carter. The previous requirement of two years' immediately active-duty military service could be substituted with a period of eight to 10 years in the reserves for athletes from any of the academies as of March 2016. Reynolds was signed and cut from the Ravens multiple times during the 2016 and '17 seasons, but never appeared in a regular-season game. Swain experienced a similar fate with the Chargers in '16 and the New York Jets in '17.

During the summer of 2017, Chris Rowley became the first former Army baseball player to play in the major leagues when he was called up to the Toronto Blue Jays. Rowley, a pitcher, graduated from West Point in 2013 and made nine minor-league appearances that summer after signing as a free agent with the Jays. Pitching in 2014 and '15 wouldn't have meshed with his deployment to Bulgaria. He was granted a release from active duty early in 2016, being placed on "individual ready reserve" that was technically still in the army. Rowley returned to Toronto's minor-league system for the entire 2016 season and, called up the following year when the Jays were short on starters, made three starts and three relief appearances in 2017 to earn a record of 1–2. He returned to the majors in 2018.

West Point Class of 2010 graduate Alejandro Villanueva, who played tight end for Army, earned a spot on the Pittsburgh Steelers' roster in 2015 at offensive tackle following three deployments to Afghanistan. He moved into the starting lineup later that season and, in 2017, was selected as a starter in the Pro Bowl.

In autumn 2017, Army fashioned its first winning streak in the series since 1992–1996, with a 14–13 win in snowy, windy Philadelphia. The Black Knights had difficulty all day containing Navy's sophomore quarterback, Malcolm Perry. Perry rushed for 250 yards, including one romp through the snow for a 68-yard touchdown in the second period. He appeared headed for another TD in the third quarter, when he broke loose on 3rd and 3 at the Midshipmen's 43-yard line with Navy ahead 10–7. Army lineman John Voit took off after Perry, clomping along like he was wearing snowshoes. The footing was also an issue for Perry. Voit drew close inside the Cadets' 20 and decided his only chance to prevent a touchdown was to dive at his target. Voit managed to get one hand on Perry's heel, which caused that foot to click with his other foot. Perry fell at the Black Knights' 11, creating something of a snow angel. Army held Navy to a field goal and a 13–7 lead. The Cadets moved ahead 14–13 with about five minutes to play and then watched warily in the closing seconds as a 48-yard Navy field-goal attempt that would have won the game went wide left.

The victory had added significance for Army in light of its early November win at Air Force. Army claimed the Commander-in-Chief's Trophy for the first time since the Ronnie McAda–quarterbacked squad of 1996. Monken's phone was flooded with congratulatory texts in the following days, some sent from officers and soldiers stationed on the other side of the globe. Soon after back at the academy, Monken told his players, West Point administrators, and a collection of military higher-ups that the trophy "ain't ever leaving again."

For an encore, Army won the Armed Forces Bowl—the Fort Worth game was played in Fort Worth this time—over San Diego State. The spectators included Ryan Kent and Brian Hill, the latter driving up from San Antonio that morning with 3-year-old son Bryce. The Black Knights didn't spare the faint of heart. They pulled within a point of the lead on a touchdown with 18 seconds left and, eschewing the conservative route of kicking a PAT to take their chances in overtime, added a two-point run to grab the lead for good. The victory gave Army a final record of 10–3, equaling the West Point record for wins in a season.

Todd Berry and John Mumford both remained in college coaching following their respective exits from the Hudson. Berry served in a handful of assistant positions across the country before becoming the head coach at Louisiana-Monroe in 2010. His 2012 Warhawks opened with a stunning 34–31 upset of No. 8 Arkansas on the road, barely lost the following week at Auburn in overtime, and came within six points of winning at Baylor in their next game. When Mumford became available in 2014, Berry brought him on his staff. ULM's team that season dropped to 4–8 and then stood at 1–9 in mid-November 2015 when Berry was fired. Taking a page from the West Point playbook for naming an interim head football coach,

Louisiana-Monroe's administration bypassed the team's coordinators and handed over the team for the balance of the season to defensive line coach John Mumford. How many football coaches step in twice as an interim head coach for the same boss? About the same number that remain on one school's staff under four head coaches.

Berry left coaching but remained in it indirectly. He was hired to become the executive director of the American Football Coaches Association—the association for college coaches—based in Waco, Texas. Mumford's stay in Monroe didn't extend beyond the conclusion of his brief term as interim head coach. He spent the 2015–16 school year back in high school, coaching at little St. John Paul II High in Huntsville, Alabama. Joe Ross, by then in private business in Huntsville, helped his friend land the position. After one season, Mumford was able to return to college football as an assistant at New Mexico State, a so-called mid-major school that had not played in a bowl since 1967. The Aggies closed the 2017 season with not only a surprising postseason appearance but also with their first bowl victory since 1960—in overtime. Mumford, still on the field long afterward amid the euphoric celebration, struggled to listen to a congratulatory call from one of his old West Point neighbors—former Army football mentor Gene Palka.

The Class of 2004's 10-year reunion was held the first weekend of October 2014, which included the Black Knights' homecoming football game against Ball State, with almost 250 graduates attending. None of the eight '04 grads who played four years of Army football were able to make it. The graduates were headquartered about 30 miles from West Point, just across the New York-New Jersey line at a hotel in Woodcliff Lake. They began checking in that Thursday afternoon, many of them arriving in SUV's with a spouse and multiple children. Skyler Munekata drove from Ohio with wife Brooke and their two children. Many of the grads became reacquainted for the first time in years at the hotel bar just off the lobby, comparing hairlines and waistlines (given that they went to West Point, some still in the military, the waistlines weren't really much different), introducing one another to their families and telling the most outlandish stories to a fellow graduate's spouse. Chartered motor coaches shuttled them to the academy for the balance of the weekend, beginning with that night's mixer in the ballroom of Cullum Hall.

Saturday was adorned in Indian summer weather when a pair of teams with 1–3 records met at Michie Stadium. Jeff Monken's Black Knights built a 27–10 lead and held off a late Cardinals rally to send away the old grads and the vast majority of the crowd happy with the 33–24 victory. Down at Buffalo Soldier Field, a huge, white tent that accommodated the 10-year reunion attendees was just one of such locations for former West Point students. The weekend concluded with Sunday brunch in Washington Hall. No one was forced to stand at attention behind his or her chair before being seated, though that was certainly optional.

Some reunion activities, like the golf tournament, were optional. But all the returning grads attended the Friday morning memorial service held in the Cadet Chapel. Dennis and Marion Zilinski sat in the front row along with relatives of the other deceased from the Class of 2004. Sitting immediately to their right was the former Marie Cicarelle and her husband, Charlie Lewis, a fellow '04 grad who was on the swim team. Among the opening remarks from graduate Anthony Martinez: "Change is a constant in our lifetime. There are changes that we can and can't control, changes that we like and we do not like. The Class of 2004 will always remember our fallen classmates for the good things they have done for the long, gray line and for our country. To our fallen, be thou at peace, for country and for corps."

The primary speaker was Chaplain Billy Hawkins. He urged the mourners not to hold in their grief: "You and your peers were those young men and women then, when you arrived some 14 years ago. And, once you began, you shared the hard times, the bad times, the good times, the challenging times. And the memories remain simply because you shared your lives together. Do you remember? That's why we're here." He referenced a Bible passage, from the Book of Lamentations, that was read earlier in the ceremony by classmate Charlsey Myers Mahle. "The scripture in Lamentations encourages and permits the opportunity to lament. It's not a word that we use very often. It's not a part of our vernacular. However, today, that's what we're here to do. We are here to remember. To mourn. To grieve. I'm asking, let the stories flow. And as they flow, so will the lumps in your throats. Those stories often cause fear because we don't want to be consumed by our sadness. Take courage in allowing those stories to arise because, as Charlsey read, because of the Lord's great love, we are not consumed, for His compassion never fails."

Another '04 graduate, Major Bridgette Bell, delivered an additional scripture reading. To another grad, Major Bradley Vance, was left the honor of calling roll for those—who died either after leaving West Point or during the class's years on the Hudson—unable to reply:

"Garrison C. Avery . . . Amos C. Bock . . . Benjamin T. Britt . . . Michael A. Cerrone . . . John R. Dennison . . . David M. Fraser . . . John E. Heinmiller . . . Jason E. Holbrook . . . John D. Hortman . . . Engelbert E. Mbog-Hob . . . Anthony B. Miller II . . . Paul W. Pena . . . Robert A. Seidel III . . . Adam P. Snyder . . . Daniel P. Whitten . . . Dennis W. Zilinski II."

A bugler played "Taps." The subsequent moment of silence laid bare the sound of the old chapel's ventilation system. Eyes were moist when the grads rose as one and sang the academy alma mater, belting out "Well done!" as they had done so many times as cadets. The attendees then walked down from the chapel to West Point's cemetery to pay respects to many of those named during the service.

Between the death of 1st Lieutenant Dennis Zilinski II on November 19, 2005, and the passing of Captain John "David" Hortman on August 8, 2011, a dozen other members of West Point's Class of 2004 became casualties of supporting the war on terrorism. That included Captain Michael Cerrone on November 12, 2006, in Samarra, Iraq. 1st Lieutenant Benjamin Britt was killed only about a month after Zilinski, on December 22, 2005, by an IED in Baghdad. 1st Lieutenant Garrison Avery was killed by a roadside bomb on February 1, 2006, also in Baghdad; his academy buddies called him "MacGyver" because of his ability to seemingly fix anything by using anything. 1st Lieutenant Robert Seidel III was killed by an IED on May 18, 2006, in Abu Ghraib, Iraq. 1st lieutenant Amos "Camden" Bock died on October 23, 2006, in Baghdad from an IED.

Captain John Ryan Dennison, who went by his middle name, died from gunfire at point-blank range in the Battle of Turki on November 15, 2006. Captain David Fraser was killed 11 days later, on November 26, 2006, in Baghdad, by an explosively formed penetrator; he was scheduled to return home two weeks later. 1st Lieutenant Jacob Fritz was one of two US officers who were kidnapped along with two US soldiers by Iraqi gunmen who accessed a meeting of the Provincial Joint Coordination Center on January 20, 2007, in Karbala, Iraq, by disguising themselves as American soldiers. All four captives were found shot to death. Captain Adam Snyder died December 5, 2007, in the same Iraqi city as Zilinski, Bayji, from an IED; he sang with the West Point Glee Club, including when the group was given a standing ovation in Boston before ever singing a note days after 9/11.

Three of the class' casualties were killed in Afghanistan. Captain Paul Pena was killed January 19, 2010, by an IED in the Arghandab River Valley. Captain Daniel Whitten was killed February 2, 2010, in Zabul Province by an IED. Captain Jason Holbrook was killed by an IED on July 29, 2010, in Tsagay. Deployed as a team leader for a special-forces operational detachment, Holbrook had been in Afghanistan less than a month.

The Class of 2004 has suffered the most casualties of any West Point graduating class since those that graduated during the Vietnam War.

BIBLIOGRAPHY

The following newspapers and other sources were used. In cases in which one or more quotes were copied that appeared to be from exclusive interviews, those sources, and some of the originating writers, were cited in the text:

Asbury Park Press (NJ), *Army Times*, The Associated Press, *The Atlanta Journal-Constitution*, *The Baltimore Sun*, *The Birmingham News* (AL), *The Boston Globe*, *The Capital* (Annapolis, MD), *The Cincinnati Enquirer*, *Clay County Progress* (NC), *Daily News* (NY), *Daytona Beach News-Journal* (FL), *Denver Post*, *Detroit Free Press*, *Detroit News*, *Enterprise Ledger* (AL), *Fort Worth Star-Telegram* (TX), *Hartford Courant* (CT), *Herald-Mail* (Hagerstown, MD), *Honolulu Star-Bulletin*, *Houston Chronicle*, *Inland Valley Daily Bulletin* (CA), *The Huntsville Times* (AL), *The Journal News* (Westchester County, NY), *Killeen Daily Herald* (TX), *Lincoln Journal Star* (NE), *Los Angeles Times*, *Louisville Courier-Journal*, *Milwaukee Journal Sentinel*, *The New York Times*, *Orlando Sentinel*, *Philadelphia Daily News*, *The Philadelphia Inquirer*, *Pittsburgh Post-Gazette*, *The Pointer's View* (West Point, NY), *Press and Sun-Bulletin* (Binghamton, NY), *The Record* (Hackensack, NJ), *Smoky Mountain Sentinel* (Hayesville, NC), *Sports Illustrated*, *The Star-Ledger* (Newark, NJ), *Stars and Stripes*, *Staten Island Advance* (NY), *Telegram & Gazette* (Worcester,

MA), *The Times Herald-Record* (Middletown, NY), *Toronto Star; U.S. Fed News, USA TODAY, The Wall Street Journal, The Washington Post.*

Atkinson, Rick. *The Long Gray Line: The American Journey of West Point's Class of 1966.* New York; Henry Holt and Company, 1999.

Barkalow, Carol. *In the Men's House: An Inside Account of Life in the Army by One of West Point's First Female Graduates.* New York; Poseidon Press, 1990.

Beech, Mark. *When Saturday Mattered Most: The Last Golden Season of Army Football.* New York; Thomas Dunne Books, 2012.

Chernow, Ron. *Grant.* New York; Penguin Press, 2017.

Feinstein, John. *A Civil War / Army vs. Navy: A Year Inside College Football's Purest Rivalry.* Boston, New York, Toronto, London; Little, Brown and Company, 1996.

Grant, John and Bailey, Ronald. *West Point: The First 200 Years.* Guilford, Connecticut; The Globe Pequot Press, 2002.

Grant, Ulysses S. *Ulysses S. Grant: Memoirs and Selected Letters.* New York; The Library of America, 1990.

Levitas, Michael editor. *A Nation Challenged: A Visual History of 9/11 and its Aftermath.* New York; *The New York Times* and Callaway, 2002.

Lipsky, David. *Absolutely American: Four Years at West Point.* Boston; Houghton Mifflin Hardcourt, 2003.

MacArthur, Douglas. *Reminiscences.* New York; McGraw Hill, 1964.

McCain, John and Salter, Mark. *13 Soldiers: A Personal History of Americans at War.* New York; Simon & Schuster, 2014.

Pfarrer, Chuck. *Seal Target Geronimo: The Inside Story of the Mission to Kill Osama bin Laden.* New York; St. Martin's Press, 2011.

Robinson, Linda. *Tell Me How This Ends: General David Petraeus and the Search for a Way Out of Iraq.* New York; PublicAffairs, 2008.

Schading, Barbara with Schading, Richard and Slaton, Virginia. *A Civilian's Guide to the U.S. Military.* Cincinnati, Ohio; Writer's Digest Books, 2007.

Smallwood, William L. *The West Point Candidate Book: How to Prepare, How to Get In, How to Survive.* Sun Valley, Idaho; Beacon Books, 2000.

Sweett, Lawrence J. *Images of America: New Smyrna Beach.* Charleston, South Carolina; Arcadia Publishing, 2007.

Wallace, Cody editor. *The Strong Gray Line: War-Time Reflections from the West Point Class of 2004.* Lanham, Boulder, New York and London; Rowman & Littlefield, 2015.

Woodward, Bob. *Plan of Attack.* New York; Simon & Schuster, 2004.

Websites for the United States Military Academy, the United States Naval Academy, the United States Air Force Academy, Boston University, Fort Benning, Fort Hood, Fort Riley, Fort Rucker and the Blue Man Group. Transcript from "The Charlie Rose Show."

"How to Survive Mountain Phase of Ranger School" by Adrian Bonenberger from Task&Purpose.com.

"Home with Honor" by Claire Knapp of the *Randolph (N.J.) Reporter* for USCHO.com, May 26, 2004.

Yearbooks for the United States Military Academy at West Point, NY; the U.S.M.A. Preparatory School at Fort Monmouth, NJ; and the following high schools: Hayesville (NC); Indian Hills of Oakland, NJ; New Smyrna Beach (FL); Nimitz of Houston; Spruce Creek of Port Orange, FL; Shaler Area of Shaler, PA; Springdale (PA); and Woodbury (NJ).

ACKNOWLEDGMENTS

The idea for this book came as I lay on the living room couch on the afternoon of December 6, 2003. The primary offerings on that day's menu of college football telecasts were the championship games of the Southeastern Conference (LSU vs. Georgia) and the Big 12 Conference (Oklahoma vs. Kansas State), plus USC's regular-season finale against Oregon State. Those outcomes would help determine which two teams would be chosen to the play in the BCS Championship Game. (Remember those days of yore?)

That afternoon's Army-Navy game was the early *hors d'oeuvre* of a different flavor. I was watching it more as a tradition observed early in the Christmas season. Navy had a solid team and was headed to the Houston Bowl. Army didn't have a solid team, though I didn't realize that before kickoff. That fact was made abundantly clear early in the CBS telecast. Soon after Navy's initial possession went for 74 yards and a touchdown, color analyst "Boomer" Esiason gave a statement that seemed more fitting for a lead of three or four TDs: "I think if I were on the Army sideline, I would be telling them, 'Listen, you're not beaten until you admit it. Hence, don't admit it.'" The score was still 7–0 early in the second quarter when a CBS technical director clicked up a graphic that noted Army was trying to avoid becoming the first 0–13 team ever in college football.

ACKNOWLEDGMENTS

I began covering college football almost thirty years before that December afternoon and understood the difference between the teams fielded by Army, Navy, and Air Force and those of other major-college programs. I also realized the seniors for Army and Navy wouldn't be headed for pro ball following graduation. I didn't realize at the time how few seniors there were on that winless West Point team.

Once I learned the number, I was determined to follow the eight young men who were likely headed off to war. You now know one of them, Brad Waudby, never made it into the military. And another, Tom Farrington, never was deployed. Of the six who went off to Iraq, some also to Afghanistan, it was a relief to me that all returned safely. And Sue Woody, too. It was a pleasure to visit multiple times with each—in their homes, present and past in most cases—at their bases, over lunches and dinners and one wedding.

They were incredibly gracious and could have reacted differently to someone whose focus was the 0–13 record "that will stay with us for the rest of our lives," as Josh Davis lamented. Actually, I'm sure you couldn't find anyone on the street who could answer that trivia question. But the point of telling their collective story was to emphasize that the football odds were stacked heavily against the eight fourth-year seniors who took the field against Navy on December 6, 2003. And that, not planning to go to war when they elected to attend the United States Military Academy, those who stayed at West Point and became officers did so with all of their heart and all of their might.

It took more than a decade for me to put the story together for various reasons. My biggest regret is that some parents whom I believe eagerly wanted to read the telling didn't live to see this book's publication—Tom Farrington Sr., Tom and Nancy Hill, Joe Petroff, and Denny Woody.

Bob Beretta and others who work or did work for West Point's sports publicity office—including Mady Salvani, Matt Faulkner, Brian Gunning, and Mike Albright—were tremendously helpful. Other academy personnel were likewise of great assistance as I shadowed a cadet for the better part of a day (I wasn't required to recite any Plebe Knowledge), sat in on Post Night festivities for field artillery and often badgered West Point people with my questions and requests through the years. I laid on the ground out in the woods at Fort Riley when National Guard troops were taught how to deal with IEDs, attended an aviation class at Fort Rucker and spent the night during a live-fire test at Fort Sill. I witnessed the joy of both the returning military and their family and friends at Fort Hood following a long deployment to Iraq. And I witnessed the sorrow of the memorial service during the class' 10-year reunion.

There was breakfast with Thomas Roberts, as he explained some of the ill-convinced decisions of youth. There was lunch with Marion Zilinski, listening to the compelling story of her late son's immense dedication to family, faith, and country. There was dinner with John Mumford, a hero of a different kind for his steadfast devotion to Army football while working at West Point for four—count 'em, four—head coaches. There were so many others who gave their time either for personal sit-downs, phone calls, or exchange of emails.

Rick Atkinson's *The Long Gray Line* proved to be something of a blueprint for this book, though I couldn't begin to replicate his quality of prose. I, like Mr. Atkinson, attempted to recreate events and sometimes conversations from years past based on at least one party's recollection. David Lipsky's *Absolutely American* proved to be my unofficial reference guide to all things West Point. I studied it long and hard before spending the day before R-Day as one of the practice dummies. Yet I still fumbled some of the replies when yelled at by the 20-something Cadet in the Red Sash. Also of tremendous value was *The Strong Gray Line*. West Point Class of 2004 graduates Cory Wallace and Jim Wilson spearheaded the book, in which they and other '04 grads honored their fallen classmates.

At Skyhorse, editor Jason Katzman was a faithful manager of this project throughout. Thanks, also, to Kirsten Dalley of the production team and to former executive editor Niels Aaboe, who saw merit in telling this story.

Thanks, also, to my wife of forty wonderful years, Frances, who had better things to do than provide moral support and to read over yet another chapter night after night.

—Jeff Miller, June 2018